TELL
TCHAIKOVSKY
THE NEWS

FOR APRIL,
Thanks for totally
rocking my world!
I hope you enjoy
the read.
Mike

TELL
TCHAIKOVSKY
THE NEWS

Rock 'n' Roll, the Labor Question, and
the Musicians' Union, 1942–1968

MICHAEL JAMES ROBERTS

Duke University Press   Durham and London   2014

© 2014 Duke University Press

All rights reserved

Printed in the United States of America on acid-free paper ∞

Designed by Courtney Leigh Baker and typeset in

Arno Pro by Tseng Information Systems, Inc.

Library of Congress Cataloging-in-Publication Data

Roberts, Michael James.

Tell Tchaikovsky the news : rock 'n' roll, the labor question,

and the musicians' union, 1942–1968 / Michael James Roberts.

pages cm

Includes bibliographical references and index.

ISBN 978-0-8223-5463-5 (cloth : alk. paper)

ISBN 978-0-8223-5475-8 (pbk. : alk. paper)

1. American Federation of Musicians—History.

2. Musicians—Labor unions—United States.

3. Rock musicians—Labor unions—United States. I. Title.

ML3795.R598 2014

331.88′1178097309045—dc23

2013026389

For Christine

CONTENTS

PREFACE

This book is a case study of a particular period in the history of the American Federation of Musicians (AFM), the labor union that represents professional musicians in the United States and Canada. My investigation has a particular spin, since it is not a comprehensive history of the institution of the union itself during the period under consideration. Rather, this book scrutinizes the ways in which the AFM responded to the emergence of rock 'n' roll music. The years I examine, roughly from 1942 to 1968, span the era from the earliest recordings of what would become rock 'n' roll music to the year that the musicians' union finally printed the words *rock 'n' roll* in their main newspaper. The implications of this history go beyond the institution of the AFM itself because the AFM's response to rock 'n' roll was one part of a much larger conflict that historians refer to as the culture wars of the 1960s. In short, this case study seeks to add to our understanding of how the labor movement went into a period of decline beginning in the 1960s, due in part to an inability to connect with the counterculture and create a viable Left politics in the decades that followed.

It would have been in the economic interests of the union to aggressively organize rock 'n' roll musicians and include them as equal members (members with equal political and cultural status) in the governance of the union, but for cultural reasons the AFM failed to do either: rock 'n' roll was not recognized as "legitimate" music, and its musicians were rarely seen as fit for membership in the 1950s and early 1960s. The case of the musicians' union points to the importance of culture as a relatively independent variable in the structuring of union identity and union policy. The emphasis on culture in this book focuses on the conditions that made it possible for a labor union to act against its own economic interests.

I also seek to emphasize the class and class conflict dimension of rock 'n' roll, because I find that it remains relatively neglected in popular culture studies compared with existing scholarship on rock 'n' roll that focuses on the race and gender-based dimensions of the phenomenon. On the one hand, there have been many very good critiques of rock 'n' roll that focus on how its culture reproduces gender norms that marginalize women, including Susan Fast's *Inside the Houses of the Holy*, Sheila Whiteley's *Sexing the Groove*, and Jacqueline Warwick's *Girl Groups, Girl Culture*. Other critiques of rock 'n' roll focus on the question of race, particularly how white musicians and fans appropriated the original black form of rock 'n' roll, rhythm and blues. Critics like Greg Tate might prefer the phrase "ripped off," because the theft of music went beyond borrowing techniques and musical forms developed by African Americans. White-owned and controlled record companies literally stole the songs written by black musicians. In their book *Rock 'n' Roll Is Here to Pay*, Chapple and Garofalo refer to this history as the phenomenon of "black roots and white fruits." These are, of course, legitimate criticisms, since there is a long history of racism and misogyny in the music industry. My intention is to add some complexity by filling in the gaps where the analysis of class in rock 'n' roll music remains underdeveloped.

When social class is considered seriously, the story of rock 'n' roll becomes more complex, because African Americans, like all Americans, have historically been divided along class lines, and this class division often turns upon differences in cultural practices, including the production and consumption of music. In his book *Blues People*, Amiri Baraka has argued that throughout most of the twentieth century, bourgeois African Americans did not embrace the culture of working-class African Americans, including blues and jump blues music. According to Baraka, "rhythm and blues became more of an anathema to the Negro middle class, perhaps, than the earlier blues forms." Following the lead of Baraka, in my own research I have found that black jazz musicians in the AFM attacked rock 'n' roll culture with as much fervor as the white musicians.

While class has been relatively neglected in the study of rock 'n' roll, there are some important works on the subject, including George Lipsitz's *Rainbow at Midnight* and Reebee Garofalo's *Rockin' Out*. I situate my perspective alongside these works as well as within the broad theoretical framework of cultural studies, building upon the work of Dick Hebdige's *Subculture: The Meaning of Style* and the collective of Marxist cultural theorists sometimes referred to as British cultural studies. Ultimately, however, I break with their position on popular culture. Against Hebdige and others from the Birmingham school, I argue that subcultural practices of the working-class provided more than imaginary or "magical" solutions to material contradictions arising from the socioeconomic structure. On the contrary, I argue that the struggle against work and its various representations in rock 'n' roll music has had tangible effects on the direction of class struggle in the United States. Recent work by scholars of popular music like Ryan Moore's *Sells Like Teen Spirit* has also pointed out this problem in the work of previous scholars in the area of Marxist cultural studies.

I also focus on the class dimensions of rock 'n' roll because I find it important to contribute to the existing scholarship that has sought to explain how and why American labor unions have, at certain times in the history of the labor movement, come to stand *opposed* to the working class, whether in terms of the conflict between the leadership structure of labor unions and rank-and-file members, or the conflict between union members and the workers who have historically been excluded from membership, namely, women and ethnic and racial minority groups.

With some important exceptions, labor historians have inadequately accounted for the decline of labor unions in American politics over the last four decades. In most accounts of this decline, the focus has been on *structural* changes in the political economy: the offshoring of jobs overseas, automation, changes in labor law, the corporate assault on labor unions, and a hostile federal government that emerged with Reaganomics. Fewer analyses look to the practices of union leadership as an important variable in the demise of labor union power. While I agree that political-economic structural changes have played a significant role in labor's waning, these analyses do not adequately account for why the labor movement went into steep decline, because they ignore how labor union *culture* has also contributed to the misfortunes of the American labor movement.

I position my work in the tradition of labor history scholarship that has emphasized that our understanding of the peculiar cultural characteristics of the American working class cannot be reduced to an examination of the institutions that are believed to be its representative, namely, the institution of the labor union. Here I situate my book in the intellectual tradition staked out by E. P. Thompson, Paul Lafargue, Herbert Gutman, Stanley Aronowitz, George Rawick, Lizabeth Cohen, Ellen Willis, George Lipsitz, and Robin D. G. Kelley as well as more recent work by important scholars like Jefferson Cowie, Jonathan Cutler, and Kristin Lawler.

In short, I hope my book will find two audiences, one in the area of popular music and popular culture studies and the other in labor studies.

There is one more reason why the musicians' union is an important case in the history of the American labor movement, beyond the fact that historians have largely neglected unions in the entertainment industry. In 1943, the AFM was able to secure one of the most remarkable labor agreements in history. By compelling record companies to take financial responsibility for musicians who were put out of work as a result of the application of innovative sound recording technologies, the union demonstrated that it was possible to oblige corporations to compensate workers for job losses that resulted from automation. The implications of this agreement pointed toward what had previously seemed impossible: a new way of living in a *post-scarcity* environment, with less work and a better material and cultural standard of living for all workers made possible by labor-saving technologies. The significance of this agreement should not be underestimated. Not only did this agreement create a precedent for other labor unions to follow, but it also had the potential to impact all working people in the industrialized world. Indeed, it is important to reconsider just how important an agreement it was, considering the dire situation of our "postindustrial" economy today, where widespread belief in the ineluctability of austerity poisons the imagination. These post-scarcity possibilities may seem like science fiction to us now, but perhaps if we continue our rigorous study of the history of our nation's working class, we can provide an alternative interpretation to what may yet come to pass. Recently, the Occupy movements around the world have begun to mount a serious challenge to the ideology of austerity. Now, more than ever, it is crucial to reexamine our nation's labor history and retrieve the forgotten discourse on the labor question. In short, we must go back to the future.

ACKNOWLEDGMENTS

This book began as a dissertation in the Department of Sociology at the Graduate School and University Center of the City University of New York. I'd like to thank the members of my committee, William Kornblum, Juan Flores, and especially Stanley Aronowitz, the chair of my committee and my mentor while I was a graduate student at CUNY. In several graduate seminars on cultural studies, Stanley and Juan drew my attention to how the rise of rock 'n' roll culture contributed to the larger project of challenging the idea of Great Art, a phenomenon that continues to arouse interest in my thinking about the relation between the culture wars and the labor question.

My dissertation grew out of multiple conversations and arguments that took place in a study group on cultural studies and the labor question that I participated in while a graduate student at CUNY. Many of the positions staked out in this book were formed while discussing these issues with my friends in that study group, including Penny Lewis, Heather Gautney, David Staples, Joshua Zuckerberg, Mark Halling, J. D. Howell, Teresa Poor, Susanna Jones, Jennifer Disney, Tracy Steffey, Joe DeMauro, Tanja DeMauro, David Van Arsdale, Jonathan Cutler, and Kristin Lawler. Jonathan's book *Labor's Time: Shorter Hours, the UAW and the Struggle for American Unionism*, and Kristin's book *The American Surfer: Radical Culture and Capitalism*, also derived much of their content from that study group, and in addition to being the best new books in their respective fields, their work inspired me to keep our study group going in print.

My intellectual soul mate since undergraduate days, Ryan Moore, has had a profound influence on everything I think about in terms of music and cultural politics. Sometimes we disagree on issues, but mostly we exist as fellow travelers, although separated now by a few thousand miles. His important book, *Sells Like Teen Spirit: Music, Youth Culture, and Social Crisis*, helped me clarify my own positions on rock 'n' roll culture and its relationship to changes in the political economy.

Other points of view found here were formed beyond formal academic settings from long conversations with the late Ellen Willis, whose essays on rock 'n' roll are still my favorite. Ellen taught us how to understand the ways in which the Left continues to struggle with the issues of pleasure, freedom, and sexuality. My reading of rock 'n' roll culture is profoundly influenced by her work. From Ellen and Stanley I also learned the importance of psychoanalysis as a framework to approach the labor question. Shout out also to Nona Willis Aronowitz and Kim O'Connell, who together with Ellen and Stanley were like family to me while I was a graduate student in New York City. They taught me how to appreciate the richness of New York culture and what it means to be in a New York state of mind. More thanks to Nona for putting together and editing the collection of Ellen's writings on rock 'n' roll in the book *Out of the Vinyl Deeps*.

Many people at the American Federation of Musicians have been extremely generous with their time in assisting me with my research, including Jay Schaffner and David Sheldon at Local 802 in New York City, and Hal Espinosa from Local 47 in Los Angeles. Many thanks to Jay in particular for his willingness to set aside many hours in order to school me on the inner workings of the political economy of the music industry. A very special thanks goes to guitar virtuoso, session musician, composer and activist member of local 802, Marc Ribot. It was Marc who got me interested in this particular topic in the first place. If it were not for him, this book would not exist. Marc is a great example of what Gramsci meant by the concept "organic intellectual." If you have not heard his music, you must go have a listen. You won't be disappointed.

My colleagues at San Diego State University have been especially supportive of my project, including Sheldon Zhang, Phillip Gay, Bo Kolody, the late Paul Sargent, Enrico Marcelli, the late George Kirkpatrick, and especially Jung Min Choi, Tom Semm, Hank Johnston, Jill Esbenshade, and Kyra Greene. Hank, Tom, Kyra, Jill, and Choi read many drafts of my chapters and articles on the topic, providing me with valuable suggestions for improvements. My graduate students at San Diego State have been especially helpful as sounding boards for my ideas in various seminars on labor and popular culture. In particular, I'd like to thank Chad Smith, Justin Myers, Ryan Gittins, Matt Kaneshiro, Graham Forbes, Amy Colony, Phil Allen, Matt Rotondi, Shannon Sellars, Kristen Emory, Somer Hall, Micah Mitrosky, Paul Cortopassi, Art Reed, Marilisa Navarro, Karen Romero, Ashley Wardle, Shey Shey, Ed Tam, Jonathan Tupas, and Benjamin Wright. Thanks also to David McHenry and Melanie Dumont for tolerating all the chaos that I sometimes create in our department.

I'd like to thank my editors at Duke University Press, Valerie Millholland, Miriam Angess, Elaine Otto, and Susan Albury, as well as my anonymous readers who have provided so many suggestions for improvement to my manuscript that I cannot begin to list them here. Any weaknesses that remain are, of course, my own doing.

I'm also lucky that my father, Nick Roberts, and my stepmother, Susan Roberts, are both English professors at Cabrillo College. Many thanks to them for all the painstaking labor they put into my manuscript correcting multiple errors that escaped my eyes. Also my mother and stepfather, Kathy and Bill Herington, showed remarkable patience and endless support throughout my graduate school career. Finally, thanks to all my siblings, Paul, Matt, Kate, Sara, and Nick, for providing feedback on my changing ideas about the history of the American labor movement over the years. My book is a much better read thanks to the support of all these people.

Christine Payne has been a great critic of my positions and a source of new ways to understand the politics of popular music. I've learned more about contemporary popular music from her than anyone else.

INTRODUCTION.
Union Man Blues

The Englishman met the West African as a reformed sinner meets a comrade of his
previous debaucheries. The reformed sinner very often creates a pornography of
his former life. He must suppress even his knowledge that he had acted that way or
even wanted to act that way. Prompted by his uneasiness at this great act of repression, he cannot leave alone those who live as he once did or as he still unconsciously
desires to live. He must devote himself to their conversion or repression.
— GEORGE P. RAWICK

In June 1969, the American Federation of Musicians (AFM), the oldest and
largest labor union that represents professional musicians in the United
States and Canada, published an article on the rock band Creedence Clearwater Revival (CCR) in their official newspaper, the *International Musician*.
The rock band from El Cerrito, California, was riding a wave of popularity
following the release of their self-titled debut album in 1968, which had
two singles, "Susie Q" and "Proud Mary," reach *Billboard* magazine's top
10 that year. The article, written by Jay Ruby, provided information about
their musical influences, as well as biographical information for all the band
members. The article also featured the broader San Francisco Bay Area
music scene of the late 1960s, which included such rock bands as the Jefferson Airplane, Country Joe and the Fish, the Grateful Dead, Janis Joplin,
and Big Brother and the Holding Company. Ruby refers to the Bay Area
music scene of that time as America's answer to the British Invasion of rock

bands from the mid-1960s. The article as a whole is a fairly interesting and informative piece but nothing spectacular in the world of music criticism and music industry reporting.

What *is* very interesting, however, about Ruby's article is that it was the first time the AFM featured a full-page article in their newspaper dedicated to a rock 'n' roll band.[1] In fact, it was only the second time that the very words *rock 'n' roll* appeared in print between the covers of the *International Musician*, a monthly newspaper that first went into circulation in 1901, five years after the AFM itself was established as a chartered craft union of the American Federation of Labor under President Samuel Gompers.[2] Prior to 1968, there is no mention of rock 'n' roll in the musicians' union's paper. Curiously, though, the words *rock 'n' roll* didn't exactly roll off Jay Ruby's typewriter; on the contrary, they appear indirectly in a quote from John Fogerty, the lead singer and songwriter for CCR. In the article, Ruby refers to Creedence as a "pop" band; it is only in a passage from the text where Ruby quotes Fogerty that the phrase *rock 'n' roll* emerges. In that quote, Fogerty refers to himself and his band mates as rock 'n' roll musicians, but that's the only instance in the entire article where that particular phrase is mentioned. It seems odd to read that article about CCR today, more than thirty years after it was written, and find that the words *rock 'n' roll*, words which seem so innocuous to us now, are almost nowhere to be found in such a relatively lengthy article about a band we now consider to be permanent members in the pantheon of classic rock music. How could anyone today *not* use the phrase *rock 'n' roll* or the term *rock* in a conversation that involved a description of Creedence Clearwater Revival?

Like many of the successful American rock bands from the late 1960s, the members of CCR grew up listening to rhythm and blues and early rock 'n' roll music on the radio, including the music of Wynonie Harris, Ruth Brown, Big Joe Turner, Roy Brown, Hadda Brooks, Amos Milburn, T-Bone Walker, Chuck Berry, and Little Richard as well as the famous Sun Records artists — Elvis Presley, Johnny Cash, Jerry Lee Lewis, and Carl Perkins and other rockabilly artists like Wanda Jackson. Indeed, a whole generation of young musicians playing in rock 'n' roll bands all over the States in the early to mid-1960s had already cut their teeth on the rock 'n' roll and rhythm and blues of earlier generations of musicians, whose careers spanned the years from the mid-1940s to the mid-1950s. That same 1940s and 1950s generation of rockers was also idolized by the "British Invasion" rock bands from 1964 including the Beatles and the Rolling Stones. Surprisingly, Chuck Berry and his generation of rock 'n' roll musicians were never fully recognized by the American Federation of Musicians, and the Beatles themselves were the subject of much controversy for the musicians' union in 1964, when the AFM attempted to ban the group from playing in the United States.[3] If a rock 'n' roll star like Chuck Berry ever had any interactions with the musicians' union, it was not because the AFM was looking to embrace him with open arms. Berry did join the union because he played live gigs at venues that were already unionized venues, organized by the AFM years before Berry performed there. Similarly, he did make recordings on labels that were union shops before he recorded there, but the AFM never actively organized rock 'n' rollers, nor did they ever recognize rock 'n' roll musicians as members of any importance, if and when any rock 'n' roll musicians became card carrying members.[4] On the contrary, rock 'n' roll musicians were the virtual pariahs of the musicians' union for nearly twenty years, and for that reason, most rock 'n' roll musicians either worked for non-union record labels and non-union venues for live music or, if they worked within union establishments, they remained second-class citizens within their union. It seems odd that rock 'n' roll, the roots of which lie in the American working class (black and white), would be shunned by the labor union that represents the interests of working musicians. . . .

Rock 'n' roll, America's most popular music, emerged as far back as the early 1940s, yet there was no mention of any of its permutations in the AFL's newspaper until nearly twenty-five years later.[5] The working-class forms of music that predated rock 'n' roll, including blues, rhythm and blues, and hillbilly (country), were all more or less dismissed by the leadership of the AFM and famous rank-and-file members who were by and large jazz and classical musicians. If one were to use the articles from the *International Musician* as a guide to what was happening in the music industry between 1940 and 1970, it would seem as if there were no such thing as rock 'n' roll in America or anywhere else. Even as rock 'n' roll records were racing up the *Billboard* singles charts as early as 1953—to say nothing of urban rhythm and blues records that topped the charts almost a decade earlier, there was virtually no recognition of the "new" music by the musicians' union. On the other hand, many famous jazz and classical musicians, conductors, composers, bandleaders, and arrangers graced the cover of the union's monthly newspaper over the same years (1947–69), including Louis Armstrong, Jascha Heifetz, Miles Davis, Zubin Mehta, Paul Whiteman, Duke Ellington, Gene Krupa, Leonard Bernstein, Dizzy Gillespie, and Aaron Copeland, to name but a few. Bernstein, Mehta, Gillespie, and Whiteman were all on the cover of *International Musician* in 1968 alone, fully one-third of all the issues in that year.

Lengthy articles were dedicated to whomever the AFM placed on the cover. Columns were devoted to reporting on the union's business affairs, national and local labor issues in American politics, sections about where the most popular jazz and classical musicians were playing, and styles and techniques in the jazz and classical idioms. Rock 'n' roll, on the other hand, did not get so much as a whisper, in spite of all the record-breaking sales figures for singles and albums in the emerging global marketplace. Other people working in the music industry had already heard the news. As early as 1953, the first year a rock 'n' roll single made it onto the charts of *Billboard* and *Cashbox* magazines, it was clear to the managers of independent record labels and their distributors that the music of the American working class was here to stay. Indeed, it already had a rich history in American culture.[6]

However, while the editors and writers for the *International Musician* ignored rock music in their own articles and columns, the companies who paid for ad space in their paper did not. There are numerous advertisements for electric guitars, the emblematic instrument of rock 'n' roll, inside the covers of the *International Musician*, starting as early as the mid-1950s. Beginning in the early 1960s, guitar manufacturers like Fender and Gibson were specifically targeting younger, "hipper" rock musicians with their advertisements for both electric guitars and state-of-the-art amplifiers that could, according to the ads, make it possible to play "really loud." Their ads also included catchy phrases like "freaked out sound," clearly aimed at rock musicians. In one example from 1968, Fender placed an ad in the *International Musician* with a picture of Jimi Hendrix playing the latest Stratocaster model of electric guitar, which was, and remains, the most popular guitar used by rock musicians.[7] By 1968, Hendrix was already an icon for up-and-coming rock guitarists, and Fender capitalized upon that as much as possible, since they knew that no honest musician or music critic could deny the profound and immediate impact that Hendrix had on American music and popular culture in general. Yet the musicians' union's own newspaper staff never formally acknowledged the contributions of Hendrix, arguably one of the greatest guitar virtuosos, in any of its own feature articles.

Clearly, the guitar companies were aware that rock 'n' roll musicians were reading the *International Musician*; otherwise, why would they place their advertisements there? It is safe to assume that at least some AFM members who received the union's newspaper were rock musicians, even though their point of view on music was grossly underrepresented in print. So why, in spite of all the conditions stated above, would the American Federation of Musicians ignore, and in many cases even condemn, rock 'n' roll well into the 1960s? How could the musicians' union ignore the significance of accomplished, talented musicians like Jimi Hendrix and the music they played, the roots of which stem from the American working class?

The answer, while complicated because of many overdetermined factors including the advancement of more sophisticated recording technologies, changes in the structure of the recording industry and changes in U.S. labor law, can be found in the culture of the musicians' union. The culture I examine includes both the leadership circles of the union and the elite rank-and-file members. There are several cultural phenomena that contributed to the marginalization of rock 'n' roll within the AFM. First, the AFM was founded as a craft union, which meant that potential members had to demonstrate certain skills in the craft of musicianship to be considered worthy of inclusion. The exclusion of unskilled workers was a defining feature of all craft unions in the American Federation of Labor (AFL). The AFM used music reading exams as the principal means to restrict membership. Because most rock 'n' roll musicians did not read music, and largely still do not, many of them were barred from membership in the union during the 1950s and 1960s. The exclusion of so-called unskilled musicians by the AFM goes further back into history, as many blues and hillbilly musicians were excluded from membership in the union. This points to a second cultural problem: the roots of rock 'n' roll stem from working-class black and white culture, which has historically been the "Other" of white, bourgeois European discourse. Because the leadership of the AFM consisted mainly of musicians trained in the classical tradition, rock 'n' roll was viewed as something Other than music, namely, entertainment. In fact, the union's leadership considered rock 'n' roll to be a mere fad with no possibility of cultural longevity. Many jazz musicians in the union were equally dismissive of rock 'n' roll, since among many circles of jazz musicians, jazz was referred to as "black classical music." Another important cultural phenomenon that contributed to the exclusion of rock 'n' roll from the AFM's purview was the medium of rock music: the record. Rock 'n' roll was and is essentially a record aesthetic, whereas the AFM has always championed the superiority of live music over recorded music. Lastly, the culture of the musicians' union was also opposed to the culture of rock 'n' roll because it was coded as "deviant" culture. It was considered deviant in the 1950s because it was largely developed by African American subcultures and embraced by rebellious working-class white teenagers, who themselves were coded as delinquents by both the musicians' union and society at large. Rock 'n' roll was recoded as deviant in the 1960s because it was at the core of the counterculture: "sex, drugs, *and* rock 'n' roll." For all of these reasons, the musicians' union kept their distance from rock 'n' roll music for roughly twenty years.

Most rock 'n' roll musicians learned to play music from listening to records rather than from reading music, and many rock 'n' roll performers emphasized "non-musical" aspects like unconventional dancing in their performances, including most infamously, Elvis Presley's gyrating pelvis. Presley's sexuality was seen by the AFM as vulgar entertainment, not musicianship.[8] There were also musical aspects of rock 'n' roll like grainy vocal timbre and infectious grooves, which were not recognized by classically trained musicians.[9] While the AFM leadership considered the rock music of the 1950s a "craze," the roots that stretch further back into rhythm and blues and country were simply dismissed and ignored by the musicians' union on the grounds that working-class musical forms were not sophisticated enough to be seriously considered by its members. Of course, not all members of the AFM were anti–rock 'n' roll, and the split over the problem of rock 'n' roll in the union was part of a larger historical struggle over the identity of the musicians' union that predates rock 'n' roll by several decades.

One of the main conflicts over the identity of the AFM turned on the question concerning the adjective in their identity, namely, *professional* musicians: how is "professional" to be understood? Are professional musicians artists or workers? If both, then under what specific conditions could they be both without conflict? Were they artists who happened to work, or workers who also made art (music)? Which mattered more, working or being an artist? Indeed, how could there not be a conflict, if being an artist meant not compromising your expression under any circumstances, including receiving a paycheck? From this point of view, receiving money for your "art" means that someone else controls your activity and therefore your art becomes a means toward an end, not an end in itself; as a consequence, your artistic integrity is compromised, not "authentic."

These kinds of questions go back to the origin of the musicians' union. In fact, at the very founding of the American Federation of Musicians in 1896, there were disagreements among the rank and file from the previous musicians' "union," the National League of Musicians, over whether they were to remain a professional *association* of "artists" and stay with the League, or become a labor *union* of "workers" by joining the American Federation of Labor under a new name, the American Federation of Musicians. Younger musicians, who typically labored at a second job to supplement their income from performing music, favored joining the American Federation of Labor, whereas older, established musicians who were able to make a living exclusively from playing music—symphony musicians in particular—opposed joining the AFL on the grounds that it would "debase" their art.[10] Musicians who opposed the proposal to be represented by the AFL argued that it would be degrading to associate with people who got their hands dirty for a living. In short, in the attempt to find their identity, the musicians' union struggled with a fundamental, hierarchical duality in American musical culture and western culture more generally: a binary opposition based upon a distinction between music as "cultivated" and oriented toward the "ideal" as well as the problem of morality, and music as "vernacular," oriented toward utility and entertainment and *not* concerned with morality and idealism. This cultural binary was and is overdetermined by another dualism rooted in the division of labor under capitalism that divides mental from manual labor.[11]

The process of "Othering" rock 'n' roll in the musicians' union, which developed along the lines of race and class, has historically been linked to these more general dualistic differences that often exist in conflict within western culture. The tiered dualism in American musical culture has operated much in the same way as Derrida has described the operations of cultural dualisms in western culture more generally. At the center of the binary lies the image of western man, while the nonwestern "Other" is banished to the margins.[12] Of course, Derrida's point was to demonstrate that the center relies on the presence of the marginal "Other" to exist in the first place, since difference is prior to being. In American society, "art" music, or classical music, exists as the center, around which popular music is marginalized. Alas, the center never holds. Not only is it the case that professional musicians struggle within particular cultural institutions in order to either police and maintain musical boundaries *or* to scramble established codes and conventions in musical forms by mixing together disparate elements; musicians also struggle for or against changes in the practices of music within a larger social and cultural context of class struggle. There are several examples from history that demonstrate how musicians decon-

eceived musical forms, as when jazz moved from the margins of the early years of the twentieth century to become popular music os, then "art" music in the 1950s and 1960s. The example I focus on in this book is how once jazz became "art," jazz musicians and classical musicians worked the *other* side of the binary by marginalizing rock 'n' roll music as "Other" and reproducing the division and opposition between art and entertainment. In short, jazz musicians, once seen as a "threat" to cultural stability, became key actors in policing musical boundaries once jazz earned the label "art." By the 1950s, it was the turn of rock 'n' roll musicians to play the part of deconstructing musical forms by disrupting the hierarchy of highbrow and lowbrow culture; in their way stood many famous jazz and classical musicians in the AFM.

In addition to the pleas of "artistic purity" that framed the craft of musicianship as a moral issue, the musicians' union also struggled over the identity markers of race and class. Indeed, the question of whether musicians were artists or workers, which was also a way of saying artists, as opposed to entertainers, has been displaced through race and class. Working-class black and white musicians have struggled against the stigma of "worker/entertainer" both inside and outside of the musicians' union, as their music has been associated with *popular* culture, which is commonly understood as mass entertainment, rather than authentic or pure art. In the pages that follow, I will argue that the struggle between different factions in the AFM over the identity of the musicians' union that followed from the questions of art (music versus entertainment) and craft (trained versus untrained musicians), explains why the American Federation of Musicians refused to recognize rock 'n' roll as a legitimate music and its performers as skilled musicians for two decades, a controversy that culminated in the union's attempt to place an embargo on the British Invasion of rock 'n' roll bands in 1964.

In some ways, the story of rock 'n' roll and the musicians' union is a repetition of the problem posed by ragtime music that drove a wedge between AFM members at the beginning of the twentieth century. The union's leadership condemned ragtime for many of the same reasons they condemned rock 'n' roll. Ragtime music was associated with deviant behavior that was viewed as essentially low class. However, ragtime developed into jazz, and jazz became the nation's most popular music. The musicians' union eventually embraced jazz enthusiastically, unlike rock 'n' roll, which was never embraced with the same enthusiasm. Jazz moved quickly up the ladder of cultural hierarchy; it took less than a generation for the musicians' union to accept jazz musicians in large numbers, and by the late 1920s, jazz was the popular music in both black and white America. Furthermore, academic musicians quickly recognized that jazz had "legitimate" aesthetic value as art, although only after jazz was pressed into a symphonic form.[13] The period of controversy over jazz was relatively short compared to the controversy over rock 'n' roll. Ironically, jazz musicians whose own music was once attacked on moral and aesthetic grounds would in the 1950s join the chorus of public outcry against the so-called depravity of rock 'n' roll music.

For many rank-and-file members as well as established leaders in the musicians' union during the late 1950s and early 1960s, rock 'n' roll was seen to be a passing fad designed by morally suspect record labels and manipulative disc jockeys specifically for impressionable teenagers, whose perceived innocence made them passive consumers and therefore perfect victims for greedy, unscrupulous record label owners. This was the official institutional explanation for why rock 'n' roll was not considered serious music by the union. Even as it was clear to industry insiders writing for the trade magazines like *Billboard, Cashbox,* and *Variety* that rock 'n' roll wasn't going away, the AFM continued to look down on the music as a short-lived fad artificially created by sleazy record label owners.

There were dissenters in the musicians' union regarding the question of rock 'n' roll. Cultural or aesthetic elitism didn't entirely dominate union politics and policy over the years, even during the period of rock 'n' roll between the years 1940–1970. There were important exceptions to cultural elitism in the history of the AFM, including the union's most popular and controversial leader, James Caesar Petrillo, who spent most of his career in the AFM fighting against the aesthetic distinction between "good" and "bad" music and the related division between trained and untrained musicians. Petrillo, who was president of the AFM from 1940 to 1958, was among those in the union bureaucracy that believed that in order for the AFM to maintain its identity as a *labor* union, and in order to be a potent labor union, the issue of taste could not be allowed to influence union policy, because aesthetic preference would inevitably divide the union and break down solidarity. He broke from the cultural elitism of the previous president, Joseph Weber, but it didn't last, because Petrillo's successor, Herman Kenin, embraced a highbrow perspective in AFM politics and policy during the years when rock 'n' roll emerged as the dominant music in America. It is perhaps no coincidence that the AFM had its most success as a labor union under the leadership of Petrillo, which included the greatest victories in the union's history, the recording bans of 1942 and 1946.[14] But a little more than a decade later, the fortunes of the musicians' union changed beginning with Kenin's presidency, when the AFM, like other unions in the United States, entered a period of decline that continues today. There were also leaders of key locals in the AFM who argued against the bifurcation of musicians into "skilled" and "unskilled" musicians, like George Cooper Jr., the president of Local 257 in Nashville, who argued against requiring musicians to pass a music-reading test as the primary basis for joining the union.

The second aesthetic issue that drove a wedge between the AFM and rock music had to do with the essential *medium* of rock 'n' roll music, namely, records. Unlike jazz and classical music, where the performance and the composition are the principal aesthetic objects, in rock 'n' roll music it is the *recording* that is the primary referent.[15] In jazz and classical music it is the performance on the one hand, and the composition on the other, that gives a piece of music its "aura." It is a different matter with rock 'n' roll. The technology of recording or the particular *sound* of a recording is what counts, which means that the instrument or *technology* of recording is an important component of the music and culture of rock 'n' roll. Sound engineers working in the studio play an important role in the construction of the record.[16]

There are two reasons why rock 'n' roll is a record culture. On the one hand, most rock 'n' roll musicians learn how to play music from listening to records rather than by reading music. Records had, to borrow an argument from Walter Benjamin, a democratizing effect on the field of music and the institutions that create musicians, insofar as it is relatively easy for people of lesser means to obtain records and use them to learn how to play music.[17] Compared to the relatively expensive and time-consuming training in formal music schools, records provided a cheap and immediate entry into the realm of music performance. Records opened the doors for droves of working-class kids who yearned to play music. In addition, once the performance of a musical score is on record, everyone can own it, appropriate it, and participate in it. In this way, records deconstruct the "aura" of a piece of music just as the photograph does to the "aura" of the painting, which is the topic that Benjamin discusses in his essay on the significance of mechanical reproduction in the field of art. Benjamin celebrates the demise of the "aura" of a work of art, because it frees us from the shackles of tradition.

For Benjamin, deconstructing the "aura" of a work of art means that *everyone* can participate in the creation and criticism of art. Specifically, it's the working class that benefits from the development of technology in the mechanical reproduction of the work of art. Benjamin's essay is a classic application of the Marxist argument that under particular historical conditions, the forces of production (technology) break down the relations of production (hierarchy and domination) within a given mode of production.

The American Federation of Musicians, however, has been, and in some cases continues to be, opposed to recorded music for two reasons. The first reason is completely understandable: the musicians' union lost tens of thousands of its members to recorded music, both on vinyl and on film. Beginning in the late 1920s, both on radio and in theaters, live musicians, the majority of whom were AFM members, were eliminated in huge numbers and replaced by "canned" music. These were very bad years for the musicians' union, and the massive hemorrhaging of membership they suffered from the improvement of recording technology had a profound impact on their collective identity, for the technology threatened their place in society. Recordings threatened both their ability to make a living and their conception of the role of music in the advancement of culture. From the union's point of view in the 1920s, recordings were a degradation of music (because the quality of the sound was still quite poor), and the displacement of the live musician with the recording would lead—in their view at the time—to the degradation of culture more generally. In short, recording technologies equaled permanent loss of jobs and the end of many careers in music. The musicians' union's fight against recorded music has been, historically, a fight to save jobs. As a strategy to obtain good favor from the public, the union has tried to present their interests as being in sync with the interests of the public at large. Since then, it has been AFM policy to promote live music over canned music in as many public venues as possible, arguing that live music provides an audience with a more complete and more authentic aesthetic experience than does recorded music. These arguments were derived, in part, from traditional European values; namely, live music is better than recorded, period.[18] It was the combination of all of these cultural factors that created the conditions for the marginalization of rock 'n' roll music by the musicians' union.

Lastly, the musicians' union was part of the larger union establishment (the AFL-CIO) that stood opposed to rock 'n' roll music because it became synonymous with the 1960s counterculture. During the era of protest in the 1960s, large segments of the white working class in America became a largely conservative cultural force, led by its representatives, the labor unions. By the 1960s, many union members had "achieved" the American dream: a house in the suburbs and a semi-middle-class lifestyle. As a result, many union members were alienated from the "radicalism" of the student-led New Left movements, the counterculture "hippies," and the militant Black Power movement. Many union workers didn't identify with the cultural radicalism of the New Left and the Black Power movements, which created the conditions for several conflicts, the most infamous being the violent assault led by construction workers against Vietnam War protesters in New York City in 1970.[19] The image of construction workers in hard hats carrying American flags and beating nonviolent demonstrators who opposed the war in Vietnam is emblematic of how some labor unions joined the conservative establishment. In popular culture, the Archie Bunker character on the popular television sitcom *All in the Family* came to be the icon for the culturally conservative white, working-class man in America. This broad context of conflict between the labor movement and the counterculture was foreshadowed by the controversy over the AFM's attempt to prevent the Beatles from touring the United States, a controversy that developed into a nationwide scandal, as legions of Beatles fans entered a very public fight against the musicians' union and its president, Herman Kenin.

The cultural reasons for why the AFM excluded rock 'n' roll from its collective identity, however, is not the only interesting issue at hand, because rock 'n' roll would eventually turn the entire structure of the music recording industry upside down. The explosion of rock 'n' roll in the 1950s restructured the recording industry in profound ways that eventually displaced the American Federation of Musicians as a major player inside the core of the music recording industry. The union itself is partly to blame for its own displacement precisely because it ignored rock 'n' roll for so long and neglected to aggressively organize its musicians. The musicians' union was once one of the most powerful labor unions in America, able to demand and obtain significant concessions from the corporations that controlled the music industry. The AFM was also a major player in national politics between the late 1930s and the late 1950s, and along with other powerful unions, it shared the space at the apex of the American economy with the dominant corporations, although as junior partners in the booming war and postwar economies.

Unfortunately, however, like other unions that were once central players in the American economy — the United Auto Workers, the United Mine Workers, and the United Steel Workers, to name a few — the AFM has, since the 1960s, lost much of its influence, especially in the recording industry. The AFM was at one time powerful enough to successfully execute a general strike that crippled the entire recording industry. Today, after decades of structural realignment in the industry, the musicians' union has lost influence and control over a significant share of the market for recorded music in America, and no longer has the means to organize a strike of any magnitude upon the recording industry. The core of the active members in the musicians' union are jazz and classical musicians, the same constituency as seventy years ago, but today jazz and classical music together are but 5 percent of the market for recorded music. Twice in the 1940s, the AFM was able to pull its members out of recording studios all across the states, conduct successful long-term strikes, and win concessions from the corporations that owned the major record labels. Beginning in the late 1950s and continuing throughout the 1960s, the years when rock 'n' roll became dominant, the major record labels developed a pattern of outsourcing the production of records to "independent" record labels that served as a kind of non-union subcontractor in the recording industry. Most of the non-union labels from that era recorded rock 'n' roll music almost exclusively, the same music that the AFM considered a fad in the 1950s. Of course, in retrospect we know that it was not a fad and that rock 'n' roll, and the music that has developed out of it, including hip-hop, totally dominated the market for records in the 1950s and has ever since. Today the multinational corporations that control the music recording industry do so through a monopoly on *distribution*; production matters little in the grand scheme of things, and the independent labels remain mostly non-union shops. The outsourcing of the production of rock 'n' roll records by the major record labels that began in the 1960s eventually became the norm for the entire music recording industry, and the effects on the musicians' union has been devastating.[20]

A strike in the recording industry by the musicians' union today would be almost meaningless, since so much of the production of records takes place in non-union shops by musicians that are most likely *not* members of the AFM. Even if those musicians are members of the union, their membership is largely the work of inertia; they are far from being active members in the union. The relative impotence of the musicians' union in the recording industry today means that the American Federation of Musicians acts more like an organization that provides services, managing pension funds and health insurance plans for its *existing* members, rather than a labor union; a labor union, by definition, is an organization that focuses on organizing *new* members and obtaining wage increases and better working conditions for its members by conducting strikes and contract campaigns designed to extract concessions from employers. In short, the AFM has shared the fate of the rest of the labor movement, as labor unions across various industries have lost their ability to flex their muscles and get results that they once could before the "great U-turn" in the economy in the late 1960s.[21]

Organized labor in America has often acted against its own interests, especially over issues about the identity of its membership as well as the identity of potential members, workers who fit the definition of their bargaining unit but are yet unorganized. Typically, in American unions and the working class generally, the struggle over collective identity—a struggle with a violent past—takes place along the lines of class (which is displaced through craft and skill), race, and gender. Racism and sexism among the rank and file of labor unions has severely damaged organized labor in the United States, problems which have only recently been addressed by the AFL-CIO.[22] In addition to the problems of racism and sexism inside the house of labor, splits within the U.S. working class have occurred between skilled and unskilled workers or between what labor historians have referred to as the split between the "labor aristocracy," which consists of skilled workers in the craft unions, and unorganized, unskilled industrial workers, who historically have been neglected by the leadership of the craft unions.

The concept of a labor aristocracy was coined by Lenin, who argued that the proletariat in the First World benefits from the hyper-exploitation of impoverished workers in the developing countries on the periphery of the world economy. Labor historians have modified Lenin's concept in order to apply it to the formation of the working class within the borders of the United States. For example, many of the older craft-based unions of the American Federation of Labor (AFL) never organized unskilled workers as a matter of *principle*. Since its inception in 1886, it was an organizing strategy of the AFL to focus specifically on craft workers, which by definition excluded millions of unskilled workers. These unskilled workers were finally organized by the industrial unions of the Congress of Industrial Organizations beginning in the 1930s after failed attempts by the International Workers of the World (IWW) in the first decade of the twentieth century.[23]

The situation of the American Federation of Musicians in the history of American labor unions is a complicated one. Like most AFL craft unions in the early years of the post-bellum labor movement, the AFM often excluded working musicians from membership on the basis of race, gender, and "skill" (through which class division is displaced). Gender was a particularly conspicuous marker, since most AFM locals barred women from membership altogether. In the economy as a whole, in 1900 fewer than 3 percent of women workers were members of unions, compared to 20 percent for men. Most women who worked in the music industry at that time worked as piano teachers in grade schools. Very few women musicians performed in commercial venues on a professional basis at the turn of the century.

The class dimension of the identity of the musicians' union was of course *overdetermined* by the first two factors, especially race.[24] In fact, I will make the case that the identity conflict over craft in the musicians' union concerning the question of rock 'n' roll was at times largely a class issue that was displaced through race.[25] In other words, the discourse of hierarchical duality between highbrow and lowbrow culture was sometimes displaced when the issue was supposedly over the craft, or the training of a musician. "Trained" musician was code for musicians, usually "white," who played in the European classical idioms and who were able to read music. As stated above, the musicians' union considered the ability to read music an essential aspect to the craft of musicianship, but this was also a veil, or displacement of sorts, since many other genres of music do not rely so heavily on the graphic representation of music in notational form as does the classical tradition of European bourgeois music. This combination of cultural markers was set against folk music as a way to "Other" American folk music and excluded large numbers of rural, working-class musicians, black and white, from the AFM.

In other instances, the term *trained* was explicitly used as code for "white" musicians, and these divisions were used to justify the institutionalized segregation in the AFM that lasted for several decades. The AFM, like most AFL unions, has a particularly poor record of race relations.[26] On the other hand, when black musicians, particularly jazz musicians who were recognized by the union as adequately trained and skilled, spoke disparagingly about other musicians, then skill was a *class* marker, and again it was a way to mask or displace the discourse of hierarchical duality of high and low culture. Cultural divisions turned on both race and class, especially in the case of bebop musicians who went on the attack against rhythm and blues and rock 'n' roll.

When rock 'n' roll upended the structure of the music industry, the musicians' union circled its wagons around its core members, the jazz and classical musicians, and clung to a withering New Deal pact between labor, capital, and the government. Rather than organize rock 'n' roll musicians and respond to the changing structure of the recording industry with new organizing strategies, the AFM chose to maintain its stronghold among its traditional base of jazz and classical musicians and hope that the major record labels would continue to renew favorable labor contracts. Their strategy ultimately proved unsustainable because the major record labels have outsourced production to record labels that do not hold a labor contract with the union.

The destructiveness of cultural hierarchy that plagued the musicians' union had far-reaching effects for the entire labor movement because not only did cultural imperialism sabotage solidarity in the musicians' union, it also sabotaged what could have been the most radical achievement of the musicians' union: the historic compromise between the AFM and the major record labels that followed the recording ban of 1942. When Decca Records agreed to terms set by the AFM in 1943, the musicians' union won one of the most significant confrontations between labor and capital in the twentieth century. By winning the strike, the AFM was able to compel record companies to create a fund to be used to compensate union musicians who had lost their jobs as a result of being replaced by records at radio stations and jukeboxes in live venues like taverns. The 1943 recording contract between the AFM and the record companies foreshadowed the very real historical possibility that the working class could have more for less: more material comforts, more material goods, more free time, *and* less work. The record companies were making enough money that they could pay the musicians who made the records *and* support musicians who did not make records, who were essentially "idle," performing occasional concerts that were free to the public. It was a truly radical achievement, and in the context of the epic struggle of labor unions to shorten working hours and push up wages, it provided a concrete example of what possibilities are waiting for us on the horizon of a post-scarcity social formation.

Unfortunately, the union itself sabotaged the historic achievement of the 1943 labor agreement. The turn against rock 'n' roll music meant that solidarity among musicians would wither, and record companies would exploit the reserve army of labor that existed among the growing pool of un-organized, non-union, working-class rock 'n' roll musicians. If the union had organized rock 'n' roll musicians rather than banish them to the margins of the industry in the early years of rock 'n' roll, the union might have been able to continue to increase its pressure on record companies and continue to set the example for the entire labor movement in the drive to realize labor's quest for more leisure time and a higher standard of living. How ironic, too, that rock 'n' roll music, which contains as its raison d'être the unequivocal affirmation of leisure and the rejection of delayed gratification, would be neglected by a labor union.

ONE. Solidarity Forever?

The Musicians' Union Responds to Records and Radio

I'm proud to be a union man.
— NEIL YOUNG

In June 1942, the musicians' union sent the following letter to record company executives in the United States and Canada:

Gentlemen:

Your license from the American Federation of Musicians for the employment of its members in the making of musical recordings will expire on July 31, 1942, and will not be renewed. From August 1, 1942, the American Federation of Musicians will not play or contract for any other forms of mechanical reproductions of music.

Very Truly Yours,
James C. Petrillo,
President, American Federation of Musicians[1]

"ALL RECORDING STOPS TODAY!" Those words ran across the front page of *DownBeat* magazine on August 1, 1942. The AFM was officially on strike against the recording industry. Session musicians and recording artists/instrumentalists all across the states walked out of recording studios and stayed out for the better part of a year. The timing of the strike was particularly significant because musicians walked off the job in spite of the no-strike pledge made by the American Federation of Labor (AFL) and the Congress of Industrial Organizations (CIO) on behalf of all union workers while the United States was at war. The musicians remained on strike in spite of numerous demands made by President Roosevelt that they return to work in the name of "national security" and "morale." The strike of 1942 was one of the most important events in the history of the American labor movement, including such notable events as the wave of strikes in 1919, the great sit-down strikes conducted by the auto workers in 1937, and the mass strikes among textile workers in the South the same year. The recording ban was significant for the organizational power displayed by the musicians as well as for the widespread implications of their 1944 labor agreement for all workers in all industries who were threatened by management's use of technology to wrest control of the shop floor from skilled workers and to replace workers altogether, as labor-saving technology steadily and dramatically reduced the demand for labor in all areas of production.

As stated above, the main issue for the AFM during the recording ban was the loss of jobs due to technological developments in music recording technology. Tens of thousands of musicians lost their jobs in vaudeville theatres, silent movie houses and radio stations as a result of the improvement of sound recording and playback technologies that allowed radio stations to drastically cut back on their staff of live musicians, while "talkie" movies eliminated musicians from movie houses altogether. The invention of the Vitaphone by Western Electric in the 1920s made it possible to sync the sound on a sixteen-inch disc recording with images on film, allowing movie theater operators to play records to accompany films rather than use a pit orchestra, as was common practice prior to the Vitaphone.[2] Seltzer estimates that by 1934 the application of the Vitaphone had displaced roughly 22,000 musicians, which accounted for almost a quarter of all the musicians in the United States who were employed exclusively (full-time) as musicians.[3] Coin-operated jukeboxes also took their toll on the musicians' union. Consumer demand for records in jukeboxes grew steadily as technologies improved the sound quality in the late 1930s and 1940s. Jukeboxes provided inexpensive pleasures for working-class "hepcats" looking for places to dance to their favorite swing tunes. By the early 1940s, some 6,000 jukebox operators had roughly 400,000 jukeboxes in operation in the United States. The AFM estimated that roughly 8,000 of their members lost their jobs as a result of the introduction of jukeboxes in taverns and hotels.[4] The demand for records also materialized in the rapid growth of home-use machines, as the number of record players manufactured for home rather than commercial application grew to 3.4 million by 1947.[5]

The story of the recording ban in 1942 begins a few years before, at the AFM convention of 1937 in Louisville, Kentucky. It was there that rank-and-file musicians turned up the heat on their leadership in the AFM to do something about the hemorrhaging of job losses. At the musicians' union's annual convention in 1937, delegates from numerous locals began pressing President Joseph Weber to do something more aggressive about the problem of the application of sound recording technologies. Although demand for musicians remained strong in the main media centers of the country, in smaller market areas professional musicians' livelihoods were devastated by the application of the new technologies. For instance, membership in the New York (local 802) and Los Angeles (local 47–767) branches was growing as a result of the emerging recording industry that increased demand for session musicians in recording studios, but for most locals across the country, membership was down dramatically. According to Kraft, by 1936 smaller market locals like Minneapolis (local 30–73) and Atlanta (local 148–462) were half the size they were in 1928, and most other locals had membership declines of 20 to 35 percent.[6] Weber had estimated that more than 13,000 members of the AFM were on public relief.[7] The drastic drop in demand for musicians meant stiff competition between musicians for waged work. In 1929, for every job opening in a symphony orchestra, more than twenty musicians applied, whereas just three years earlier, symphony managers had struggled to fill such positions.[8] Of course, the Great Depression accounted for the rise in unemployment among musicians, but the loss of jobs in movie theaters at the hands of movies with sound predated the Depression by a few years. While Weber realized the magnitude of the problem, he was slow to move toward doing something about it, angering many rank-and-file members, and this eventually led to his removal from office.

The AFM's first response to the commercial use of mechanical recordings in the late 1920s was to conduct a public relations campaign that touted the superior quality of live music over recorded music. Weber made this argument on the grounds that records simply sounded bad. He did not foresee the radical improvements made possible by electronic recording technology. For the consumer of music looking for quality entertainment, it was argued by the AFM leadership that there was no doubting the priority of live music to records.

The AFM's public relations strategy had two other dimensions. First, it was claimed that the cultural experience of live music was a far more enriching and "uplifting" experience than listening to "canned" music. The strategic move here was to appeal to high-culture sensibilities; the desire among music listeners to ascend the cultural status ladder was targeted as a way to try to boost consumer demand for live music. This particular strategy was part of the union's history of positioning itself as a taste-making institution, "educating" the "masses" on matters of music as art. Here, Weber was arguing a case for what Walter Benjamin refers to as the cultural significance of the "aura," or the presence and authenticity of the piece of music that follows from the specificity of time and place of the live music performance.[9] However, in opposition to the position taken by cultural theorists like Benjamin, Weber took the position that maintaining the "aura" of live music is an important cornerstone in the protection and advancement of "culture." He made this case in two ways: on the one hand, he argued that the public would benefit from the experience of listening to live music—jazz and classical music in particular. It was argued that live performances of music were educational because they allowed people who lacked cultural capital to develop the skills necessary to understand and adequately experience "true" art. Once educated, music consumers would be able to begin the accumulation of cultural capital and climb the status ladder. Recorded music, on the other hand, was portrayed by Weber and the union's leadership as a simulacrum, lacking aesthetic value, a poor substitute for the real thing. The mechanical reproduction of the work of music was a "perversion, which constituted a fatal blow to musical culture," the union insisted.[10]

Second, the AFM argued that it was in the national interest to protect musicians from the threat of recorded music. It was claimed that if records reduce the demand for live music and if, consequently, potentially talented musicians find that they cannot make a living playing music because there is no demand for their labor, then music with true aesthetic value ceases to exist, which in turn leads to the decline of high art and the degradation of civilization into moral depravity. It was on these grounds that Weber argued that America could not afford to allow its most promising musicians to fail. He appealed to nationalism and the desire for upward mobility. True patriots, according to Weber, would never allow the culture of their nation to degenerate, and individuals who desire access to the discourse of the middle and/or upper class must first learn how to recognize authentic art. Knowing the difference between "art" and "entertainment" is a principal ritual of upward mobility in the American class structure. The musicians' union's first strategy to save their jobs was to appeal to that ritual tradition.

It is important to note that Weber didn't believe that it was realistic or desirable to resist the advancement of sound recording technology, which he saw as inevitable. Rather, for Weber, the musicians, like all workers, had to find ways to adapt to the new technologies. "The development of machinery cannot be hindered," argued Weber in 1930. "There is no force on earth—or ever will be—able to do this."[11] The task was to negotiate an arrangement with record companies that could be beneficial to both labor and capital. The question was: which strategy should the union pursue, a strike or some other means? Weber sought to appeal to the public interest as a means to gain leverage in AFM negotiations with employers rather than use the threat of strike. Rather than risk the perceived possibility that union members would simply be fired if they went on strike, Weber hoped to build up public support for the AFM in the hope that public pressure would bring record companies to the bargaining table.

Weber's position was in stark contrast to James Petrillo, who at that time was president of Local 10 in Chicago but would eventually replace Weber as AFM president. Petrillo was calling for a ban on recording as a means to create a bargaining chip with the record companies. Petrillo and his circle in Chicago felt that it was absurd for one group of union members to put another group out of work, which was essentially the case with session musicians working in recording studios who were making it possible to eliminate the jobs of other musicians who played either on radio or in live venues like taverns, hotels, and movie houses. Weber didn't have the confidence that Petrillo had, since he was concerned that the union might be defeated if they went on strike and that defeat would end in disaster. Accordingly, Weber's strategy was to pursue a publicity campaign on behalf of the superiority of live music, because he thought consumers of music would agree that live music was better than canned music. Ultimately, Weber and other leaders in the musicians' union believed that in the long run there wouldn't be any conflict between records and live music, since they be-lieved that records would be a passing fad, more a curiosity for hobby en-thusiasts than legitimate entertainment. Weber was not alone in this be-lief. Many professional musicians—with the exception of Petrillo and his circle—believed records were a temporary craze. For example, members of the Los Angeles Theater Organists' Club believed that mechanical music would never be a viable money-making enterprise, claiming that owners of theaters that played "talkie" movies would "lose their shirts in this latest folly." Organist Gaylord Carter said, "We thought it [talkies] was just a fad . . . we all thought it would pass."[12]

In late 1929, the AFM embarked on an advertising campaign to boost de-mand for live music, a campaign that cost them close to $1 million. Rather than take control of the issue at the point of production via a strike, as Petrillo had already done in Chicago, Weber's plan was to give consumers the power to save live music. Indeed, Weber claimed that he would "spare no expense" in his appeal to consumers. Most of the money was spent on advertising space in 798 newspapers and 24 magazines. In the ads, the AFM warned about the impending doom associated with the "debasement" of art if live music were to fall victim to recorded music. The AFM also ap-pealed to the federal government to save live music, in order to preserve a legitimate, robust national culture. Writing to the Federal Radio Com-mission in 1929, the union argued that "the invasion of the radio field by canned music is destroying the advancement of art at its base by depriving musicians of the necessary means of livelihood."[13] It seemed at first that the ad campaign was gaining momentum since many of the newspapers that ran the ads also supported the AFM with editorials that argued for the superior cultural value of live music. Part of the advertising campaign in-volved the establishment of the Music Defense League, an organization created by the AFM for the public. The union printed membership coupons inside their ads so that anyone concerned with saving live music could clip the coupon from the ad, sign it, mail it to the union, and become mem-bers of the League. In all, the union collected over 3 million membership coupons, which led Weber to argue that he had made the right choice in rejecting the plan to organize a general strike on the recording industry.

Meanwhile in Chicago, Petrillo began to make it public that the Chicago local would pursue a recording ban in the city if necessary. On New Year's Eve in 1931, Petrillo threatened to call a strike on local radio stations, which led to a minor victory as radio stations agreed to terms with the local before a strike materialized. In 1935, Petrillo was able to get radio stations in Chicago to agree to keep full staff orchestras on hand, as well as to agree to destroy some records after just one use. In addition to music, the other main use of records on radio was advertising; most radio stations used recorded "transcriptions," which were recorded commercials that often used music. Petrillo was able to get Chicago stations to use these recordings one time only, discarding them after one airplay. This was Petrillo's first attempt to find a way to regulate the use of records on radio. In 1936, Petrillo also led a nationwide legal campaign by the AFM, which brought a series of lawsuits that attempted to establish the rights of musicians to restrict the use of commercial recordings to "in-house use only," a legal strategy that mirrored the successful regulation of the use of records in Chicago.[14]

Petrillo's reputation for not backing down from fights made him a popular figure in the union. He always considered himself a union man first and a musician second. He did play the trumpet, but he described himself as a mediocre musician who was better suited to negotiating labor contracts with employers than playing trumpet. Petrillo had also been a saloon owner and a cigar stand owner, which gave him a familiarity with the harshness of street life, a skill set that he used effectively in his negotiations with management in the broadcasting and recording industries.

By the mid-1930s, in spite of the positive response to the Music Defense League, the AFM lost an additional 4,100 jobs nationwide since the beginning of the ad campaign for saving live music.[15] The campaign did relatively little to stem the tide of massive job losses. As a result, Petrillo's circle in the union was attracting more attention and more followers. In 1937, Petrillo had successfully led a recording ban in Chicago, which contributed to a growing militancy among the rank-and-file at the union's 1937 convention, forcing Weber to take a more militant stand. Many proposals for action were considered at the convention, ranging from striking radio and/or the record companies, to enforcing minimum size limits for staff orchestras at radio stations, a system that would impose a tariff on affiliate stations that carried network shows, to the creation of a royalty system for the union that was based on record sales. Weber's tenure as union president was becoming tenuous as early as 1934, when the union lost 50,000 members and $60,000 of annual revenue as a result of declining membership, which was down to around 100,000. Weber did take a more aggressive posture at the convention by hinting he would be willing to consider using the strike. He was pushed in that direction because more and more locals like Local 174 in New Orleans were backing Petrillo's call for an industry-wide recording ban. Weber moved cautiously by exploring the strike option in radio before a strike on the recording industry. He argued that if radio stations did not maintain staff orchestras, the AFM should strike all of radio. But a ban on recording was already underway in other locals besides Chicago, including Local 802 in New York. Both locals required their members not to take recording engagements in their jurisdictions, a sign that Weber was beginning to lose control of the international.

To Weber's credit, in the last days of his presidency he reached out to the other organization struggling to get recognition from the radio broadcast industry, the American Society of Composers, Authors and Publishers (ASCAP), as the AFM prepared for a conflict with the National Association of Broadcasters (NAB), which represented the interests of radio stations. Weber held AFM strategy meetings in the offices of ASCAP in New York City to show NAB that the AFM and ASCAP were united. ASCAP had been struggling with radio companies who refused to recognize the performance rights of ASCAP members in the use of music by radio station broadcasts. Before their conflict with NAB, ASCAP won a series of legal battles with other music users, including owners of hotels, restaurants, cabarets, and vaudeville and movie theaters. In key court cases, ASCAP was able to demonstrate that these businesses were making profits through the public performance of music copyrighted by members of ASCAP. Therefore, under an interpretation of the Copyright Act of 1909, members of ASCAP established that they had a legal claim to a share of revenues generated by the public performance of their music.[16]

Songwriters, composers, and publishers formed ASCAP in 1914 in response to major structural changes in the music industry that occurred with the emergence of new technologies and the explosion of the entertainment industry. Prior to the improvement of broadcast radio and sound recording technologies, the music industry revolved, in large part, around the sales of sheet music for the piano, which had been the anchor of entertainment in the bourgeois home. When musical entertainment moved from the privacy of the home into public venues like cabarets and hotels, and as radios and record players competed with pianos in the home in the 1930s, sales of sheet music plummeted. According to Ryan: "In the 1920s, songs considered to be 'good sellers' sold 500,000 copies of sheet music compared to 50,000 in the 1930s. So called 'smash hits' often sold 2 million copies in the 1920s compared to 300,000 copies in the 1930s." Radio had been the last industry to recognize performance rights, but eventually ASCAP was able to negotiate an agreement with NAB that obligated radio stations to share revenues generated by the use of music with ASCAP. The agreement secured by ASCAP specified that radio stations would pay a blanket fee for a catalog of songs and music owned by ASCAP members.[17] Their allegiance with the AFM during these years was more than a symbolic gesture, because many of the famous bandleaders of the era were members of both organizations.[18]

Weber retired in 1940 citing reasons having to do with his health. Even if Weber had not retired, Petrillo would have taken over the reins of the union. He was more popular among the rank and file than Weber because he had made a reputation for himself as an effective and aggressive labor leader in Chicago and had led a successful strike. Petrillo exposed the weakness in Weber's strategy that depended on consumers and the federal government to solve the union's problem, rather than rely on the union itself through the use of the strike. Petrillo understood that the union had to take its agency back from consumers and the government and develop a new strategy for action. Only the union itself—by focusing on the point of production as the means to gain leverage—could launch a sustainable response to the problem of mechanization and job losses. That meant going to the source of the problem, the recording studio. Petrillo's first move after taking office was to pick up where Weber had left off at mounting a strike on radio. He seized upon one of the first opportunities he had, a labor conflict at radio station KTSP in St. Paul, Minnesota.

On June 28, 1940, contract negotiations between the St. Paul local of the AFM and KTSP, an affiliate of the National Broadcasting Company (NBC), reached an impasse when management at the radio station broke off talks with the union. At that time, KTSP was one of 250 affiliates that held labor contracts with the AFM, as thousands of orchestra musicians, most of them union members, were still barely hanging on to full-time employment at radio stations. The issue that caused the breakdown in contract negotiations was the number of musicians on the staff orchestra at KTSP. The St. Paul affiliate, like many network affiliates during the early 1940s, was attempting to "downsize" its staff. The consolidation and reorganization of network radio by the big three—NBC, CBS, and Mutual Broadcasting System (MBS)—in the early 1940s had dramatically reduced demand for flesh-and-blood musicians at radio stations in small markets. At the time when talks between the union and KTSP broke down, the radio station was using network programs from NBC, shows that were produced and performed in places like New York City and then broadcast via station affiliates to more "remote" areas like St. Paul. Industry insiders referred appropriately to these network shows as remotes.[19] Many of these programs included concerts performed by the most popular swing bands of the era, like Duke Ellington, Count Basie, and Benny Goodman.

Prior to the reorganization and consolidation of network radio, musicians all over the country, especially union musicians, were able to find relatively good jobs playing live music for broadcast at smaller market radio stations. Radio in the 1920s was a chaotic patchwork of more than five hundred stations that were sponsored by individuals, various organizations, and private companies, and even as late as 1934 there were still several "independent" radio stations that were content with producing and broadcasting their own regional and local programs. The enormous popularity of radio created a sustained demand for musicians, even as the country struggled to get through the Great Depression, because radio provided free entertainment to its listeners.

The 1930s and early 1940s was the era of swing music, which was all the rage in the after-hours hot spots and in the homes of swing fanatics who had radio sets. By 1940 there were some 15 million radio sets in American homes, as listeners tuned in to hear the big band swing concerts aired every evening. The record industry, which at this time was still in competition with radio, was reeling from the Depression as people preferred radio to records. At the time, records could not adequately reproduce the sound or experience of live music.[20] The issue for record producers was to try, as much as possible, to accurately re-create the experience of live music on a record. Record companies were experimenting with electronic recording technology to improve the quality of recorded sound, but it wouldn't be until after World War II, when the Allies seized magnetic tape recording technology developed by the German military, that the recording industry would be able to dramatically increase the quality of sound recording. Consequently, the AFM enjoyed a relatively tight labor market for live music, despite the bad economic times of the Depression.

Corporate consolidation and monopolization of the airwaves challenged the power of the AFM. By the early 1940s, expansion of remote broadcasts threatened to displace thousands of musicians all across America.[21] On the other hand, network radio was a boon to the superstar musicians working in the major media centers, especially New York and Los Angeles. Bandleaders like Duke Ellington, Count Basie, Chick Webb, Woody Herman, Tommy Dorsey, Paul Whiteman, and Benny Goodman all benefited enormously from the network broadcasts of their shows. However, for the staff orchestras at radio stations in smaller markets, network programming was a disaster, because it threatened to render them superfluous. Network affiliates like KTSP could save money by broadcasting remotes, because the remote programs allowed them to use their own staff orchestras much less frequently. Remotes also brought local affiliates a larger audience.

Frustrated by negotiations with management, and concerned that their members would soon be out of work, the St. Paul local asked Petrillo to intervene. He agreed. His strategy was to pull the plug on network broadcasts of popular, big name concerts if KTSP refused to retain its staff orchestra and agree to the remaining contract demands of the local. Petrillo gave KTSP twenty-four hours to agree to the union's demands or else he would halt the remotes by calling out the big name bandleaders and their orchestras and asking them to stop playing for remote broadcast. When KTSP refused, Petrillo made good on his word, and on the following day he called for ten bands, including Tommy Dorsey, Gene Krupa, and Woody Herman, to stop playing at NBC. So, on June 29, 1940, when radio listeners in several small market areas like St. Paul tuned in to NBC, they found that their favorite remotes were not on the air that evening. Petrillo was willing to gamble that the networks—NBC in this case, but there would be more cases involving the other networks, especially CBS—would put pressure on their affiliates to capitulate to the union because the networks depended on the popularity of the remotes, especially the big band shows, for lucrative advertising contracts. Petrillo's gamble paid off when the strike on remotes succeeded in squeezing the network and the affiliate. Eventually, NBC persuaded its St. Paul affiliate to agree to the union's demands. All the jobs in the staff orchestra at KTSP were saved.

In July, a CBS affiliate in Richmond, Virginia, station WRVA, attempted to lower the wages of its staff orchestra. When the Richmond local was unable to negotiate a contract that would satisfy its members, they, too, asked for Petrillo's assistance. Petrillo intervened in the same manner and with the same strategy he used with success in the KTSP case. Petrillo ordered thirty traveling bands to halt performances for remote broadcasts on both CBS and MBS. Just as Petrillo had hoped, CBS pressured their Richmond affiliate to sack its plan to trim wages. Over the next few years, Petrillo and the AFM waged similar struggles in Scranton, Nashville, Akron, and a few other cities, denying those affiliates the music of big bands, including Duke Ellington, Lawrence Welk, and Artie Shaw, until they agreed to union demands.[22] It was a dramatic show of solidarity among the rank-and-file members of the AFM, especially on the part of the celebrity bandleaders that they were able to secure a series of victories over recalcitrant management. The famous bandleaders had much more to lose than the relatively unknown musicians who played in staff orchestras at small market radio stations, but nonetheless they were willing to stick their necks out. Encouraged by the successful strike against the broadcasting industry, Petrillo would soon call for a general strike on the recording industry, but first he had to organize instrumental soloists into the AFM.

Instrumental soloists, including the famous violinist Jascha Heifetz, were, by and large, members of a competing union, the American Guild of Musical Artists. The AGMA was formed in 1936, and it focused mainly on organizing opera singers, but the union also encouraged instrumental soloists who played in operas and symphonies to join, creating competition with the AFM. Petrillo realized that if the AFM were to have any chance at winning a general strike on the recording industry, the instrumental soloists would have to be on board. So in August 1940, Petrillo took action by forbidding AFM members to play any shows with soloists who were not members of the AFM. He gave all instrumental soloists until Labor Day to join the AFM, or they would be unable to perform, since nearly all the symphonies and orchestras were already organized by the AFM. The only exception was the Boston Symphony Orchestra, and it was only a matter of days before their musicians would join the AFM. The dispute between the two unions received national attention, since many of the soloists that Petrillo was attempting to organize were household names. In fact, Petrillo was ridiculed when he asked, rhetorically: "Since when is there any difference between Heifetz playing a fiddle and the fiddler in the tavern? They're both musicians."[23] Of course Petrillo knew the difference, but it was a smart rhetorical move, because he understood that the union was less likely to win a general strike if it could not bridge the high/low divide and promote solidarity among all members regardless of "talent" or fame. Unlike Joseph Weber, Petrillo never took the highbrow line, refusing to try to legitimate the musicians' union by positioning the AFM as a gatekeeper of American highbrow culture.

The representatives of the AFM, along with the other powerhouse unions of the time, like the United Auto Workers, the United Mine Workers, and the longshoremen's union, were riding the crest of rank-and-file militancy, which began in the early 1930s and would take them well beyond the end of World War II. The United States was racked by labor conflicts from coast to coast, including sit-down strikes, wildcat strikes, sick outs, and work stoppages.[24] Rank-and-file militancy was so strong that the federal government scrambled to find measures to contain it, beginning with the National Labor Relations Act, also known as the Wagner Act, which was passed in 1935. The NLRA was designed to bring labor into the fold of capital accumulation by officially recognizing the institutionalization of unions, and by creating stability for investment and growth by giving labor a "voice" in the structure of government and corporate control over the economy. But workers could not be easily appeased and controlled, even if they were invited to the table as "junior partners" in the planning of the economy. When the United States entered the war in 1941, President Roosevelt asked for, and received, a no-strike pledge for the duration of the war from the AFL and the CIO. Roosevelt had hoped he could count on labor's cooperation because steady production schedules at full capacity were the key to winning the war, but he was unable to secure the cooperation of stubborn workers in industrial unions who refused to abide by the pledge. The AFM was one of the few craft unions that also violated the no-strike pledge.

Two years after the strike on remote broadcasts and a year into the war, Petrillo called an industrywide recording ban, pulling all AFM members out of all recording sessions, including media centers like Los Angeles and New York. For more than a year, no instrumental recordings were made in the United States.[25] This time the issue for the musicians' union was the use of records by radio stations and in jukeboxes at places like bars and hotels that previously used live musicians. The musicians' strategy was to conduct a secondary strike. The aim of the recording ban was to save union jobs at radio stations and taverns. Recording technology was improving with the invention of electronic recording processes, and more and more radio stations, taverns, and hotels were playing records as a means to trim their budgets.[26] Management voices in the movie houses and radio stations were explicit in their declarations that the new sound technology was designed to cut back on labor costs.

In 1941, the AFM held its annual convention in Dallas, and delegates urged Petrillo to take action. They demanded that the union "draw the line" against its real enemy, namely, the unrestricted practice of recording and the unregulated use of records. Petrillo agreed, and at the annual convention in June of the following year, Petrillo declared that the union would no longer "play at their own funeral." A strike on recording was called, and Petrillo's speech was received with vigorous cheers and applause from the audience of delegates. Petrillo sent out his letter to the major record labels and transcriptions companies announcing the beginning of the recording ban.

The aim of the strike was not to eliminate the use of records. Petrillo was not that naïve, despite the relentless editorials that portrayed him as a Luddite. Attacks against the union came from the right and the left. The *New York Times* wrote: "Mr. Petrillo is grossly mistaken, for example, when he assumes that if he forbids radio stations and restaurants from using records they will have to use orchestras and bands." On the contrary, the *Times* argued that the recording ban would only end up creating an environment of less music in those venues. Even the left-leaning *Nation* attacked the AFM in a rather nasty editorial. "Chances are," argued the editors, "that [audiences] will continue to choose first-rate recordings in preference to second or third-rate 'live' music." Regardless of actions taken by the musicians' union, they would not be able to "restore the musician to his pre-jukebox position. Small-time musicians have become as obsolete as the Indian." The *Nation's* editorial, "Mr. Petrillo's Hopeless War," unfairly and inaccurately framed the union's position as a reactionary Luddite perspective. The *Chicago Tribune* also attacked the AFM, arguing that Petrillo wanted to return "the United States back to the days before Thomas A. Edison."[27]

While many in the union opposed the use of the strike, Petrillo believed it was the only way to save jobs, and the strategy was to persuade recording companies, especially the major record labels, to agree to a plan created by the AFM to account for jobs that were lost as a result of the use of records. Going to the source of the problem in the recording studios also dealt a blow to the radio companies who depended on records, because by 1942 the radio and recording industries were no longer in competition. On the contrary, they had merged into gigantic corporate media conglomerates with tentacles reaching into every medium: radio, records, film, publishing, and eventually television.

In spite of the size and scope of their adversary, the musicians' union was able to mount a successful campaign. Petrillo argued that musicians were in a unique position to control the application of technology to their craft, because unlike production workers in factories, management interests depended on the musician to make a record in the first place. The division of labor in the recording industry at that time was unusual: in most other craft production work, engineers working for the interests of management were and still are able to design machines to replace factory floor workers without their consent or knowledge.[28] With the craft of music making it's a different matter altogether. In order to replace a live musician, some other flesh-and-blood musician must do the work to make the recording possible. If musicians who perform the labor of recording refuse, then capital is unable to replace other musicians who perform in live venues.

Petrillo counted upon the solidarity among all union members to wrest some control from the record companies over the use of records. He was banking on the solidarity displayed during the radio broadcasting strikes of 1940, hoping that the cooperative mood would last long enough for the AFM to emerge victorious.

At first, the major record companies held out and refused to negotiate, anticipating that President Roosevelt and the War Labor Board would rule against Petrillo and force the union back to work. They also enjoyed positive press coverage. The news media had already established an anti-union perspective during the great labor upheavals of the 1930s. It was only a matter of time before newspapers began grinding their anti-union axes against Petrillo and the musicians' union. Papers like the *Washington Post* and the *Buffalo News* referred to Petrillo as a "dictator," a "tyrant," and a "czar," making hay out of the irony that his middle name was Caesar. One of the major newspapers from Petrillo's hometown referred to him as "the inflated little nonentity who strong-armed himself into dictatorial power."

The thought of a labor union suggesting that workers have some say in the decisions about the conditions where they work, or the security of their jobs, was never really seriously entertained by the mainstream media, since they sided with management's position that only management has the right to make those kinds of decisions. Editorials never presented a coherent argument that justified their labeling of Petrillo as a tyrant for exercising the union members' rights not to cause their own destruction. Rather, the editorials that attacked Petrillo appealed to knee-jerk jingoism, making the case that a strike during the war was unpatriotic. The NAB financed its own anti-union public relations campaign, paying the New York–based public relations firm Baldwin and Mermey $2 million to smear the AFM. The attack on Petrillo also used the tactic of red-baiting, which was a typical public relations strategy used during most labor disputes. In addition to violating the no-strike pledge, which was allegedly illegal, NAB made the case that because "music plays a vital role in war morale," the United States could not afford to allow the musicians to stay out on strike.[29]

In spite of all the negative press, Petrillo and the musicians' union stood their ground, insisting that union members would not make the very products that were threatening the destruction of their craft. They did make one concession, however, when they agreed to allow limited recording under the Victory Disk Project, created by the army to make records specifically for soldiers fighting overseas. Petrillo allowed records to be made under the v-Disc project as long as the army agreed to destroy the records after the war rather than sell them as surplus. The federal government agreed to the terms, and Petrillo was allowed to sidestep the patriotism issue momentarily, because he allowed union members to make records as part of the overall effort to boost the morale of troops overseas. The move gave Petrillo and the AFM some latitude in the ongoing discussions with, and appearances before, the War Labor Board in 1942 and 1943.

With the patriotism issue somewhat resolved, the major record labels and NAB turned to a legal assault against the AFM, filing an injunction against the musicians' union, claiming the strike created a restraint on trade, thereby violating the Sherman Anti-Trust Act. Before the passage of the National Labor Relations Act, employers embroiled in labor disputes often used the Sherman Anti-Trust Act to leverage court-ordered injunctions against striking workers on the grounds that strikes were unlawful restraints on trade. Ironically, even though the act was written to curb the power of capital, or the power of monopoly on the part of giant corporations, it was more often used against workers than corporate monopolies, since the U.S. legal system as a whole was ideologically opposed to labor's cause until the passage of New Deal legislation in the 1930s.[30] The NAB and the record companies thus waged the battle on two fronts. On the one hand, they attempted to get the judicial branch to rule against the union on the grounds that the strike violated the Sherman Anti-Trust Act. On the other hand, they appealed to the executive branch, asking the Roosevelt administration to bring Petrillo to testify before the War Relations Board and force him to abide by the no-strike pledge forged by the leaders of the AFL and CIO and the Roosevelt administration. While the legality of the recording ban was being argued over in court, Petrillo called musicians out of radio as well, banning remote broadcasts as he had done in 1940. Petrillo planned to match the intensity of NAB and the major record labels step-by-step by calling more musicians out on strike while legal proceedings dealing with the recording ban dragged on in court.

Good news for the union came first in Chicago, where the NAB was pressing their case. Judge John P. Barnes eventually threw the case out of court on the grounds that he had no jurisdiction since it was a labor matter. Barnes ruled that the matter applied to the National Labor Relations Act, not the Sherman Anti-Trust Act. His written account of the issue was a major boost to the union, because it was one of the first times in the twentieth century that companies were foiled in their attempt to use the anti-trust laws, and also because he challenged the argument made by the NAB attorney Thurman Arnold, who attempted to demonstrate that musicians did not face any serious threat of unemployment as the result of the use of records. Judge Barnes flatly denied that records did not threaten musicians' jobs. On the contrary, he argued that the evidence demonstrated the converse, namely, that half of the professional musicians who had second jobs outside the music industry held those second jobs because "they were not able to make a reasonable living in their chosen field." "This is a controversy between masters and servants," wrote Barnes, "a question of whether the servants must make music as the masters direct."[31] Barnes's ruling was a significant victory for the AFM, not only because they beat the anti-trust rap but also because the ruling bought them more precious time to conduct their strike. While the AFM and NAB waged their battle in the courts, Petrillo was called before the War Labor Board, a move that backfired badly for radio and record companies because they underestimated Petrillo's oratory skills. Petrillo's actions were represented by the press and by management public relations groups as the actions of an unreasonable tyrant because he refused to buckle under pressure. Roosevelt himself asked Petrillo to send the musicians back to work, but Petrillo refused, and when Petrillo went before the War Labor Board in July 1943, he denied that the federal government had the authority to force musicians to work, calling it "involuntary servitude." Petrillo was able to improve his public image when he appeared earlier that year to testify before a special congressional committee.

Petrillo was the first labor leader called to testify before Congress, and he made the most of it, capitalizing on his leadership skills and charisma. As various senators peppered Petrillo with questions about the purpose of the strike, he was careful not to answer that the strike was designed to coerce radio and live venues to hire more musicians, because the union could be found guilty of conducting a secondary boycott. Rather, Petrillo argued that the strike was about musicians getting their "fair share" of the profits from the record industry, and he suggested that Congress draft legislation to alter the Copyright Act to create a royalty system for session musicians who work in recording studios, a system that would give them similar copyrights enjoyed by composers and publishers of music. It was a clever move by Petrillo to introduce the idea that the union had a moral and legal case for demanding property rights in recordings, because he couched the demand in a larger context that described the threat that giant corporations and unbridled capitalism posed to the public's well-being. Petrillo argued before Congress that instead of investigating the musicians' union, the Congress could better spend the taxpayers' money on an investigation of the "few giant corporations" that had too much power over the industry "at the expense of the live musician."[32] Petrillo also emphasized that the AFM was helping with the war effort, pointing out that union members made records for overseas troops in the V-Disc program. Petrillo also reminded Congress that 25,000 AFM members were in the armed forces and that the union itself had purchased war bonds valued in the thousands of dollars. Petrillo took a risk by telling Congress he would end the strike if Congress could demonstrate that the recording ban posed a serious threat to the war effort. It was Petrillo's way of showing that he was reasonable and willing to negotiate, and it contradicted the image portrayed by the mass media that painted him as a tyrant. Petrillo's skill at responding to tough questions and transforming the matter from an issue of an illegal strike to an issue of the dangers posed by giant corporations gone awry was a victory for the musicians' union. Petrillo's rhetorical skills changed the minds of enough senators that they recommended, upon the urging of chief counsel Senator Bingham, that Congress enact *no* legislation against the union or the recording ban. The NAB admitted that Petrillo's testimony was a turning point in the conflict. In the trade magazine *Broadcasting*, editorials admitted that the radio industry had made a mistake in their assessment of Petrillo. In the January 18 issue, the magazine begrudgingly concluded that Petrillo "made a far better witness than was anticipated." One editorial read, "We understand why the AFM elected him president."

The stars finally lined up for the musicians' union when certain record companies began to show signs of coming to terms. Ultimately, the record companies were not able to mount a united stand because in September 1943 Decca records signed a four-year agreement with the musicians' union agreeing to Petrillo's royalty plan, referred to as the "fixed fee" plan. After his testimony before the War Labor Board in July 1943, Petrillo had sent a proposal to the major record companies, including RCA Victor, Columbia, and Decca. Copies of the proposal also made their way to the radio networks NBC and CBS, companies that had controlling interests in RCA Victor and Columbia. The radio/recording conglomerate promptly rejected Petrillo's proposal that record companies pay the union a royalty, the amount of which was negotiable, to be used to create jobs for unemployed musicians. Decca was the only record company not tied to radio, so it seized the opportunity to come to terms with the union and get a head start on gaining market share by signing recording artists who left RCA Victor and Columbia. Decca already had 25 percent of the market for records and saw a chance to get more of it as long as the other majors adhered to their stubborn position that opposed the right of the union to ask for a royalty system. Decca was able to strengthen its position in the market, in part by recruiting the violinist Jascha Heifetz, who by then had become a member of the AFM, away from RCA Victor, a move that gave Decca enormous publicity.[33] The signing of Decca was followed by scores of important independent labels, who were also hoping to capture more market share while the other major labels continued to hold out against the union. Eventually, RCA Victor and Columbia, along with their family of subsidiary labels, came to terms with the AFM because they were losing too much money. RCA and Columbia mustered one more unsuccessful attempt to lobby Roosevelt to lift the ban, but Roosevelt refused, citing Decca's willingness to work out a deal with the union as a model that should be followed. Thus in November 1944 RCA Victor and Columbia agreed to the AFM's demands by accepting the royalty system.

It was truly remarkable that the AFM prevailed in the face of so much adversity from both the record companies and the federal government. Petrillo remarked in an interview, "I believe the chains are beginning to realize that when I say a strike will be called, it will be called."[34] The aftermath had implications far and wide for the labor movement in the United States. The agreement that followed the strike included the establishment of the Recording and Transcription Fund (RTF), which raised money from the sale of recordings to underwrite free concerts for public consumption. The fund employed jobless and underemployed members of the AFM to perform at these free venues. The fund proved to be quite successful during the length of the labor contract held between the AFM and the record companies, raising more than $4.5 million to conduct 19,000 free concerts in parks, schools, and other public venues.[35]

The labor agreement secured by the musicians' union established a model for unions in the mining, automotive, steel, and printing industries, where workers' jobs were threatened by the application of labor-saving technology. All of the agreements between labor and capital that followed the war, agreements that have become known collectively as "welfare capitalism," were successful due in part to the musicians' strike because the labor agreement secured by the AFM helped to establish a pattern of relations between labor and capital that required capital to take more responsibility for the well-being of their workers, both those who were currently employed and those who were replaced by machines and subsequently unemployed. Arrangements like pension plans, workmen's compensation insurance, and unemployment benefits are all based on the premise that the social costs of technological advances (especially labor-saving technologies) have to be carried by capital; such social costs should be the burden of capital, *not* labor. This profound change in social relations of production between labor and capital was a huge ideological and structural victory, but capital would fight back through Congress with the passage of anti-labor legislation beginning in 1947.

In fact, the AFM conducted a second strike in 1948 in order to save the royalty plan, which was declared illegal under the Taft-Hartley Act, passed by a Republican-dominated Congress in 1947. After the war, business went on the attack against labor, lobbying Congress to pass both the Taft-Hartley Act and the Lea Act, which were major setbacks for organized labor.[36] The strategy that Petrillo and the AFM used in times of labor/management conflict was a classic example of a secondary strike, where a union uses one employer to coerce another employer to accept the contract demands of the union. The key to winning the strikes on the broadcasting industry was the AFM's ability to use the union's star members, the most popular recording artists of the day, including Duke Ellington, Gene Krupa, Tommy Dorsey, and Lawrence Welk, as effective leverage in persuading network affiliates to come to terms with the union because the networks themselves depended on the popularity of the super star musicians for lucrative advertising contracts, while the affiliates, in turn, depended on the remotes. Petrillo and the AFM were so successful in leading work stoppages that the union became a major target of the architects of the Taft-Hartley Act, which made the secondary strike illegal. The musicians' union was also the target of the Lea Act, which prohibits the practice of "featherbedding," where a union establishes a labor agreement that obliges an employer to hire more workers than management believes are deemed "necessary" for the task at hand. Many radio stations had complained that the AFM forced them to hire musicians who were almost never used. According to NAB, many AFM members simply loitered around radio stations, basically getting paid for doing nothing. The Republican Congress agreed with NAB and passed the Lea Act as a direct attack upon the AFM. When the labor agreement that followed the 1942–44 recording ban expired in 1947, the AFM planned a second strike in part to save the RTF, which became illegal under the Taft-Hartley Act.[37] The fund was saved by creating a trustee who was independent of both the union and the recording industry to oversee the fund, which after 1948 was renamed the Music Performance Trust Fund. The MPTF continues to raise money today, underwriting roughly 10,000 concerts a year that remain free to the public.[38]

It is important to emphasize just how incorrect the media was in portraying Petrillo and the AFM as Luddites. In fact, it could be effectively argued that the opposite was the case, because the union made a point of discussing the possibility of moving beyond economic scarcity, given the proper application of technology to the production process in the music industry. The position on the application of labor-saving technology taken by the AFM could apply to other industries equally as well.[39] The AFM made their argument in an editorial in 1947: "Discs — those culprits that were in the course of convincing an all-too-acquiescent public that music can be divorced from musicians embarrassingly possessed of stomachs to feed and fingers to warm — are put to work collecting this revenue to be turned back to the source of all music — the "live" musician. Thus this fund system, as a sort of alchemy of Modern human relationships, transforms records from potential destroyers of living musicians into their partial sustainers."[40] The language used in the editorial, especially the choice of the term *alchemy*, points to new possibilities of tackling the age-old problem of economic scarcity, both in the job market and in the economy more generally. In the labor agreement forged by the AFM, we see the very tangible possibility of technology *creating* income for unemployed musicians, rather than the opposite, which unfortunately is how we have to come to view the application of labor-saving technology today in virtually all industries. Herein lies the extraordinary significance of the legacy of the musicians' union.

The solidarity experienced among union musicians in the 1940s that produced a string of victories over radio and record companies began to diminish in the 1950s with the arrival of rock 'n' roll. Camaraderie collapsed as a result of the union's marginalization of rock musicians on the basis of aesthetic preference and membership auditions that were based on the ability to read music. In less than two decades, just as rock 'n' roll was racing up the *Billboard* charts, the union was no longer the powerhouse that it was in the 1940s. The erosion of unity within the musicians' union following the rise of rock 'n' roll seems especially curious, if not ironic, considering that rock 'n' roll emerged out of the leisure spaces of the American working class, and it is to that story that we now turn.

TWO

**Have You Heard the News?
There's Good Rockin' Tonight**

Wildcats, Hepcats, and the Emergence of Rock 'n' Roll

Rock 'n' roll is about freedom.
— CHUCK BERRY

We were the first working-class singers that stayed working-class and pronounced it
and didn't try to change our accents, which in England were looked down upon.
— JOHN LENNON

In 1943, the popular jump blues bandleader Louis Jordan and his band, the Tympany Five, recorded a hit single for Decca Records called "Ration Blues." Through the use of risqué double entendres, the lyrics of the song present a humorous satire of the experience of the sudden and serious misfortune of enforced austerity implemented by the War Production Board, an agency created by the federal government to assist in the colossal effort of reorganizing the economy after the entrance of the United States into World War II. In the third verse, Jordan sings, "They reduced my meat and sugar / And rubber's disappearing fast / You can't ride no more with poppa / 'Cause Uncle Sam wants my gas."[1] In the song, Jordan plays the part of a lamenting profligate who once enjoyed the good life but who now has to cope with lowered expectations given the shortages of certain goods that prevailed during the war. In addition to complaining about giving up "meat," Jordan laments giving up his "jelly." These two terms were com-

"high roller"

monly used in the vernacular of the urban working class as code for indulging in the carnal pleasures. "I like to wake up with my jelly by my side," sings Jordan. "Since rationing started, baby, you just take your stuff and hide." At the end of the song, Jordan's character resorts to appropriating the "meat" of his partner as a means of coping with the problem of government-enforced austerity. "I'm gonna steal all your jelly, baby / And rob you of your meat / I've got the ration blues, blue as I can be."

The use of sexual innuendo in the lyrics of rhythm and blues songs from the 1940s and early 1950s has been duly noted by historians of rock 'n' roll music who have chronicled the ways in which rhythm and blues and rock 'n' roll culture contributed to the transformation of the norms that govern sexual relations in American society.[2] Much less attention has been given to the ways in which the situation of class and class conflict mediated the formation of sexual practices within rhythm and blues culture. In "Ration Blues," however, we see how risqué double entendres are layered within a discourse of working-class grievances about enforced scarcity upon workers, a situation which was widely seen as unjust at the time, since big business was allowed to enjoy large, very lucrative contracts with the federal government during and after the war. Jordan recorded "Ration Blues" in the midst of widespread discontent among the American working class over the double standard set up by the federal government that allowed corporations to garner windfall profits during the expansion of the wartime economy, while the working class was expected to renounce wage increases and cut back on "luxury" goods, including food items like meat, butter, and sugar and clothing material like silk, nylon, and wool.

Between the years 1940 and 1944 the government turned over more than $175 billion in military contracts to approximately 1,800 companies, marking the beginning of the phenomenon that Eisenhower, in his famous speech from 1960, referred to as the military-industrial complex. The money was far from evenly distributed among the 1,800 companies that held contracts with the Pentagon. Of the 1,800 companies involved, 100 walked away with $117 billion. The U.S. economy almost doubled in size during the war, and yet President Roosevelt called for a wage freeze for workers, while companies were allowed to raise prices — in spite of so-called price regulations — during the wartime era of increasing aggregate demand.[3] Widespread awareness among workers of these severe inequities led to the largest working-class revolt in American labor history.

"Ration Blues" is a good example of how rhythm and blues culture during the 1940s presented sexual practices as part of a *totality* of pleasures that constitute the construction of working-class identity, a totality which exists in *opposition* to surplus repression and unjust austerity, conditions which follow from the unequal distribution of wealth and power. Jordan cut a similar hit record in 1946 called "Inflation Blues," which also lampooned the federal government for allowing corporations to raise prices and garner huge profits during and immediately after the war, while workers were forced to cope with stagnant wages and while returning soldiers were dealing with the problems associated with finding relatively "meaningful" and well-paid work during the reconversion of the American political economy from a war-oriented system to a peacetime market.

Among the American working class in general, a significant pent-up demand was beginning to put pressure on the establishment to respond to their growing expectations for both more income and more leisure. The tension was particularly acute during 1945–46 as workers in the millions went on strike all over the country in response to the problems associated with restructuring the economy. At the end of the war, as production was severely curtailed, nearly one-quarter of all workers lost their jobs, many of them women who were unfairly expected to give up their relatively well paying jobs to men returning from war. By October 1945 some 2 million workers were unemployed, and they would have to compete for jobs with the 10 million service men and women returning from overseas.[4] Mediating the general tension between workers and capital during this period was a growing impatience among the black working class with the status quo of racial discrimination in the United States. Black soldiers returning from the war—in addition to civil rights activists who did not fight overseas and young men who refused to fight and found ways to dodge the draft—were even more critical of the stark hypocrisy of the government, which was willing to fight a war abroad, ostensibly in the name of saving democracy and defeating racist ideology, while allowing racism to thrive at home. The general mood of American workers that included pent-up demand and the grievances having to do with economic injustice, combined with the more specific grievances of black workers having to do with racial discrimination, gave shape to the content and form of rhythm and blues music during the 1940s. The music of Louis Jordan and his influence on the development of rhythm and blues and rock 'n' roll provides us with a good example of this phenomenon, since much of his music and that of his peer group expressed resistance to the pressures of the changing conditions of capital accumulation and racial injustice. Rhythm and blues culture also provided the working class with images produced by utopian desires for a better future based on more leisure time and an improved material standard of living.

Jordan's two records were part of a string of hits between 1941 and 1947 that would lead to Jordan being dubbed the "King of the Jukebox." Jordan's domination of the jukebox and the pop charts during the 1940s is significant in part because he popularized a new type of arrangement of musicians that would become the template for rhythm and blues bands. But Jordan also solidified the *recording*—rather than the live performance—as the new cultural signifier for consumers of popular music. The uniqueness of rock 'n' roll as a record culture can be traced back to Jordan's dominant presence in jukeboxes. Jordan was also the first crossover recording artist to sell over a million records. He did this with at least four singles. *Billboard* magazine placed Jordan fifth on the list of most successful black recording artists in terms of total records sold. To this day, Louis Jordan still ranks as the top black recording artist of all time in terms of the total number of weeks at the number one spot on the rhythm and blues charts. His records spent 113 weeks in the number one position on the R&B charts between 1941 and 1947. Jordan also had nine records in the top twenty of the pop charts.[5] In 2004, *Rolling Stone* magazine placed Jordan at number 59 in the top 100 recording artists of all time.[6]

Jordan and his generation of rhythm and blues musicians of the 1940s created a culture that was mediated by class and class conflict. Rhythm and blues in turn shaped the development of the content of rock 'n' roll music during the 1950s, giving the new music a form and content that continued to express the struggle against work and authority. The influence of class on the emergence and expansion of rock 'n' roll remains relatively neglected in most historical accounts of the music. Class as a concept that signifies "status" as a position in the hierarchical social structure often figures as an important background context in many histories of rock 'n' roll, but class *conflict* rarely does. Usually class as *status* figures as a biographical detail associated with an individual who may struggle against poverty and finally make it as a recording star in the music business. In these histories, class is important as an indication of the status of an individual, but not as a structural phenomenon that shapes the organization of social relations in society. In short, class coded as status usually follows the familiar American myth of rags to riches in most histories of rock 'n' roll that address the phenomenon. Class conflict and class as a collective phenomenon are rarely considered, especially as forces that shape the music, rather than merely describe the status of the individual musician. The consideration of class conflict as a variable that contributes to the creation of popular culture provides a framework to interpret Louis Jordan's music and the rhythm and blues culture of his era as a form of resistance.

Of course, popular culture is always constituted as a contradiction: it is never "pure" in the sense that it is either a form of resistance or a form of domination. Certainly the culture industry — the corporate powers that dominate the network of production and distribution of records is one example — is a major player in the creation of popular culture. Popular culture is also often an enclave of racism and conservatism. In short, the space of popular culture is and has been a site of domination, where conservative values find expression, where reification of social relations takes place, and where sometimes commodified leisure functions as distraction and diversion rather than resistance and liberation. But these are all half-truths at best. It is more accurate to portray the site of popular culture as one of negotiation and struggle. As Stuart Hall argues, dominant values can just as easily be *dis*articulated in popular culture as they can be articulated. The reception of cultural messages, which have been encoded by the culture industry, are never correlated perfectly with the production of the codes, since reception always involves de-coding, which invariably changes the meaning. At the very least, the production and reception of popular culture always involves negotiation and struggle. According to Hall, "In the study of popular culture we should always start here: with the double-stake in popular culture, the double movement of containment and resistance, which is always inevitably inside of it."[7] Hall makes the case that historical periodization is crucial in any analysis of popular culture, because popular culture has historically been a problem for capital in the long processes of the societal transition to agrarian capitalism and then to industrial capitalism.

Historians of American labor like Herbert Gutman have demonstrated that popular cultural traditions that were formed in preindustrial times presented a serious obstacle to merchant capitalists who were seeking to impose a new way of life on agrarian workers who filled the first factories in the United States, a life oriented toward endless work and the hours on the clock rather than the natural rhythms of the day and of the seasons.[8] Workers who were unwilling to give up their leisure time activities developed in preindustrial times resisted these changes, and although proletarianization and industrialization eventually destroyed the agrarian way of life, certain features of preindustrial working-class culture—especially resistance to the Protestant work ethic—continued to exist in the forms and images of popular culture. The development of rhythm and blues in the 1940s presents a good case study of this phenomenon, because as workers left their agrarian way of life in search of work in the urban areas of the country during the war, they brought their culture with them, one that has consistently been at odds with the demands of capital accumulation. Structural changes in the economy during the war provided a unique opportunity for workers to gain leverage in their struggle with capital during this period, and the increasing political power of workers is reflected in the urban music of both rhythm and blues and honky-tonk. Older, preindustrial images of leisure remained in the culture, but a new popular culture developed in the urban areas as rural cultures from different parts of the country collided in the cities. The structural opportunities that followed from the changing economy gave the urban working class a reason to develop rising expectations, and these new expectations made their way into the utopian images of the new popular culture. This chapter is an investigation of working-class images, both old and new, in the popular music of this period, through the analysis of key figures in the emergence of rhythm and blues and honky-tonk music and how these forms influenced the shape and content of rock 'n' roll music.

Before launching his own recording career in 1941, Jordan had been the lead alto saxophonist in the Chick Webb Orchestra, the house band in residence at the famed Savoy Ballroom in Harlem during the heyday of the big band era of swing music. Webb fired Jordan in 1939 when he heard that Jordan was attempting to start his own band by recruiting members from his orchestra, including Ella Fitzgerald. Fitzgerald remained with the orchestra and eventually she took over the eighteen-person band when Webb died after a lifelong struggle with spinal tuberculosis. When Jordan left Webb's band, he embarked on one of the most remarkable and financially successful careers in the history of American popular music. With the decline of swing music and the demise of the big bands beginning in the early 1940s, the music industry pivoted on the extraordinary career of Jordan, as rhythm and blues became the new dance music. When the big bands broke up, musicians formed smaller groups and took jazz music in two distinct directions, one that led to the formation of bebop and one that led to the emergence of rhythm and blues.

Jordan's lineup for his new band consisted of just five members: Courtney Williams (trumpet and arranger), Lem Johnson (tenor sax), Clarence Johnson (piano), Charlie Drayton (bass), and Walter Martin (drums). Jordan named his band the Tympany Five because Martin often added two kettle drums—also known as timpani drums, which are commonly used in symphonies—to his trap set. Jordan called his new style of music, which drew from both swing jazz and rural blues, "jump blues" because the distinctive marker of the new music was a shuffle rhythm, a four-in-the-bar rhythm where each of the four beats is divided into two notes. The first note is two-thirds of a beat long and the second is one-third of a beat long and lightly accented, which gives the rhythm a legato feeling. When Jordan combined the shuffle rhythms with his humorous lyrics and flamboyant dress—the entire band was outfitted in brightly colored suits that resembled the zoot suit style and Jordan often donned huge glasses and a top hat when he performed a character dubbed "Deacon Jones"—he had created something new and very successful in the pop music industry. Jordan's lyrical delivery often involved the spoken word style, what we call rap today, and he used the technique to add humor to his repertoire. Many of his tunes involved very funny and ironic narratives that poked fun at class distinctions in American society.

Jordan's move was bold because he broke from the popular model of the dance band, which at the time typically included fifteen to eighteen instrumentalists. While the size of Jordan's band was an important development—as was the arrangement, which included an electric guitar on many recordings and performances—Jordan's leadership was key to the success of the band, because his performances combined comedic entertainment (which included humorous antics he learned from his vaudeville experiences as a young man performing with the Rabbit Foot Minstrels) with dance music. Jordan's performances, which expanded the repertoire of what a band could do on the stage in addition to playing instruments, had a significant influence on the creation of the stage personas of other key figures in the history of rock 'n' roll. Jordan's success at pushing the limit of what was possible in a musical performance opened the door for rock 'n' roll artists like Chuck Berry to experiment with nonmusical performance practices like the duck walk. Elvis Presley's nickname, "Elvis the pelvis," which he earned as a result of his notorious pelvic gyrations, is also indebted to the groundbreaking repertoire of Louis Jordan's nonmusical practices onstage. Indeed, many of the nonmusical elements of rock shows

[handwritten margin note: Jordan was in a minstrel group.]

that we now take for granted, including light shows, outrageous costumes, etc., can be traced back to the relatively outrageous performances of Louis Jordan and His Tympany Five. Today Jordan is widely acknowledged by rock 'n' roll historians as one of the key figures in the origins of rhythm and blues music. Many of the rock 'n' roll stars of the 1950s, including Chuck Berry and Bill Haley, have argued that case. Berry said, "I identify myself with Louis Jordan more than any other artist."[9] Bill Haley, who shared the recording studio at Decca Records with Jordan, purposely modeled his music on Jordan's.

Images of Work and Resistance in Rock 'n' Roll

Historians of rock 'n' roll (including Altschuler, Miller, Tosches, Palmer, and Marcus) frequently make use of terms like *dangerous, mysterious,* and *rebellious* to describe what it is that is unique to rock 'n' roll during the early years in the development of the music and culture, but these terms are usually used in a context that focuses on the subversion of norms that govern race and sexual relations, or the conflict between generations, at the relative expense of an analysis that considers class conflict. In other places in these texts it seems that the "danger" signified by rock 'n' roll culture seems to hang in the air all by itself with no adequate explanation for what gave content to the menace posed by rock 'n' roll culture. The relative mystification of the early years of rock 'n' roll can be explained in part as *reification,* which follows from either a complete erasure of class conflict from the history of rock 'n' roll or a displacement of class onto other categories like race. I use the phrase "class struggle" very broadly to include not only the clash between labor and capital during these years but also the struggle for racial equality and the specific ways in which black workers had to fight on two fronts. On the one hand, they fought alongside white workers for better working conditions, better pay, and more leisure time. On the other, they fought over these issues within a larger social context of racial discrimination and violence, making their struggle against capital much more complicated and difficult than that of their white contemporaries.

In short, there is no scholarly account of the history of rock 'n' roll that approaches the topic of class in a rigorous manner such as Bill Malone's excellent book on country music, *Don't Get Above Your Raisin': Country Music and the Southern Working Class.* Malone's book is the only sustained analysis of the impact of social class on the formation of popular music in the United States. For Malone, country music was particularly relevant for people like his father, whose "life as a tenant farmer on the worn-out cotton fields of East Texas, working on someone else's land and under someone else's terms, did not permit much in the way of self-assertion."[10] Country music was and continues to be, according to Malone, a means for working-class people to cope with, and at times escape from a life working under someone else's terms.[11] I find a similar phenomenon at work in the history of rock 'n' roll. The image of cotton picking is one of the primary signifiers in early rock 'n' roll music as it serves to frame a backdrop for the struggle against work and the rebellion against authority within rock culture. Other images of rebellion in rock 'n' roll emerged a decade earlier in the urban, rhythm and blues culture of the war years and the late 1940s.

In the 1950s, social critics of "mass" society, from both the left and the right side of the political spectrum, considered popular culture—which included most importantly rock 'n' roll music—to be an anathema to cultural progress. For the left, pop culture was viewed as part of an "industry" of culture, a corporate creation designed to control or co-opt the working class, whereas for the right, it was seen by conservative critics as the decline of culture in general. For the cultural right-wing, popular culture was viewed as a version of the tyranny of the masses phenomenon, where the uneducated, savage masses are seen destroying the cultural achievements of society, sending western culture back toward chaos and disorder.[12] Since the late 1960s, cultural critics on the Left have responded to both criticisms of popular culture, making a case that rock 'n' roll, as popular culture, is a legitimate aesthetic worthy of serious criticism as well as an agent of progressive social change.[13] Still, the working-class roots of rock 'n' roll have yet to be clearly understood by social critics. Rock 'n' roll historians usually point to the 1950s as the origin of rock 'n' roll and typically argue that rock 'n' roll emerged specifically as a phenomenon of youth culture.[14] While it's true that rock 'n' roll in the 1950s was central to the formation of a youth-oriented subculture that developed into a counterculture in the 1960s, it would be a mistake to reduce rock 'n' roll to exclusively a phenomenon of youth culture.[15]

In 1941, the year that Jordan began his successful recording career, 8.4 percent of the U.S. workforce had been on strike. The overwhelming majority of the strikes were wildcat strikes—strikes that were not authorized by the leadership of the union bureaucracy—conducted by rank-and-file workers who struggled against both their employers and their own union leaders, who had pledged not to strike for the duration of the war, an agreement that FDR was desperate to obtain at the outset of war. In 1941, there were 4,288 strikes involving 2,362,620 workers.[16] As Jordan's career skyrocketed during the 1940s, so did labor disputes between workers and management. Thousands of work stoppages involving millions of workers occurred in every year during the war, and they continued the year after the end of the war. When Jordan recorded his second crossover hit, "Ration Blues," in 1943, which reached number 11 on the pop charts and stayed at number 1 on the "Harlem Hit Parade" for six weeks, there were 3,752 strikes involving 1,980,000 workers.

The 1940s were also the spike years of the "great migration" of African Americans from the South to the urban centers in the North and Southwest. Between the years 1916 and 1960 approximately 6 million blacks left the South and moved to urban areas both in the North in places like Chicago, New York, and Philadelphia, and the West, including Kansas City and St. Louis, as well as further west to Oakland and Los Angeles. The long-term migration of blacks from the South was due in part to the spectacular failure of Reconstruction, but the significant spike in the demand for labor that followed from the entry of the United States into the war also had a huge effect on the structure of demographic change. After the war, demand for labor remained relatively strong in the southwestern areas of the United States as new defense-related industries continued to grow after the war. The push of Jim Crow and the pull of relatively well paying jobs in the manufacturing areas created new opportunities for African Americans. As a result of the relative improvement in their job prospects, African Americans in urban areas became a new class of consumers as well, as they helped to support the increase in record sales of rhythm and blues music in the mid- to late 1940s.

In spite of racial segregation in the music industry, Louis Jordan scored a number 1 hit on the pop charts with "Is You Is or Is You Ain't My Baby" in 1944 when 2,120,000 workers were involved in 4,956 strikes. After the war, the waves of wildcat strikes in the United States continued. The year 1946 marked the most tumultuous year in the history of the American labor movement, when 14.6 percent of the workforce went on strike, setting a record with 4,985 work stoppages. That year Jordan recorded his biggest hit with an interpretation of a country song titled "Choo Choo Ch'Boogie," which sold over 2 million copies. Many of the hits Jordan recorded during the war were directly aimed at problems facing the American working class, including the tunes mentioned above, like "Ration Blues," "Inflation Blues," and "Re-conversion Blues."

In addition to expressing the grievances of workers, however, Jordan's music also embodied the feeling of power and leverage that the working class enjoyed during the labor shortages that prevailed during the war. Songs like "Let the Good Times Roll" and "Saturday Night Fish Fry" are indicative of the phenomenon, where Jordan's lyrics reflect the more Dionysian side of life, as opposed to songs like "Ration Blues" and "Inflation Blues," which emphasize grievances. The main themes of "Saturday Night Fish Fry" and "Let the Good Times Roll" are the rejection of delayed gratification and confrontation with authority figures that attempt to put an end to the "good times." In "Saturday Night Fish Fry," partygoers end up in fisticuffs with the cops who try and break up their party, while in "Let the Good Times Roll," the emphasis is on spending lots of money in pursuit of immediate gratification. As in most of Jordan's songs, both themes are portrayed through humor and irony. Indeed, it was his ability to capture the rebellious and irreverent mood of both the black and white working class through humor that partly explains his significant crossover success during the 1940s.

The example of Louis Jordan points to what Theodor Adorno refers to as the ways in which "music . . . sketches in the clearest possible lines, the contradictions . . . which cut through present-day society."[17] My appropriation of Adorno's position on the situation of music in the modern world is not true to the original argument, since Adorno wrote very disparagingly about jazz and popular music, which he viewed as a problem that stemmed from the commodification of music, which in turn leads to standardization and alienation, key features of the totally "administered" society under the rule of capitalist exchange value. In my view Adorno, who was writing about popular culture while in exile in the United States during the war, was mistaken in arguing that "the current musical consciousness of the masses can scarcely be called Dionysian." While Adorno did not have popular music in mind when he argued that music revealed certain contradictions at the core of modern capitalist society, it remains the case that popular music during this period was mediated by the pervasiveness of class struggle that enveloped American society during the 1940s, and for this reason Adorno's aesthetic theory remains useful for an analysis that seeks to uncover the class content of rhythm and blues and rock 'n' roll.[18]

To make Adorno's aesthetic theory work for popular music of the time (rhythm and blues in particular), I take his critical Marxist argument that the economic base mediates the cultural superstructure and shift the analysis away from the universal domination of exchange value over use value, or from the analysis of how in everyday life all human products are subjugated to the rule of exchangeability and the universality of the commodity form, to an analysis of how *class struggle* mediates, but in no direct way determines, the cultural superstructure. Contrary to Adorno, commercial and popular music provided the working class of this era a means to express utopian hopes and Dionysian desires.

Rather than see the essential antagonism in the culture industry as that of the struggle between the individual attempt to realize their individuality in musical creation and the structural requirements of capital to realize exchange value—which destroys individuality and allows alienation to reign supreme—I focus on the class struggle as the crucial antagonism that is revealed in the music. The category of *mediation*—how the object (music) is a moment of the totality—is a crucial concept offered by Adorno, and I find it very useful in revealing the class content of popular music in the 1940s, in spite of Adorno's own pessimism about the possibility that anything produced by the culture industry could have any political value for the working class.

In short, while Adorno focused on the relatively hegemonic logic of capital and the struggle of the avant-garde musicians (like Schoenberg and Berg) against that logic, I see rhythm and blues music of the 1940s as a mediated cultural form that expressed a *counterlogic* of labor, which signifies a struggle against work as well as the playful deconstruction of highbrow and lowbrow cultural sensibilities. Both of these elements are present in the rhythm and blues of the 1940s, as well as rock 'n' roll during the early and mid-1950s. Appropriating Adorno's critical Marxist analysis addresses the problem of reification that prevails in most histories of rock 'n' roll that mystify the "danger" and "rebelliousness" of the atmosphere that characterized the early years of rock 'n' roll.

The working-class cultural struggle against work stretches back to the songs of slaves working in the cotton fields. The white working class also has a musical tradition that is oriented around the cultural resistance to work and exploitation which stretches as far back as the eighteenth century.[19] This particular cultural struggle connects the music of the slaves to the Delta Blues of Robert Johnson's generation and all the way through to the jump blues of Louis Jordan and the rock 'n' roll of Chuck Berry and Little Richard. The struggle against work that animates blues music also influenced white honky-tonk musicians like Hank Williams and white rockabilly musicians like Carl Perkins, Johnny Cash, and Elvis Presley.[20]

The epic labor struggles of the 1940s that erupted in the industries which had grown up during the war contributed to the form of a new kind of music which developed out of a unique mixture of diverse cultures as millions of people migrated out of rural areas in search of manufacturing jobs in the southwestern and in the northern areas of the United States when the war jump-started an economy mired in depression. For the people who did not leave the rural South in search of work, the labor question still figured prominently in the popular culture, including the formation of blues and country music, although in a different way, primarily within the context of cotton picking. These two distinct ways in which the labor question became a focal point in country music, honky-tonk, blues, and rhythm and blues—the desire to escape the sorrows and suffering of field labor and sharecropping in the rural South, and the dramatic collision of capital and labor in the manufacturing industries in urban areas in the North and Southwest—gave substance to much of the music that became rock 'n' roll. It is in the lyrics and in the form of the music as well as the arrangement of the instruments. It is also expressed in the reflections of the musicians themselves, when they situate their music in their everyday lives of that period.

Historians of rock 'n' roll disagree about which was the first rock 'n' roll record or which recording artists constituted the first rock 'n' roll group, but I take Jim Miller's cue that the late 1940s marks the emergence of rock 'n' roll as a reasonable estimate.[21] Miller goes so far as to pinpoint Wynonie Harris's recording of Roy Brown's song *Good Rockin' Tonight* in 1947 as the first rock 'n' roll record and the beginning of rock 'n' roll music as such. While I make the case that rock 'n' roll can be traced even further back in the history of jump blues to Louis Jordan, I accept Miller's assertion that rock 'n' roll is at least as old as the late 1940s, a unique period of social unrest in the United States. The key issues that triggered this period of turbulence were the spatial and social transformation of the labor process, which led to a popular focus on the labor question and the race question, which in turn found acute expression in the early years of rhythm and blues music. Tight labor markets created by wartime production allowed all workers to enjoy a rising standard, which followed the increasing leverage with which to negotiate with their employers. Increasing demand for labor also provided black workers the opportunity to challenge racial segregation, both in terms of the distribution of jobs and in terms of political and spatial marginalization in society more generally.

Workers during this period were both advancing their right to a larger slice of the pie and openly demonstrating their willingness to spontaneously walk off the job as a means to secure a hold on their stake. The spike in wildcat strike activity combined with the rowdy atmosphere of urban, working-class leisure spaces demonstrated a peculiarly ostentatious lifestyle, which was most visible in styles of clothing and openly sexual dance styles. Sometimes working-class pretensions were made explicit in the lyrics of jump blues tunes, but even when it is not in the lyrics, it is in the music itself: the shuffle rhythms, the heavy backbeat, pounding boogie-woogie piano, walking bass lines, the noisy, growling, and "honking" saxophones, and especially the electric guitars, which together with the saxophones produced so much noise that the singers had to shout to be heard, ushering in a new genre of singers in the late 1940s known collectively as the blues shouters, which included Big Joe Turner, Jimmy "Mr. Five by Five" Rushing, and Wynonie Harris.

Because rock 'n' roll emerges during this period and not in the mid-1950s, some historians call this phenomenon the "secret" history of rock 'n' roll. The secret, however, is presented by historians like Nick Tosches as a "secret" simply because rock 'n' roll is older than Elvis. It may be relatively unknown to the casual fan that rock 'n' roll did not start with Elvis Presley, but Tosches neglects to examine the social content of that largely unknown pre-Presley social history. In his book *Unsung Heroes of Rock 'n' Roll*, Tosches emphasizes the controversial nature of the rhythm and blues artists of the late 1940s, referring to the era as a "forsaken time of relentless excess" and "the wild years before Elvis." While Tosches has adequately captured the rebellious mood of early rock 'n' roll perhaps better than any other writer/critic, it remains the case that in his account, the rebellious spirit of rock 'n' roll seems to hang in the air all by itself, like a rebel without a cause. Tosches is correct to describe the era as a time of "relentless excess" and the attitudes as "forsaken," but there is no adequate analysis of where that rebelliousness or "forsaken time of relentless excess" comes from. Another good example of this phenomenon is Robert Palmer's book

Rock & Roll: An Unruly History, which like Tosches's book is an excellent *internal* history of rock 'n' roll, but it also fails to adequately capture what is "unruly" about this history. The "unruliness" of rock 'n' roll seems to float in the air, unsupported by any edifice.[22]

The rebellious character of rhythm and blues music was sustained by the increasing political power of the American working class, which benefited significantly from structural changes in the economy. Steep increases in the demand for labor during the war drove the unemployment rate down to an insignificant 1.3 percent of the population by 1943, which was less than a tenth of the unemployment rate in 1937, the most "prosperous" year of the Great Depression.[23] Perhaps the most important indication of the increasing leverage that workers were enjoying in the tight labor market was the reason behind why workers were separated from their jobs. In a stunning reversal of fortune, by 1943 fully 72 percent of job turnovers were accounted for by *voluntary resignation*, whereas in 1937 *layoffs* accounted for 70 percent of job turnover.[24] One-third of the workforce (approximately 15 million workers) was able to move into higher paying jobs with better working conditions. Weekly earnings in manufacturing jumped up 65 percent after 1941, rising from $32.18 to $47.12 by 1943.[25] For most workers who left rural areas for a defense job in the urban factories, the new environment of better wages encouraged rising expectations. When factory workers who were working in the defense plants got a taste for the improved lifestyle that went along with a relatively good paycheck, they developed a desire for more. The issue was how to get the companies that held the defense contracts to share the newfound wealth with their workers.

Just before and during World War II, more than 16 million people joined the armed forces, and in the effort to ramp up production for war, American companies drew upon 15 million new workers from the reserve army of labor, millions of whom were people who migrated from rural areas to urban production centers that were located primarily in the North and Southwest, but also in urban areas in the South like the shipyards in Mobile, Alabama, where Hank Williams found work during the war. Among the new wartime workers were 6 million women and over 1 million African Americans. The massive migration of workers was the largest ever seen in America. All told, more than 4 million people had left rural areas from thirty states for production centers in urban areas in eighteen other states from 1940 to 1946. According to the U.S. Census Bureau, the overall increase in population within the cities that served as wartime production centers was around 19 percent, whereas for African Americans the increase in population was close to 50 percent!

The working-class migration to urban centers where factory work was located also included groups of African Americans who formerly worked as domestic workers in white, upper-middle-class suburbs. In his autobiography, Chuck Berry recalls:

> The effects of the war were felt quickly throughout the home front. Materials such as rubber, copper, gasoline, and soap became scarce, and some were even rationed. There was a shortage of goods, but there was an abundance of jobs and everybody worked for the war effort. The suburban rich people were panicking because the maids and domestic workers were all leaving them for higher-paying jobs at the defense plants. . . . As a result, maids, gardeners, and garbage technicians got the chance to revisit their former employers in the suburbs where they tooted their Cadillac horns while driving by, "Just coming out to say hello!"[26]

Berry's construction of the image of African Americans cruising white, upper-middle-class suburbs in order for their former employers to see them driving fancy new cars nicely captures the mood of working-class pretensions during that period.

Huge demographic shifts as the result of the steep increase in the demand for labor meant that workers had the upper hand even in the face of a hostile business community, the presidential administration, *and* a union bureaucracy that demanded sacrifice and obedience in the name of patriotism and national "emergency." The years between 1941 and 1946 were unique for American workers because they displayed an unusual willingness to use their main weapon, the wildcat strike. Worker pretensions among the rank-and-file were at an all-time high in the history of the American labor movement. Many of the wildcat strikes were playful and celebratory. In Fairfield, Alabama, in 1944, wildcat strikers held a jitterbug dance in the street just outside of the windows of the management offices at the mill where they were on strike. In 1943 workers in Stamford, Connecticut, conducted a general wildcat strike that shut down the entire city, where a reporter recalled that the atmosphere felt more like a carnival than a strike.[27] The wildcat strike data from the early to mid-1940s are truly remarkable numbers. They reveal significant turmoil within the United States during the war in spite of the efforts by the Roosevelt administration to create a stable climate of production for the war. Mine workers were able to force concessions from both the mine companies and the Roosevelt administration, a truly remarkable feat. Roosevelt threatened to conscript mine workers when they went on strike in 1943, and in response to the president's threat, the United Mine Workers union pulled *more* workers out on strike. They continued to pull workers out of the pits until the Roosevelt administration gave in to their demands and forced the mine companies to capitulate.[28] It was no coincidence that these were also the years that gave birth to rock 'n' roll music in America.

The seed elements of rock 'n' roll, which took root in Louis Jordan and his generation, developed and were nourished within a cultural milieu that I refer to as the working-class pretensions of the 1940s. To appreciate the class dimension that colors the history of rock 'n' roll music is to examine how rhythm and blues musicians took the electricity of the wildcat strike movement of rank-and-file workers during the 1940s and plugged it in through amplified guitars and blew it hard through growling and honking saxophones.[29] While the wildcat strikes reverberated through the structures of power in American politics, rhythm and blues music gave American popular culture a shot in the arm. By pretension I mean both the advancement of a claim on something — a certain material standard of living, a cultural lifestyle, a demand for equal rights, etc. — as well as ostentation in the presentation of self.[30] The period of years between the outbreak of war and the end of the decade is truly remarkable in that workers routinely walked off the job due to many issues that might seem trivial today. For example, in 1944, 300 auto workers at a GM factory in Detroit walked off the job when management attempted to ban smoking, and shortly before the end of the war workers at a Cadillac factory in Detroit walked off the job when they found out that they would not be allowed to play checkers at work! Imagine workers trying something like that today. The wave of wildcat strikes was punctuated by a massive general strike, which occurred in Oakland, California, in 1946.

Department store workers, members of the Department Store and Specialty Clerks Union Local 1265, went on strike at Hastings' and Kahn's department stores in November 1946. Teamsters supported the strike by conducting a secondary boycott, by refusing to carry any "hot" cargo on their trucks, that is, by refusing to make deliveries to the two stores. The department stores responded by hiring non-union truck companies to deliver their goods. When news traveled that the police were called in to protect trucks that were crossing the picket lines, workers all over Oakland took to the streets to block traffic and create gridlock. It took less than twenty-four hours for more than 100,000 workers all over Oakland to join in the general strike, which was eventually approved by the Alameda County AFL Labor Council. In addition to closing most stores downtown, workers prevented anyone who didn't have a union card from entering downtown. Workers walked the streets of downtown and struck all stores except for the grocery stores, pharmacies, and bars! Keeping the bars open was their way of ensuring the general strike would maintain a playful, raucous atmosphere. Striking workers also pulled jukeboxes out onto the streets so that people who could not fit inside of the bars also had a chance to partake in the dancing and festivities. It is very likely that on those jukeboxes were many records by Louis Jordan.

In short, the increasing power exercised by American workers during the 1940s was the basis for keeping the culture of rhythm and blues aloft during the 1940s and into the 1950s. To focus on these issues is to give a reason for the rebellious attitudes of those intimately connected to the rhythm and blues and rock 'n' roll culture that figure in the historical accounts written by critics like Tosches and Palmer, who have been unable to give a reason for why rhythm and blues and rock 'n' roll took an oppositional stance to the status quo during this period in American history.[31]

Louis Jordan presents a particularly good example of this phenomenon because the word *tympany* in Jordan's band's name, the Tympany Five, means "pretentious style." As stated above, Jordan dubbed his band Tympany Five because his drummer sometimes used kettledrums, which are also known as timpani when they are used in symphonic arrangements. It is unclear whether or not Jordan intended to have a double meaning in his band's name. According to Jordan's biographer, the spelling of the band name was a mistake, but they kept the name anyway.[32] It seems a most fortuitous error because Jordan's performances and recordings were nothing if not pretentious.

The choice of costume was a very important ingredient in the nascent rhythm and blues culture that was developing out of the big band scene, which had dominated the late 1930s and early 1940s, because clothing style can be read as a text embedded within a subculture, where style "signifies" a particular lifestyle and also a particular politics. As Dick Hebdige argues:

The tensions between dominant and subordinate groups can be found reflected in the surfaces of subculture — in the styles made up of mundane objects which have a double meaning. On the one hand, they warn the "straight" world in advance of a sinister presence — the presence of difference — and draw down upon themselves vague suspicions, uneasy laugher. . . . On the other hand, for those who erect them into icons, who use them as words of curses, these objects become signs of forbidden identity, sources of value.[33]

The clothing style of working-class subcultures in the 1940s is a prime example of this phenomenon.

The dominant fashion of the urban, working-class subculture of African Americans, Chicanos, and (to a somewhat lesser extent) Italian Americans of the early and mid-1940s was a controversial style of suit that became known as the zoot suit. Louis Jordan took his fashion cue from Cab Calloway, whom Jordan respected as a musician and as an entertainer. Calloway can be seen wearing a zoot suit in the 1943 film *Stormy Weather*. Although Jordan himself never wore a zoot suit like Calloway did, the fact that Jordan and his band made use of relatively outrageous clothing styles points to the larger subculture of the zoot-suiters of the time, a subculture that overlapped the big band era and the newer rhythm and blues subculture. Reading the cultural politics out of the code inscribed within the zoot suit subculture involves what Robin Kelley describes as solving the "riddle" of the zoot.

The zoot suits were distinct for their very wide-legged pants, which were worn high above the waist and pegged at the bottom with a tight cuff. The pants could be as wide as forty inches at the knee before being pegged tight at the ankle, where they were no more than ten inches around. On top, the coat, which was worn very long, had wide lapels and shoulders that contained extra padding to make the coat very broad on top. Typically men would wear a hat with a very long feather to complement the suit. The shoes were usually pointy to complement the pegged ankles of the pants. The final accessory to adorn the zoot suit was a long chain that dangled from the belt, which was high above the waist, to down below the knee.

The cultural politics inscribed upon the zoot suit derived from two factors: first, the zoot suit signified the collective resistance among young African American and Chicano men who publicly challenged racial segregation by drawing attention to themselves in the popular dance clubs in Los Angeles and New York. Young African American and Chicano men who were emboldened by the rising expectations that followed from relatively good jobs in the war economy refused to remain trapped within the segregated areas of their cities. The rising incomes among all workers allowed young African American and Chicano men to spend their money on the ostentatious zoot suit. Displaying the zoot suit in the downtown areas of major cities like Los Angeles and New York was a way for young men to signify that they were no longer willing to accept the status quo of racial segregation of city spaces. Part of their refusal to go along with racial discrimination and inequality included a refusal to join the war effort. Many young zoot-suiters actively dodged the draft on the basis that it would be hypocritical, if not absurd, to fight for democracy and an end to racism abroad, while at home African Americans and Chicano(a)s faced discrimination and inequality on a daily basis.

Second, the zoot suit was linked to a more general working-class resistance, what Kelley refers to as the "refusal to be good proletarians." Refusing to be obedient workers was the primary signifier encoded in the zoot suit, which was embedded within a subculture where individuals constructed an identity *outside* the workplace, in the dance halls and after-hours leisure spaces, an identity that was at odds with the workplace identity insofar as the meaning of these leisure practices emphasized pleasure through the *escape from work*. In both cases, the zoot-suiters refused to perform deference, whether it was the deference that nonwhites were supposed to perform for whites in the public spaces of the city or the obedience expected by employers at the workplace. Zoot suits draped the rebellious body in an unmistakably extravagant way that said "no" to racial discrimination, austerity, and the alienation of work in the modern capitalist world.

As stated above, a key to deciphering the code or "riddle" of the zoot suit is to place the fashion style within the context of the working-class affirmation of leisure over work. The baggier the pants and the more outrageous the color of the suit, the more it signified individuality and prestige, two things sorely lacking while at work on the assembly line in the factory. Zoot suits and the culture that spawned them emphasized the construction of identity *beyond* the workplace. Factory work was alienating, but life after work in the nightclubs provided workers with an opportunity to create themselves anew, and the best way to signify to others what you were all about was through the spectacular threads that adorned the rebellious body and how well you could dance. According to Kelley, the "zoot-suiters who sought alternatives to wage work and found pleasure in the new music, clothes, and dance styles were 'race rebels' of sorts, challenging middle-class ethics and expectations, carving out distinct generational and ethnic identity, and refusing to be good proletarians."[34]

The Savoy Ballroom in Harlem was a prime example of how a worker could become someone *other* than a worker. Dressing up in a zoot suit and cutting up the dance floor was a way to reduce the severe status gap that existed in the spaces of work. The Savoy Ballroom in Harlem was a favorite spot for the young Malcolm X in the early 1940s. Kelley emphasizes the passages in the *Autobiography of Malcolm X* where Malcolm speaks about how in his youth he was always shedding his work clothes to escape his work identity, as a way to interpret the political significance of the zoot suit, including Malcolm's description of how, when he worked as a porter on the railroad, he would change into his zoot suit *before* the train reached the final destination. Leaving the train as the best-dressed person challenged the middle-class expectations that porters perform the identity of the subservient worker. The workplace identity was always something for workers like Malcolm to leave behind as they embarked on the nightly journey to the dance halls where they could be someone else, construct an identity formed by pleasure rather than subservience, deference, and alienation. Taking off your work clothes was symbolic; it was a way to step out of your identity as "worker." Why I hate uniforms, so degrading.

Seeking out alternatives to wage work and finding pleasure in new music, dance styles, and clothes that collectively challenge middle-class norms about work and pleasure can also be found in the 1950s rock 'n' roll subculture. Indeed, the struggle against work and the discovery of pleasure in new music, clothes, and dance is the cultural undercurrent that links rhythm and blues to rock 'n' roll as the music developed and changed from one decade to the next. As Kelley persuasively argues, it is not that the zoot suit per se was a direct political statement, but when it was worn in the particular social context in the public spaces of the 1940s — an environment of heightened racial and class tensions following the structural changes in the wartime economy — it became so because it spoke the subversive language of the refusal to perform deference.

Another reason why zoot suits became controversial for middle-class white society was that the zoot suit was an active refusal to obey the rationing codes set by the War Production Board (wpb). Men's suits were included in the government rationing program, along with all clothing items that used wool. The WPB called for a 26 percent reduction in the production of suits, which included regulations that specified the dimensions of what kinds of suits should be manufactured. *Esquire* magazine referred to these WPB regulations as "streamlined suits by Uncle Sam."[35] WPB regulations effectively put an end to the production of zoot suits by the major clothing manufacturers as well as the sale of zoot suits at most retail outlets, but the demand for and production of zoot suits did not diminish during government rationing. A bootleg network of tailors working underground stepped in to continue the production of zoot suits. Displaying the zoot suits in spite of government rationing signified the working-class pretensions of this period, signifying a refusal to acknowledge the perceived ineluctability of wartime austerity. The phenomenon can be linked to Jordan's expression of the working-class critique of rationing in his song "Ration Blues." The appropriation of the suit by working-class subcultures also demonstrates how, in Dick Hebdige's words, "commodities can be symbolically repossessed in everyday life, and endowed with implicitly oppositional meanings, by the very groups who originally produced them. The symbiosis in which ideology and social order, production and reproduction are linked is neither fixed nor guaranteed. It can be prised open."[36]

Donning a zoot suit in predominantly white spaces of the city became particularly controversial once the style of suit became associated with antipatriotism. The controversy surrounding the zoot suit culture reached a climax during the zoot suit riots in Los Angeles in 1943, when U.S. servicemen and Mexican American youth battled each other on the city streets for more than a week. In Los Angeles, the zoot suit was primarily associated with the *pachuco*—which translates roughly into "punk"—subculture of young Mexican Americans. Some of the white rioters who joined the servicemen in the riots claimed they were "helping with the war effort" by attacking pachucos. Part of what angered white servicemen was what Robin Kelley refers to as the "hipsters' laissez-faire attitude toward work and their privileging of the pursuit of leisure and pleasure, holding the view that one should work to live rather than live to work."[37]

After the riots ended when the U.S. military brass made most of Los Angeles off-limits to the servicemen, the city banned zoot suits within its boundaries.[38] While the zoot suit was much less commonplace after the city council banned it, homage was paid to the zoot suit subculture in the 1947 rhythm and blues recording of "Pachuco Boogie," by Don Tosti, a talented bass player and session musician from Los Angeles. Tosti was part of the generation of musicians living in Los Angeles, including Johnny Otis, Wynonie Harris, and T-Bone Walker who were following in Louis Jordan's footsteps in transforming the big band sound into more compact combinations of musicians. "Pachuco Boogie" was a hit record within the pachuco subculture in Los Angeles, but it also got crossover radio play on KFWB's popular radio show "Make Believe Ballroom." It has been estimated that the record sold over a million copies.[39] "Pachuco Boogie" is an important record because it demonstrates both the Mexican American contribution to the creation of rhythm and blues music as well as how the zoot suit culture overlapped the transition in dance music from the big band era to rhythm and blues. Too often the Mexican American contribution to the creation of rhythm and blues culture is overlooked. Typical histories of rock 'n' roll acknowledge contributions by figures like Richie Valens. But the *pachuco* zoot suit subculture of the 1940s that developed in Los Angeles was a key ingredient in the expansion of rhythm and blues music on the West Coast.

By the late 1940s, rhythm and blues was an integral part, if not the principal vehicle, of this new interracial urban working-class culture of pretension that continued to grow after the war ended in 1945, and again the music of Louis Jordan was at the center of the rebellious subculture. When Louis Jordan recorded his smash hit "Inflation Blues" in 1946—a song about the injustice of government freezes on wage increases while private businesses were allowed to raise prices on their goods—workers all across the United States were on strike over the very same issues that Jordan was singing about. Louis Jordan cut the right record at the right time. In "Inflation Blues" Jordan sings:

Now listen mister President and all you Congressmen too,
You've got me all frustrated and I don't know what to do,
I'm trying to make a dollar and can't even save a cent,
It takes all my money just to eat and pay my rent,
That's why I got the blues, got those inflation blues . . .
I'm not one of those high-brows; I'm average Joe to you
I came up eatin' cornbread, candied yams, and chicken stew
Now you take that paper dollar, it's only that in name,
The way that paper bucket shrunk, it's a low down dirty shame,
I got the blues, got those inflation blues

Hey, Prez, please cut the price of sugar so I can make my coffee sweet,
I like to smear some butter on my bread; you know I like my meat;
When you started rationing you really played the game,
Things are going up and up but my check remains the same.[40]

The content of Jordan's lyrics and the form of the music, which included a hard driving backbeat behind Jordan's rapping, and his growling, honking saxophone emphasized aspects of life that mainstream "pop" music typically shied away from. Pop singers, especially white pop singers who performed tunes written by the Tin Pan Alley songwriters, usually did not sing about controversial subjects, nor was the structure or form of the songs in any way threatening. There were some important exceptions, of course, including songs like "Brother, Can You Spare a Dime?" and "Hello, Central, Give Me No Man's Land," but for the most part, mainstream pop songs coming out of Tin Pan Alley painted a rosy picture of American life devoid of conflict, whether racial tensions or class conflict. The "happy" formula that Tin Pan Alley songwriters developed in the 1920s had changed very little by the 1940s. Tin Pan Alley was more and more out of touch with working-class life in the big cities. It was rhythm and blues music that told the truth about racial tensions and class conflict in America during the 1940s. Jordan also made use of the call-and-response techniques that are part of the rich tradition in the history of African American music, a history which stretches back to the work songs of field slaves in antebellum America, where the lead singer would call out lyrics and receive a responding set of lyrics from other field slaves. Many of Jordan's tunes were performed in storytelling modes in the call-and-response style. In addition to the form of call-and-response, the lyrical content of jump blues also has roots in the work songs of field slaves and the blues music that developed from that context.

The history of country blues is rooted in the experience of suffering endured by slaves and their descendants who endured the oppressive sharecropping system that prevailed between the end of the Civil War and the early twentieth century. These conditions of abject poverty and backbreaking labor are what produced "the blues" in the first place. According to the legendary electric bluesman Howlin' Wolf:

Well I was broke when I was born, that's why I grew up howlin.'
We talk about the life of human beings [in our music], how they live. A lot of people wonder what the blues is, and I'm gonna tell

you. When you ain't got no money you got the blues. . . . A lot of people holler, "Well, I don't like the blues," but when you ain't got no money to pay the rent and when you can't buy you no food you damn sure got the blues. When you ain't got no money you got the blues cuz you're thinkin' evil. . . . If you gettin' everything you need [and more] you don't have no right to worry about nothin. But when you don't got nothin, you got to worry about something, and that's when the blues comes in. You say, "I don't have this and I don't have that." When you look around and you see these other people have this and they have that, and in your heart you feel like you're nobody, then you got the blues.[41]

Blues music was distinct in the way in which the music was intimately bound up with everyday life. Unlike much of the music that was produced by Tin Pan Alley, which was distinctly separated from the everyday life of the producers and consumers of the music, blues music was oriented toward textures of daily life, the problems and the pleasures that individuals directly experienced. Life and art were not separate in the culture that created blues music. The blues is a set of feelings produced by a stark existence, and blues music was developed in order to cope with those bad feelings or even as a means to chase those feelings away. Music critic and historian Albert Murray refers to this as the difference between the blues "as such" and blues music. The function of chasing away the blues in music is referred to by Murray as "Stompin' the Blues." Master bassist and singer/songwriter Willie Dixon claimed blues music "relaxes the mind about bad feelings." Pianist Memphis Slim, another key figure in the development of blues music during this era, put a slightly different spin on the meaning of the blues. For Slim, in addition to being about coping with identity crises that follow from abject poverty and alienating work, blues music is also about resistance and fighting back. "The blues goes back to slavery," according to Slim. "When slaves wanted to say things that they couldn't say, that would get them in trouble, or [when they wanted to] *get back at the boss*, they would sing" [emphasis mine].[42]

Getting back at the boss, as well as getting back at authoritative figures that working-class people face in their everyday lives is a central theme that connects blues, jump blues, and rock 'n' roll. One way that slaves coped with not being able to say what they wanted to say was to use code to fool the slave masters. The use of code and deception became part of African American folklore through the trickster tales, the best known of which is perhaps the Brer Rabbit character. Brer Rabbit stories were typical of slave stories that told of magical animals or lesser gods that were able to use deception to overcome the superior strength and power of their opponent. The stories usually tell of small victories, but the rich tradition of the trickster-hero tales demonstrates how the slaves kept alive their utopian desires to overcome slavery. The key to understanding the figure of the trickster is in how the trickster must make use of cunning and deception, which becomes possible only through a profound fluency in knowing how and what the slave master—or the boss, or other figures of authority— thought about themselves and the Other.

You can see the trickster-hero figure used in Louis Jordan's hit record "Ain't Nobody Here but Us Chickens," which appropriates the lyrics of an old field song that was popular among slaves. The lyrics of the song, which tell a story about a farmer investigating a disturbance in the hen house, are a metaphor for a victory of the powerless over the powerful by fooling the authority figure. In the song, when the farmer asks what is going on in the hen house, he hears the response, "There's nobody here but us chickens." The voice inside the hen house goes on to tell the farmer that laying eggs is serious business, which requires plenty of rest and sleep, and that the farmer should therefore leave them alone so they can get back to sleep. In this way, the thief inside the hen house uses the farmer's knowledge and interests against the farmer. The voice can appeal to the farmer's greed as a way to get the farmer to leave the hen house. Of course, when the farmer leaves, the thief goes about his/her mischievous ways.

Louis Jordan probably did not intend to make a political statement with "Nobody Here but Us Chickens"; however, placed within the social context of the time, the song does take on political meaning. It may seem obvious that Jordan, an African American, would be familiar with and draw upon the figure of the trickster-hero in his music, but "Ain't Nobody Here" was also a huge cross-over hit. As George Lipsitz has argued, Jordan's hit records frequently crossed over to the white pop charts because "white people turned to black culture for guidance, because black culture contains the most sophisticated strategies of signification and the richest grammars of opposition available to aggrieved populations."[43] Jordan's music points to the way in which commercially produced popular culture provided working-class individuals ways to position themselves to resist authority and create novel identities.

In Louis Jordan's songs, we see how both Howlin' Wolf's and Memphis Slim's definition of the *meaning* of the blues can also be found in rhythm and blues, although the *mood* of rhythm and blues was significantly different, as it made more use of humor and more often emphasized the Dionysian side of life rather than the sorrows of work. The form of the blues changed with the development of jump blues in the late 1940s because urban working-class pretensions injected a more affirmative, positive outlook on life into the music as the speed of everyday life and the mixing of cultures in an environment of low unemployment created a new sense of excitement. The fast tempo of urban life provided the cultural stuff needed for jumping the blues. Life in the city signified a material existence of upward mobility for workers who fled the misery of sharecropping that prevailed in the South, as Howlin' Wolf himself said after he moved from Mississippi to Chicago in order to begin a recording career at Chess Records. While the older blues music provided a way of coping with the backbreaking, alienating work, the newer jump blues signified a break from work and the affirmation of the pleasures found in the new working-class leisure spaces. When you "jump" the blues, as Louis Jordan used to say, then you're not so sad, at least not in the way that Howlin' describes in the quote above where he says you look at yourself and you think you're nobody. Jordan's music did include working-class grievances, but many of his hit records also emphasized the celebration of a rising standard of living.

Jordan claimed that "when you come to hear Louis Jordan, you hear things that make you forget what you'd had to do the day before and just have a good time, a great time."[44] In the spirit of escaping work, one of Jordan's big hits was "Let the Good Times Roll," a song with obvious connotations for workers enjoying an atmosphere of more leverage in the labor market. "Let the Good Times Roll" was written in 1946, the same year that workers were on general strikes all across America. The first two verses of "Let the Good Times Roll" read: Hey everybody let's have some fun / You only live once / And when you're dead you're done / So don't sit there mumblin' and talkin' trash / If you wanna have a ball you gotta go out and spend some cash.[45] The rejection of delayed gratification is a central theme to the song, and it is repeated in the second to last verse, where Jordan sings: "Hey tell everybody Mr. Jordan's in town / I got a dollar and a quarter just rarin' to clown / But nobody play me cheap / I got fifty cents more that I'm gonna keep / So let the good times roll." The bravado of Jordan's performances and lyrics, where he announces that he's come to town to spend money, have a good time, and make sure everyone else at the club also has a good time, reflects the rejection of delayed gratification and the Protestant work ethic, norms which prevailed among middle-class white society.

Such bravado in rhythm and blues music mirrored the outrageous audacity of bombastic workers who were able to abruptly part ways with employers deemed unacceptable or unfair. In many cases, a better job was literally around the corner. Jordan's emphasis on spending lots of money signified that workers were not embracing the bourgeois norm of delayed gratification and sacrifice. By and large, American workers understood that the war was used as an excuse by the power elite to squeeze excessive amounts of surplus value from their labor, while attempting to impose false austerity on the working class.[46] Rank-and-file workers who led the wildcat strikes saw through the ideology of delayed gratification and sacrifice as still more attempts by the bourgeoisie to impose austerity on workers, while capitalists consumed most of the wealth produced by economic growth.[47] By the 1950s, the cultural staying power of the working-class rejection of delayed gratification and the emphasis on spending money can be seen in records like Little Richard's 1956 hit, "Rip It Up," where Richard exclaims, "Saturday night and I just got paid / I'm a fool about my money, don't try and save!" "Rip it Up" was one of the most important compositions of its era, as it was covered by the likes of Bill Haley, Buddy Holly, Elvis Presley, Wanda Jackson, Gene Vincent, and Pat Boone, demonstrating the widespread cultural resonance of the rejection of delayed gratification in popular culture.

The actual phrase *rock 'n' roll* comes from this atmosphere of working-class cultural resistance, as it was a vernacular that appeared in most early rhythm and blues songs. Years before rock 'n' roll became the music industry's name for rhythm and blues — once it was being consumed and performed by white youth in large numbers — rock 'n' roll was a phrase used in the everyday life of the urban working class to describe sexual activities and more general pleasures. In rhythm and blues songs, "rock 'n' roll" sometimes refers to sexual intercourse, as in "my baby rocked and rolled me all night long," and sometimes it refers to having a good time, as in it was a "rockin'" good time. Typically, in an R&B song, a rockin' good time ends up with partygoers and the police in fisticuffs as the cops attempted to break up the party. Both of these meanings are used in Louis Jordan's smash hit record "Saturday Night Fish Fry." Written in 1947, "Saturday Night Fish

Fry" is a rocking tune with a boogie-woogie piano, a walking bass line, a heavy backbeat, and a very funny narrative about rowdy partygoers who end up fighting with the police and going to jail. In addition to being one of the first rhythm and blues tunes to feature the electric guitar, it was also one of the first tunes that emphasized the term *rockin'* in the chorus. The last few verses describe in humorous style how the rowdy party gets shut down by the police:

> Now, the women was screamin' and jumpin' and yellin',
> The bottles was flyin' and the fish was smellin';
> And way up above all the noise they made,
> Somebody hollered, "Better get out of here; this is a raid!"
> Now, I didn't know we was breakin' the law,
> But somebody reached up and hit me on the jaw,
> They had us blocked off from the front and the back,
> And they was puttin' 'em in the wagon like potatoes in a sack.
> It was rockin'! It was rockin'!
> You never seen such scufflin' and shufflin' till the break of dawn!
> It was rockin'! It was rockin'!
> You never seen such scufflin' and shufflin' till the break of dawn!
> I knew I could get away if I had a chance,
> But I was shakin' like I had the St. Vitus dance,
> Now, I tried to crawl under a bathtub,
> When the policeman said, "Where you goin' there, bub?"[48]

In mainstream, white, middle-class popular music of the late 1940s, it would be very unlikely hear a tune boasting about going to a party to get drunk, get in a fight with the police, and end up in jail. On the contrary, pop music portrayed a more wholesome image of everyday life in America, but in many corners of urban America, the middle-class norms did not apply.

While Louis Jordan helped create the template for rhythm and blues in the early 1940s, a new group of artists took advantage of the growing demand for the new music toward the end of the war and immediately after the war, including influential black recording artists like Wynonie Harris, Big Joe Turner, T-Bone Walker, and Amos Milburn, as well as white musicians like Hank Williams, who contributed to the development of honky-tonk, and Bob Wills, whose Western Swing music, together with honky-tonk, influenced the development of rockabilly in the 1950s.

Among the African American rhythm and blues musicians, Wynonie

Harris in particular embodied the audacity of working-class pretension after the war. Harris had made a name for himself as an outrageous entertainer on the West Coast during the war. Like Louis Jordan, Wynonie Harris had a background in vaudeville, entertaining people at minstrel shows that traveled the Midwest between Nebraska and the Dakotas. He got his start in the nascent rhythm and blues culture while in Kansas City in the mid-1930s, where he used to socialize with the other great blues shouters, Big Joe Turner and "Mr. Five by Five," Jimmy Rushing. At that time, Turner worked as a bartender and bouncer in Kansas City. The wide-open anything goes night life in that city exposed the three men to the exciting lifestyle of entertainers as well as an opportunity to learn from the masters of the swing era. Turner and Harris were in Kansas City when Count Basie and Charlie Parker were rocking that town, and Rushing joined Basie's band in 1935. The blues shouters were particularly influenced by Count Basie's style of swing. In fact, Basie's hit record "One O'Clock Jump" gave the new genre of music developed by Jordan, Harris, and Turner its name: *jump* blues. Basie's famous rhythm section — bassist Walter Page, guitarist Freddie Greene, and drummer Jo Jones — were particularly influential in the construction of the "jump." Years later, Page and Jones were idolized by the Rolling Stones' rhythm section, drummer Charlie Watts and bassist Bill Wyman.

When the scene in Kansas City waned, Harris made his way out to Los Angeles to take advantage of the new economic opportunities associated with the rising demand for rhythm and blues music in urban areas where factory workers were eager to enjoy the night life. Harris soon found an audience for his rowdy and sometimes raunchy brand of music. Los Angeles was the scene of major labor unrest. One of the first wildcat strikes of the 1940s occurred in Los Angeles when workers from local 683 of the United Auto Workers (UAW) walked off the job at North American Aviation in Inglewood on June 5, 1941. According to Glaberman, that strike helped to set the tone for workers during the war, as it demonstrated that rank-and-file workers were much more radical than union leaders.[49]

Black workers led several of the wildcat strikes in the 1940s, especially over issues having to do with the rights of blacks, including a famous strike at Dodge Motors in Detroit when the Chrysler Corporation refused to allow black workers to transfer to new plants on the same basis as white workers. Workplace discrimination had been a seriously contested issue when, in 1940, A. Phillip Randolph, the leader of the Brotherhood Sleeping

Car Porters labor union, threatened a march on Washington if the Roosevelt administration did not take a more aggressive stand against the problem of racial discrimination in war-related industries. FDR, facing pressure from Randolph and other civil rights and labor leaders, responded by creating the Fair Employment Practices Committee, which had as its mission the eradication of workplace discrimination. It was this combination of Roosevelt's position against workplace discrimination and relatively tight labor markets that provided opportunities for black workers to take more political risks at work, including the instigation of wildcat strikes. According to Glaberman, it "was a fairly common expression of black workers that they had Hitler and Tojo to thank for their better-paying jobs in industry. Patriotism was of much less significance among black auto workers."[50]

Wynonie Harris found regular work in Los Angles around Central Avenue, which had already become a major cultural center for African Americans, rivaling both Harlem and New Orleans.[51] In some ways, Los Angeles had taken over for Kansas City as the preferred locale for hipsters looking for wild times. Historian R. J. Smith has captured the exciting mood:

> Walled off by segregation and custom, black L.A. built an infinitely rich world. Once upon a time black L.A. was a stand-alone city within a city. . . . Once upon a time, everything was connected: the civil rights leader Clayton Russell was good friends with the R&B artists. He appears fictionalized in one of the early L.A. books of black novelist Chester Himes. On Central Avenue the jazz musicians were civil rights champions; the actors were tied to the gangsters; the gangsters courted the crusading newspaper who was allied with the Communist Party; the renegade communist was a member of the gay subculture; the gay subculture's meeting place, Brother's after-hour club, was also the site of fabled jazz sessions.[52]

Most of the major big bands including the Count Basie Orchestra, Duke Ellington's band, Benny Goodman's, and Billy Eckstine's band made numerous appearances in the area, as it was the major hub of music activity in the Southwest. Others who had an important influence on the creation of rhythm and blues were the pianist, vocalist and composer Hadda Brooks, who was dubbed "Queen of the Boogie," for compositions like "Swingin' the Boogie," and Nell Lutcher, pianist and vocalist, who recorded "Hurry on Down," and "He's a Real Gone Guy." In his memoir, Buddy Collette, one of the most famous musicians to come out of the Central Avenue area, recalled that "the war years had brought a booming economy and also an awareness that people could do more than just what they were doing before. The black community began to expand and venture out."[53] Trumpeter Art Farmer, who arrived in Los Angeles in 1945, referred to the boisterous cultural atmosphere of the Central Avenue area as "the Wild West."[54] Central Avenue, which stretched south from downtown Los Angeles through the neighborhoods of Watts and Compton, showcased several clubs that served as key venues for the development of rhythm and blues as well as bebop. These included the Elks Auditorium, the Jungle Room, the Club Alabam (a regular venue for Harris), the Cosmo Club, the Downbeat, the Last Word, and a handful of clubs run by Billy Berg, including the Club Capri and the Trouville. Many bebop musicians frequented the clubs managed by Berg, conducting late-night jam sessions that rivaled the famous jam sessions at Minton's in New York City. Blues shouters like Harris and Big Joe Turner as well as the singer/songwriter T-Bone Walker shared venues with leading local jazz musicians like Charles Mingus, Lester Young, Buddy Collette, and Joe Lutcher, as well as beboppers from out of town, like Dizzy Gillespie and Charlie Parker, who introduced Los Angeles to bebop in 1945.

It was in this social and political environment that Wynonie Harris created an identity for himself as a brash, raucous, good-looking rock 'n' roll star. Harris was one of the most outrageous of the blues shouters from the late 1940s, with a notorious reputation as a hard drinker and big spender. In the book *Central Avenue Sounds*—a collection of oral histories from many of the important musicians who lived and worked in the area during that time—the pianist Gerald Wiggins recalls that "T-Bone Walker was around. Wynonie Harris. Bad news. [laughter] Whew! Yeah, Wynonie. Now, that was a character, if you wanted a character. He got into fights everywhere he went."[55] Harris was renowned for announcing to the patrons of his favorite clubs as he entered, "Mr. Blues is back in town, and I have enough money to air-condition Hell!"[56] Eventually Harris rose to fame after a string of hits in 1946–47, including "Good Rockin' Tonight." It was written by Roy Brown, but the record was never a hit for Brown as it was for Harris. Harris's recordings perfected the function of blues music, which according to music historian Albert Murray "is not only to drive the blues away and hold them at bay at least for the time being, but also to evoke an ambiance of Dionysian revelry."[57] "Ambiance of Dionysian revelry" is a good way to describe the influence Harris had on the formation of rhythm and blues.

According to rock critic and historian Jim Miller, "Harris and his combo transformed the song into a celebration of everything dance music can be: an incantation, an escape, an irrepressible joyous expression of sheer physical existence."[58] Decades before Mick Jagger announced to the world that he was Beelzebub in the Rolling Stones classic recording of "Sympathy for the Devil," Wynonie Harris was causing serious mischief and Dionysian mayhem among his generation of postwar GIs.[59] In "Good Rockin' Tonight," Harris uses the term "rockin'" in all its connotations: a rocking good time, the house is rocking from all the dancing, and somewhere in the house somebody is surely rock 'n' rolling with his/her partner. Many of his songs include narratives about promiscuity and excessive drinking.

Harris cut "Good Rockin' Tonight" in 1947 for King Records, based in Cincinnati, Ohio. King records was one of the key independent record labels of the 1940s that filled the void left by the major record labels that had turned a collective deaf ear to rhythm and blues and country music. King records was founded by Syd Nathan, a former jazz drummer. In addition to recording Wynonie Harris, Nathan helped launch the careers of Hank Ballard, (who recorded the hit "Work with Me, Annie"), Little Willie John, Billy Ward and the Dominos, and Bull Moose Jackson. The biggest star to come out of King Records was James Brown, whose *Live at the Apollo Vol. 1* hit number two on the album charts in 1963.[60] Together with other labels like Queen, Deluxe, Federal, and Glory, Nathan used King Records to respond to a growing demand for both country music and rhythm and blues. Situated in Cincinnati, and observing the migration of both working-class whites from the Appalachia region and working-class blacks from the South to cities like Detroit, Cleveland, Chicago, and Cincinnati, Nathan was in a position to produce recorded music previously neglected by the major labels. In doing so, Nathan also contributed to the crossover phenomenon, selling records to white and black consumers, playing a key role in the emergence of what would become rock 'n' roll.

While it is true that many of the independent record label owners did exploit the recording artists on their rosters, it is also the case that the independent labels were willing to take risks on music that the major record labels did not consider a viable business opportunity. King was a good example, by making a star out of Wynonie Harris and James Brown. Historical scholarship on the role of the independents has tended to be polarized to some extent between those who take the position of Chapple and Garofalo that the indies phenomenon can best be understood in terms of racial discrimination and exploitation—what they refer to as "black roots and white fruits"—and cheerleaders like Kennedy and McNutt who tend to portray the independent record label owners as *hero* entrepreneurs who made rock 'n' roll possible thanks to their ability to foresee trends that nobody else was able to understand.[61] Of course, to some extent, both of these representations of the indies are accurate. Many did exploit the recording artists on their rosters, and much of the exploitation was racially motivated. But it is also true that rock 'n' roll music might not have emerged when and where it did, if it were not for the structural openings in the music industry that were exploited by independent record label owners who were willing to take a risk by recording the music that the majors considered an unviable business opportunity. Recent scholarship by Broven has corrected the error of the one-sidedness of previous interpretations of the role of the independent record labels in the history of rock 'n' roll.[62]

The phrase "rock 'n' roll" had long been in use in the African American community, but the jump blues musicians like Harris helped to make it a mainstay in postwar, urban working-class culture. In addition to "Good Rockin' Tonight," Harris cut two tunes in 1949 that helped introduce the term "rock" to popular music and popular culture. First was a tune that he wrote himself called "All She Wants to Do Is Rock," and the second record was "I Like My Baby's Pudding." Both records were not so subtle tributes to the pleasures of carnal indulgences, but perhaps the one record that went over the top with sexual double entendres was "Keep on Churnin,'" also on King Records, cut in 1952. "Keep on churnin' til the butter comes" is the main refrain on the record, followed by "wipe off the paddle and churn some more." Raunchy double entendres like these did not raise many eyebrows in middle-class, white society as long as recording artists like Wynonie Harris were coded as "race" artists. Controversy regarding the suggestive and raunchy lyrics did emerge, however, when white teenagers began enjoying rhythm and blues in large numbers in the early 1950s.[63] On Harris's records that are still available on the King label today, including some of the recent compilations, there are warnings of "explicit lyrics," although Harris never actually cursed on any of his records. On "Good Morning, Judge," recorded in 1950, he sings about getting arrested for dating a fifteen-year-old girl who just so happens to be the daughter of a policeman, then having to explain himself to the judge.

"Good Rockin' Tonight" solidified Harris's place in the rock 'n' roll hall of fame. In June of 1948 *Billboard* magazine listed "Good Rockin' Tonight" as both the "best-selling" and "most played" race record in jukeboxes. While Harris's version of "Good Rockin' Tonight" was a huge hit in the "race" jukeboxes across America, and although Harris was marketed as a black entertainer, his music was eventually heard by white teens via radio, which led to white teenagers crossing the tracks to the black side of town to buy copies of "Good Rockin' Tonight" and other "race" records. Beginning in the early 1950s, southern working-class white kids who tuned into radio stations like WDIA in Memphis, got turned on to rhythm and blues music. In fact, one of Elvis Presley's first big hit records was a cover version of "Good Rockin' Tonight," a song he had heard on radio in Memphis while working as a truck driver.

In addition to the blues shouters like Wynonie Harris and Big Joe Turner, other key musicians from the postwar era who had an important influence on the formation of what I refer to as working-class pretension in rock 'n' roll culture were T-Bone Walker from Texas, Guitar Slim from Greenwood, Mississippi, who had a hit tune on the label Specialty Records (produced by a young Ray Charles and later covered by Stevie Ray Vaughn) titled, "The Things That I Used to Do" in 1954, and Hank Williams from Alabama.[64]

T-Bone Walker was closer to the classic blues than the "shouting" rhythm and blues style of Wynonie Harris and Big Joe Turner, but he is a key figure in the history of rock 'n' roll because of his astonishing guitar work, which emphasized single notes through picking as opposed to the strumming style of rhythm guitar. Walker helped to establish the guitar solo as a key feature in rock 'n' roll music. He also developed unconventional performances that incorporated outrageous bodily contortions into his guitar solos. Years before Chuck Berry was doing his duck walk across the stage, and more than a decade before Jimi Hendrix was playing guitar with his teeth, T-Bone Walker was playing electric guitar behind his head, jumping up in the air with his guitar, landing on the ground in the splits. T-Bone was a close friend of Charlie Christian, the guitarist who played in the Benny Goodman band. Together with Christian, Walker demonstrated the enormous potential of the electric guitar. In the jazz idiom before Christian, guitar was seen as primarily a rhythm instrument, and in the traditional blues, guitar was largely understood as an acoustic instrument. When Les Paul developed the electric guitar, everything changed. After

Charlie Christian's and T-Bone Walker's innovations, the guitar rivaled the saxophone as the preferred instrument for the skilled instrumental soloist in rhythm and blues music.

T-Bone Walker's biggest hit was "Call It Stormy Monday," recorded on Black and White Records in 1947 and perhaps the most important blues guitar record ever cut. It became a pop standard virtually overnight, and it has been covered and performed by countless bands since, including Count Basie, Muddy Waters, Isaac Hayes, Albert King, B.B. King, Eric Clapton, and the Allman Brothers, who recorded it for their famous live album that captured their signature performance at the Fillmore East. The virtuoso guitar playing in "Stormy Monday" redefined what was possible on guitar, profoundly influencing younger guitar geniuses like Chuck Berry and Jimi Hendrix.

Apart from the classic guitar licks played masterfully by Walker, the song is famous for its lyrics. The lyrical refrain of the song is about work, or rather the flight from work. The term *stormy* refers to the juxtaposition—via metaphor—of the paradise of the weekend to the bad weather endured during the workweek. Monday is signified as "stormy" because many workers begin the workweek with a hangover from the heavy drinking and partying that took place during the night, if not the entire weekend, before. Walker's record signifies a popular tradition from the nineteenth century when workers would take an extra day off work without the official recognition or permission of the employer. Beginning in the early decades of the nineteenth century, nearly a century before the labor movement achieved the two-day weekend, factory workers referred to Monday as "Saint" Monday, because they often stayed home or came in to work very late due to the fact that they were recovering from a hangover. In short, "Saint" Monday, became an unofficial holiday of sorts. Before the Fair Labor Standards Act of 1938, which instituted the forty-hour workweek, there was no weekend as we now know it, but thanks to nearly a century of fighting for shorter hours of work, the labor movement finally delivered another day for the weekend. Walker's famous tune signifies the history and tradition of "Saint Monday" in the following lyrics:

> They call it stormy Monday,
> But Tuesday's just as bad.
> Yes, they call it stormy Monday,
> But Tuesday's just as bad.

Wednesday's worse, and Thursday's also sad.
Yes, the eagle flies on Friday and Saturday I go out to play,
Yes, the eagle flies on Friday, and Saturday I go out to play . . .
They call it stormy Monday.[65]

Although workers won an extra day off each week in the 1930s, it was still the case, as T-Bone Walker signifies, that Monday through Friday remained sheer misery. Friday night, however, the eagle flies! The anti-work/pro-leisure theme from "Stormy Monday" is the continuation of "stomping the blues," as described by Albert Murray. Walker's record helped keep alive the counterlogic of labor, which animates both rhythm and blues and rock 'n' roll. In fact, this central image in working-class culture was recorded a generation after T-Bone's record, on Fats Domino's smash hit record "Blue Monday," originally cut for Imperial Records in 1956. "Blue Monday" made it to number five on the "pop" charts and number one on the rhythm and blues charts. The lyrical content of the song is virtually the same in "Blue Monday" as it is in "Stormy Monday." In "Blue Monday," Fats Domino declares how much he despises "blue" Monday because he has to "go to work and slave all day." In the middle of the week Domino complains that he is "so tired" that he has "no time to play." And as if to tip his hat to T-Bone Walker, he sings, "Sunday mornin' I'm feeling bad, but it's worth it for the time I've had," and "I've got to get my rest, 'cause Monday is a mess." Louis Jordan and his generation of black musicians — including Wynonie Harris, Big Joe Turner and T-Bone Walker — were the most influential recording artists in the development of rock 'n' roll, but other genres like Western Swing and honky-tonk were also important influences in the construction of what would become rock 'n' roll in the 1950s.

Honky-tonk was the rough equivalent of rhythm and blues in the country music genre, since honky-tonk developed in urban areas as working-class white musicians versed in country music migrated to cities in search of work during the war. Hank Williams was the biggest country music star to emerge out of Nashville. Between 1948 and 1953, Williams had eleven records that sold more than a million copies each. He was especially influential for the group of Sun Records musicians from Memphis, including Elvis Presley, Carl Perkins, Jerry Lee Lewis, and Johnny Cash. Like the rhythm and blues musicians from his generation, Hank Williams was part of the great migration of workers to war production centers during the war. Williams found work as a welder in a shipyard in Mobile for the Alabama Drydock and Shipbuilding Company, which at the time held a contract with the Department of Defense for manufacturing ships for the war. And, just as was the case with the rhythm and blues musicians of his era, Hank Williams found an eager audience for his music among the workers who had recently arrived from the countryside. But unlike the more playful, affirmative content of most jump blues music, many of Hank Williams's tunes were sad, dark songs about the pain and suffering that came from hard work at low pay. Williams once said that in order to understand his music, you had to have an intimate knowledge of the relative brutality of certain kinds of work.[66] Williams also saw into the dark side of relationships between lovers and in family life more generally, topics that Tin Pan Alley tunes kept at bay. Many of his songs exposed the lie of domestic bliss in America in songs like "Your Cheatin' Heart," "I'm So Lonesome I Could Cry," and "Long Gone Lonesome Blues."

Williams's father was an itinerant laborer, and William's childhood experiences were filled with hard times, as his father sometimes went long stretches of time without work. As a child, Williams suffered from malnutrition, and a severe case of hookworm damaged his eyesight. As a young man he suffered an accident while trying out for a rodeo that caused a serious back injury that gave him problems for the rest of his life. Like other poor kids from his generation, Hank Williams viewed entertainment, whether as a rodeo star or as a country music star, as the only way out of a life of grinding poverty and back-breaking low-wage jobs.

Williams was profoundly influenced by blues music. The pain and suffering Williams experienced as the child of a poor working-class southern family helps explain the cross-pollination of blues music into country music more generally. He was exposed to blues as a boy and also when he worked as a welder. His first music lessons were with a black singer and musician, Rufus Payne. When Williams organized his own band, he used traditional hillbilly instrumentation and arrangements, including steel guitar, fiddles, and the four-line rhymed couplet verses that were typical in country music, but he also sang in falsetto style and used call-and-response techniques that he learned from listening to blues music and from his training with Payne.

While many of his songs portrayed a feeling of loneliness and alienation that accompanied his personal life, others were more upbeat tunes that celebrated leisure and emphasized the value of immediate pleasure over delayed gratification. One of the best examples is "Honky-tonkin,'" a song about stepping out on the town and spending lots of money. In "Honky-tonkin,'" we can see a theme similar to that of Louis Jordan's "Let the Good Times Roll." The song holds its own with any of the rowdy jump blues tunes of the same era. In the first two verses Williams sings: "When you are sad and lonely and have no place to go / Call me up, sweet baby, and bring some dough / And we'll go honky-tonkin,' honey baby / When you and your baby have a falln' out / Just call me up sweet mama and we'll go steppin' out / And we'll go honky-tonkin.'[67] Williams also flirts with the topic of infidelity—as he does in many of his songs—when he tells his date not to worry about a falling out with her boyfriend because Williams will show her a good time to get her mind off of her failing relationship. Another good example is the song "Settin' the Woods on Fire," perhaps Williams's most rambunctious, again emphasizing the importance of spending lots of money and having as much fun as possible. In "Settin' the Woods on Fire," Williams (2002) sings:

> Comb your hair and paint and powder, you act proud and I'll act prouder
> You sing loud and I'll sing louder, tonight we're settin' the woods on fire
> You're my gal and I'm your feller, dress up in your frock of yeller
> I'll look swell but you'll look sweller, settin' the woods on fire
> We'll take in all the honky-tonks tonight we're having fun
> We'll show the folks a brand new dance that never has been done
> I don't care who thinks we're silly, you'll be daffy and I'll be dilly
> We'll order up two bowls of chili, settin' the woods on fire
> I'll gas up my hot rod stoker, we'll get hotter than a poker
> You'll be broke but I'll be broker, tonight we're settin' the woods on fire
> We'll sit close to one another, up one street and down the other
> Tonight we'll have a ball oh brother, settin' the woods on fire
> We'll put aside a little time to fix a flat or two
> My trey and tubes are doin' fine but the air is showin' through
> You clap hands and I'll start howlin,' we'll do all the law's allowin'
> Tomorrow I'll be right back plowin,' settin' the woods on fire

The key lines in "Settin' the Woods on Fire" are the lines about acting proud, competing to see who can spend more money in order to become "broker," not caring what anyone thinks about how they look; indeed, looking fine and acting silly is the point. Williams's emphasis on spending as much money as possible and pushing the law to the limit clearly demonstrates the counterlogic of labor that developed out of the postwar working-class culture of pretension.

Williams and his contemporaries were performing for an audience that was taking advantage of growing economic prosperity after the war, and since their generation had fulfilled their patriotic duty by sacrificing their labor and lives for the war effort, the music incorporates a particular entitlement to the good life earned by years of sacrifice. The soldiers who returned home from the horrors of war, and the factory workers who worked extra-long hours with no increase in pay were looking to cash in on the political and moral capital they had accrued during the war. You can hear these sentiments in Williams's tune "Rockin' Chair Money," from 1947, a song that became an anthem for working-class servicemen and servicewomen returning from the war.

> Now I got rockin' chair money
> But I got it the hard, hard way
> I fought in every battle
> From the start to the VJ day
> And now I'll rock . . . yeah rock . . .
> Oh baby rock . . . rock on down the line
> I'll soon get my big check, baby
> And then we'll have some fun
> This rockin' chair money, honey
> Is better than totin' a gun
> Cause I love to rock, yeah rock
> Baby, rock, let's rock on down the line
> Now, honey, let's go honky-tonkin'
> Let's honky-tonk all night
> Let's lollygag and smooch and love
> and do it all up right
> Cause I love to rock, yeah rock
> Baby, rock, let's rock on down the line

Like Louis Jordan, Williams was among the first recording artists to popularize the term *rock*. "Rockin' chair money" refers to the GI Bill and along with it the improving lifestyles afforded by soldiers who took advantage of government programs to buy a house, attend school, secure access to healthcare, etc. Williams also uses the term *rockin'* to signify having a good time by spending some of that money from the GI Bill. Williams use the hillbilly slang words *honky-tonkin'* and the blues slang word *rockin'* interchangeably to describe the pleasures found in the leisure spaces of the city. In "Rockin' Chair Money," Williams says that after he gets his big check he's going to "lollygag" and "smooch," signifying the desire to idle away the hours indulging in the various pleasures at hand.

Hank Williams sang, and continues to sing, for workers who dream about better pay and more leisure time. The ideological categories of scarcity, discipline, and delayed gratification that permeate bourgeois cultural forms were largely rejected by the culture of the American working class during Williams's tenure as the king of hillbilly music. In songs like "Settin' the Woods on Fire" and "Rockin' Chair Money," Williams helped shape the working-class culture of resistance that challenged the main bourgeois ideological categories. This was his legacy that the 1950s rockabilly stars like Elvis Presley, Carl Perkins, Wanda Jackson, Johnny Cash, and Jerry Lee Lewis would embrace. In turn, the British invasion bands like the Beatles and the Rolling Stones revived that legacy in the 1960s.

Honky-tonk and rhythm and blues music developed from everyday life experiences, as opposed to much of the mainstream popular music from Tin Pan Alley, which came from the top down, so to speak, from corporate media centers like New York. In large part, the music from Tin Pan Alley, called pop "standards," was influenced by the European bourgeois traditions of separating music from everyday life. Tin Pan Alley songs generally described life in America as peaceful bliss. Most songs were ballads about falling in love or happy songs devoid of any references to the very real tensions and conflicts that existed between the races and classes in America. As Charles Hamm has argued, "Tin Pan Alley songs were for white, urban, literate, middle- and upper-class Americans. They remained practically unknown to large segments of American society, including most blacks . . . and the millions of poor, white rural Americans."[68] For honky-tonk and rhythm and blues music, on the other hand, the musicians and the music were intimately linked to the experiences of everyday life, and live performances usually included the audience in the show via call-and-response practices, a tradition that extends back in time to the field songs of the slaves. In sum, within the history of country and blues music, we see the survival of the preindustrial culture of the working class, a culture which celebrates leisure and which has struggled against the imposition of the

Calvinist work ethic since the early years of the transition to capitalism in the United States during the nineteenth century.[69]

With the exception of Hank Williams and Louis Jordan, many of the country and jump blues from the mid-1940s to the early 1950s remained marginal to the pop charts and the core of the music industry as well as from mainstream society. The music was recorded almost exclusively on independent record labels, and it wasn't played much on the radio either, which meant the only place you could hear it was on the jukebox in an out-of-the-way working-class tavern. The main reason why blues and hillbilly music remained on the margins of radio in the 1930s and 1940s is because it clashed with middle-class bourgeois values and it represented a very different version of life in America. In addition to these cultural differences, there were structural reasons for the marginalization of blues and country music: most of the music on the radio consisted of songs licensed by the American Society of Composers, Authors and Publishers (ASCAP), which routinely excluded blues musicians and country musicians from membership, ostensibly on the grounds that their music was not worthy of airplay, nor were the songwriters sufficiently trained in the cultural capital necessary to join the exclusive membership of ASCAP, which dominated Tin Pan Alley. In spite of these barriers, the working-class culture of blues and hillbilly music thrived, and two developments in the music industry would soon expand the boundaries of jump blues and country. The first was the significant improvement of electronic recording technologies, and the second was the invention of television, which completely restructured the format of radio in favor of previously neglected segments of the music market.

Rhythm and Blues Crosses Over to the Pop Music Market

In the late 1940s, before the era of television and before the civil rights movement challenged racial segregation, there were relatively few opportunities for a record by Wynonie Harris, Amos Milburn, T-Bone Walker, and many other rhythm and blues musicians to get on the radio stations that catered to large markets of mainly white listeners. Not only was radio more or less dominated by content marketed for middle-class whites, but the bawdy content of rhythm and blues records, which consisted of stories about hard drinking and casual sex, was much too controversial to be considered for radio play. Explicitly bawdy content was strictly off limits. Rhythm and blues lived and thrived in the jukeboxes, which partly explains why rock 'n' roll became a record culture. The improvements in recording technologies that resulted from the invention of electronic recording, which replaced the older acoustic techniques of recording, combined with the discovery of magnetic tape recording technology captured by Allied forces during the war, dramatically improved the technique of recording and the quality of records and helped to elevate the recording artist to pop icon during the 1940s. The new technologies also made record production in general more efficient, which made it possible for record companies to drop their prices on records.[70] Even smaller independent record companies could turn a decent profit on relatively small budgets. For the major record labels, sheer volume of sales created an economy of scale that allowed them to significantly drop prices. By 1946 record sales had reached more that $165 million. That revenue came largely from the sales driven by the demand from jukebox operators in working-class juke joints.[71]

Radio had made stars out of white musicians and performers, as well as black musicians like Louis Armstrong, and the big bands of Duke Ellington and Count Basie, but records opened the door for working-class black and white musicians who had been completely shut out of radio, since radio was controlled by taste makers who preferred jazz dance music and Tin Pan Alley pop ballads. After the development of and sustained demand for jukeboxes, working-class musicians and aficionados could produce, distribute, and consume their own culture relatively independently from the virtual monopoly held over the music industry by ASCAP, the major record labels, and the National Association of Broadcasters (NAB). The enormous popularity of jump blues and hillbilly music on jukeboxes in working-class bars and dance halls continued to drive up record sales for the music in spite of receiving virtually no airplay on the radio. By the early 1950s, record sales topped the $200 million mark.[72]

Jukeboxes were particularly significant in the growth of rhythm and blues. In the late 1940s there were some 750,000 jukeboxes in America. Jukeboxes were key technological factors that fostered the expansion of rhythm and blues music that provided cultural support to the political battle for racial equality. Many black recording artists like Wynonie Harris and T-Bone Walker became big stars in spite of not being heard on the radio because of the enormous popularity of the jukebox. Working-class African Americans who visited juke joints had considerably more purchasing power after the war, which helped to drive up record sales. More important, the jukebox made it possible for the working class to develop its own culture during the 1940s, because a night out at the juke joint was relatively inexpensive compared with paying to see live music. Bars have always been an important social space for the American working class to develop its own, autonomous culture, and the jukebox significantly improved the atmosphere and quality of life in working-class bars.[73] With the jukebox, the relatively inexpensive "talking machine" (record player), and cheap records, the working class was able to create a distinct cultural tradition separate and sometimes in conflict with middle-class norms.

Records were a means for learning how to play instruments. Working-class aficionados could purchase a record they first heard in a jukebox, take it home, put it on the turntable, pick up their guitar, and learn to play. The social and cultural significance of the new recording technologies can be found in Walter Benjamin's prophetic vision outlined in his 1936 essay, "The Work of Art in the Age of Mechanical Reproduction."[74] Benjamin predicted that technologies that made possible the reproduction of art by mechanical means (which included sound recordings) would profoundly alter the social relations of production in capitalist society. Specifically, he predicted that the working class stood to benefit from the transformation of art at the hands of the camera and the talking machine, the phrase used for record players at the time when Edison first invented the device. While Benjamin focused mostly on the camera to make his case, it is equally the case with records.

Benjamin believed that with mechanical reproduction two profound shifts in the production and consumption of art take place: first, the distinction between artist and audience becomes blurred. Second, common folk become critics and experts in the field of aesthetics. Benjamin made his case by arguing that mechanical reproduction erodes the "aura" of a work of art by freeing it from its "parasitic" dependence on tradition and ritual, a process that gives a work of art "cult" value. The aura of a work of art refers to its uniqueness stemming from the particular time and place of its origin. With mechanical reproduction, not only is it relatively meaningless to speak of an original, but also the work of art is no longer embedded in the context of its origin. It becomes portable. With records, you can take a performance of Beethoven, or whomever else, with you to whatever context you choose. As a result, Benjamin argues that art loses its status as a cult object, and it becomes political because the "masses" have *access* to it. Furthermore, mechanical reproduction means that because the masses have access to the work of art, they are given the opportunity to become critics of art, ~~a role~~ *and artists?* previously enjoyed exclusively by the bourgeoisie. According to Benjamin:

> The technique of reproduction detaches the reproduced object from the domain of tradition. By making many reproductions it substitutes a plurality of copies for a unique existence. *And in permitting the reproduction to meet the beholder or listener in his own particular situation, it reactivates the object reproduced.* . . . The camera that presents the performance of the film actor to the public need not respect the performance as an integrated whole. Guided by the cameraman, the camera continually changes its position with respect to the performance. The sequence of positional views which the editor composes from the material supplied him constitutes the completed film. . . . Hence, the performance of the actor is subjected to a series of optical tests. . . . Also, the film actor lacks the opportunity of the stage actor to adjust to the audience during his performance, since he does not present his performance to the audience in person. This permits the audience to take the position of a critic, without experiencing any personal contact with the actor.[75]

The same is true with records, because they meet the listener in his/her own particular situation. In addition to providing the working class with the means to become art critics, records also break down the distinction between performers and audience, because the masses are provided with the means to learn how to play music. Benjamin also makes his case with the example of print media:

> With the increasing extension of the press . . . an increasing number of readers became writers — *at first occasional ones.* It began with the daily press opening to its reader's space for "letters to the editor." And today there is hardly a gainfully employed European who could not, in principle, find an opportunity to publish somewhere or other comments on his work, grievances, documentary reports, or that sort of thing. Thus, the distinction between author and public is about to lose its basic character.[76]

This is precisely what happened with the emergence of rock 'n' roll music: aficionados from the working class became critics of music by amassing huge record collections. By the early 1950s, working-class kids were purchasing more records, enjoying an improving lifestyle in the after-hours juke joints, and becoming skilled musicians in their own right by listening to their favorite records. When discussing how his generation of musicians learned about the existence of blues music and also how to play it, Felix Cavaliere, from the rock band The Young Rascals, recalled that "nowadays the people have schools they can go to and study all that music. In those days we had records. People all over the world could study that music on records. Those records were like gold."[77] George Harrison of the Beatles studied the B sides of records by Carl Perkins in order to learn how to play rock 'n' roll.[78] Between 1948 and 1954, a thousand independent record companies went into business, and by 1952 record sales for independent companies soared past $15 million.[79] All this took place with hardly any airplay on the radio. To paraphrase Benjamin, there was hardly a gainfully employed American who could not, in principle, find an opportunity to record and publish music.

At the same time that the new technologies were improving the process of recording, the big radio networks were developing a new medium called television. When NBC, CBS, and later ABC began broadcasting on television they transferred their variety shows from radio to television. As a result, local radio affiliates lost much of their programming. After television, music and recorded music in particular became the dominant format for radio, as many local stations found market niches in particular kinds of music, like rhythm and blues, which at last made its way onto radio in the early 1950s. A new network developed in the periphery of the music industry that connected independent record companies to local radio stations and their fan base of black and white working-class people and young aspiring rock 'n' roll musicians.[80] This first occurred in the South in places like Memphis and Nashville.

WHBQ in Memphis was one of the most popular radio stations, and the most popular show was Dewey Phillips's rock 'n' roll radio show, *Red Hot 'n' Blue*. Phillips is less well known today than Alan Freed, another disc jockey, but Phillips was one of the first white disc jockeys to play black records, and he was the first modern disc jockey to become a star in his own right. Phillips, who began his broadcasting career in 1949, developed an on-air routine that made himself as much a part of the show as the music, which significantly influenced the development of the role of disc jockey on radio. After Phillips, radio stations that used music programming as their dominant format made the disc jockey personality a main feature of their programming content as a way to attract larger audiences. Eventually, the disc jockey became just as important a draw as the music itself. Dewey Phillips had a fiery personality with a thick southern drawl that he combined with a hip attitude that was reflected in his taste for cutting-edge rhythm and blues music. He also talked over the beginning and the end of songs and would throw in all kinds of playful nonsense catch phrases that made his style unique.

More important, Phillips served as a role model of sorts for his working-class audience, proving to them that it was possible for the child of a tenant farmer to become a "hip" and "cultured" person. He demonstrated that working-class kids could be a part of an exciting new culture, representing a break from historical traditions that made "culture" the exclusive domain of the middle and well-to-do classes. Phillips was allowed to experiment with his show, since local radio stations were struggling in the late 1940s to find new content. The first night he had seven callers request records, and in less than a week, he had over 100 calls a night. The listening audience averaged over 100,000 each night. Phillips's first show in 1949 ran for just thirty minutes, but soon it ran two hours on weeknights and on Saturday from 9 to midnight. His show generated significant revenues from advertisers who were targeting a new, relatively affluent black working class in Memphis.

Memphis was one of the main destinations for blacks and working-class whites who left the Mississippi Delta area during the war in search of work and in desperation to escape the misery of the collapsing sharecropping system. Many who left the Deep South remained in Memphis, which had a growing economy as a result of the war and which remained strong after war's end. Chicago, New York, and St. Louis were also principal destinations for migrant workers. Marketing research via surveys revealed that like the other destinations, African Americans found a better life in Memphis. One survey showed that blacks consumed 80 percent of the rice in Memphis, 70 percent of its canned milk, and 65 percent of the all-purpose flour in that city. The same marketing study revealed that 93 percent of blacks in Memphis owned radios and that 30 percent of households had two radio sets.[81] Advertisers were eager to reach this new audience of consumers. With a show like *Red Hot 'n' Blue*, WHBQ enjoyed significant financial success. *Red Hot 'n' Blue* was one of the first programs to air black music almost exclusively, and as a result of the demand for the music and for the personality of the disc jockey, the show was a key ingredient in the advance of rock 'n' roll.

Dewey Phillips helped launch the careers of the recording artists at Sun Records, owned by Sam Phillips (no relation). Initially Sam Philips would let Dewey know about which records were hot sellers in the stores and popular in the jukeboxes. With this information in hand, Dewey Phillips would play those records on his show in order to attract an audience and advertising money. Eventually, the arrangement began working in reverse, when Sam Phillips requested that Dewey promote one of his artists on the Sun label.[82] Before television, the radio and recording industries existed largely in competition, but beginning in the late 1940s, independent record companies, independent record distributors, and local radio stations all worked together in promoting their business interests.

As disc jockeys like Dewey Phillips, Zenas "Daddy" Sears on WAOK in Atlanta, John R. Richbourg on WLAC in Nashville and Hunter Hancock on KFVD in Los Angeles soon found out, white teenagers were listening to their shows as well, creating a new interracial working-class culture of music that included self-educated aficionados, self-taught musicians, and creative constructors of identity. Hunter Hancock started his show *Harlem Matinee* in 1947, and like Dewey Phillips, Hancock's show was popular among black and white teenagers. Hancock's show was also popular with Chicanos. Hancock played mostly jazz music when he first began working at KFVD in 1944. In early 1947, Jack Allison from Modern Records, a small independent label that specialized in rhythm and blues, told Hancock that he was playing the wrong kind of music and that if he wanted the radio show to succeed he should try rhythm and blues records, including some that were cut on Modern Records. As a result of *Harlem Matinee*, sales of rhythm and blues records in southern California skyrocketed. John Dolphin, owner of the Dolphin record shop in Hollywood, which also specialized in rhythm and blues records, noticed that after Hancock went on the air, 40 percent of his buyers were white teenagers. Black, Chicano, and white working-class kids who listened to shows like *Red Hot 'n' Blue* and *Harlem Matinee* amassed large record collections that reflected their knowledge of all kinds of music.

The working-class youth culture that developed among young record buyers in the early 1950s was an appropriation of the working-class culture of pretension that emerged during the war. The working-class teenagers of the early 1950s were putting their stamp on the already existing culture, but what was different was the increasing interracial aspect of the culture. Dewey Phillips's and Hunter Hancock's radio shows were among the first manifestations of the interracial aspect of the developing culture because radio waves crossed over the segregated spaces of the city. In many cases, listeners were unable to determine the race of the disc jockey or the recording artist being played on the air. As the Memphis-based blues singer/songwriter Rufus Thomas noted, "Dewey was not white. Dewey had no color."[83] As a result of the popularity of the DJs, white kids who loved Dewey Phillips's radio show were more frequently shopping in black record stores and peeping in the windows of black clubs on Beale Street, while also attending live venues where they were prone to violate the separate seating areas rules that were typical in the late 1940s and early 1950s.

One of the young, white working-class rhythm and blues and country music aficionados at the center of the new record collecting culture was Elvis Presley. As a young man, Elvis made a reputation for himself with his gigantic record collection. Many of his childhood friends, as well as fellow rockabilly stars like Wanda Jackson, commented on the enormity of Elvis's collection, which contained records in the jazz, blues, jump blues, hillbilly, and Western Swing genres.[84] Elvis was just one example of how inexpensive records of relatively good quality allowed working-class youth to break down the barrier between artists and audience in the manner that Benjamin describes above. By combining the elements of different songs from their favorite records, which came from the diverse backgrounds of many kinds of musical traditions, Elvis, together with the other famed recording artists like Carl Perkins, Johnny Cash, and Jerry Lee Lewis, created rockabilly.

Like many from his generation of southern rock 'n' roll musicians, Elvis came from a family of failed sharecroppers, victims of the mechanization and consolidation of the cotton industry. Presley's father had moved his family from Tupelo, Mississippi, to escape grinding poverty in hopes of finding better opportunities in Memphis. Once in Memphis, Elvis hustled to scrap together numerous irregular jobs in order to help the family make ends meet. Elvis sold his blood, drove trucks, and ushered at movie houses to help the family get by, but he also made a point to keep some extra cash for himself to enjoy the musical culture offered by their new life in Memphis. The Presley family moved into a racially mixed, working-class neighborhood in Memphis, where black and white working-class teens spent much of their free time listening to records and hanging around the cornucopia of music clubs on Beale Street, America's capital of blues music.

Poor and working-class whites like Elvis Presley and other young white rock 'n' roll recording artists from Sun Records were attracted to the blues musicians because the blues music was steeped in the history of African American cultural resistance. In the antebellum South, blacks sang work songs to cope with the misery of slavery, and after the dismal failure of Reconstruction, they sang the blues to ease the burden of sharecropping, a system of labor exploitation perhaps second only to chattel slavery for its extreme brutality. Poor whites also toiled under the sharecropping system for starvation wages. Work in the cotton fields is the main point of reference for most of the first generation of southern rock 'n' roll musicians from the early 1950s, black and white.

Tina Turner worked in cotton fields as a young woman and recounted that the experience influenced the formation of the content of her music, as well as her career choice, in the first place. "I hated picking cotton," she said. "The sun was so hot. I dreaded it. It was those times that made me change my life. As a child, I knew I couldn't do that. It was the beginning of my . . . dislike and hatred for that kind of work and I decided I would not do that anymore."[85] Perhaps the most famous story about a rock 'n' roll star escaping the prison house of alienating labor is the story of Little Richard. He was working as a dishwasher at a bus station in Macon, Georgia, when, as legend has it, his boss barked at him to work faster. Richard slammed the dishes down and exclaimed, "Awop bop-a lop bop-a-wop bam boom, take 'em out!!" That, according to Little Richard, was the inspiration for one of his biggest hits, "Tutti Frutti."[86] This story of escape inspired young musicians who immersed themselves in rock 'n' roll history while they learned their craft. Joe Strummer, guitarist singer/songwriter from the 1970s British punk rock band The Clash, recalled, "I think of Little Richard working that shitty job in Macon, Georgia, and saying to himself, 'I'm going to get the fuck out of here. I'm going to be a rock star. And he made it. He got out of that kitchen. Man that's great, that's fucking great. His records are great. They still sound great and they always will sound great."[87]

Sam Phillips, the owner of Sun Records, also picked cotton as a young man, and he too fled cotton picking as if it were the plague. Although Phillips was hardly a role model for the good employer or model citizen—since he had a notorious reputation for mistreating some of his recording artists—it remains the case that Phillips was correct in surmising that in the South, rock 'n' roll culture was largely influenced by the flight from indentured servitude within the sharecropping system. Indeed, all the Sun Records artists, black and white, understood that the referent which framed their music was the refusal to work the most recent incarnation of the plantation. Sonny Burgess, one of the artists from Sun Records who — while never having had the chart success as his more famous peers — is credited with helping develop the rockabilly sound on guitar.

> We were all a bunch of country guys from this little area in the South, most of us anyways. Elvis was from Memphis, but everybody else lived out in the country. . . . Most all of us picked cotton, and that's one thing that makes you wanna play music. One day of picking cotton will make you *really* wanna play music. Everything is better than picking cotton.[88]

Johnny Cash, who also worked as a cotton picker, explained that his experience in the fields gave him a new perspective on blues music. "I love and understand the blues," said Cash in an interview. "I was born and bred on them. I'm from the Delta farmland on the Mississippi."[89] One of his popular records was "Pickin' Time," a song he wrote about the hand-to-mouth existence of workers in the cotton fields. He performed the tune with Tennessee Ernie Ford on Ford's television show after it became a hit. In short, working-class whites in the South were attracted to blues music because African Americans had developed the most sophisticated cultural response to oppression and exploitation. Blues music has provided one of the most effective means for aggrieved communities to cope with or resist exploitation. The history of African American culture is particularly rich in its creation of practices that provide oppressed populations the means to carve out spaces of autonomy within the structures of domination in everyday life.

The image of the struggle against work in country and blues musical culture often involved the affirmation of leisure and pleasure in addition to being a means of coping with the brutality of work in the cotton fields. Greil Marcus convincingly argues that the southern rock 'n' roll culture of the early 1950s expressed the Dionysian side of life. As a means to interpret the cultural significance of early rock 'n' roll, Marcus quotes from W. J. Cash's book, *The Mind of the South*, where he argues that the prototypical image in rock 'n' roll music is this:

> To go into the town on Saturday afternoon and night, to stroll with the throng, to gape at the well-dressed and the big automobiles, to bathe in the holiday cacophony . . . maybe have a drink, maybe to get drunk . . . to go swaggering into the hotels with the corridors satu-

rated with the smell of dichloride, of mercury, or the secret, steamy bawdy houses; maybe to have a fight, maybe against the cops, maybe to end, whooping and god-damning, in the jailhouse.[90]

Like other working-class musical forms, rock 'n' roll developed in leisure spaces, but it did not remain a segregated culture trapped in Saturday night. Marcus argues that the point of rock 'n' roll with Elvis and the other recording artists from Sun Records was to transform and extend the excitement of Saturday night into the everyday, in order to make it a *way of life*.

> Now, that Saturday night caught by Cash . . . would get you through a lot of weekdays . . . [but] the key dividing line that made Elvis 'King of Western Bop' [rather than] just another country crooner or a footnote in someone's history of the blues . . . [was] the idea that Saturday night could be the whole show. You had to be young and a bit insulated to pull it off, but why not? Why not trade pain and boredom for kicks and style? Why not make an escape form a way of life—the question trails off the last page of *Huckleberry Finn*—into a way of life?"[91]

Marcus also describes quite accurately the environment that Elvis and other rock 'n' roll musicians as well as their fans struggled against:

> The central facts of life in Elvis' South pulled as strongly against the impulses of hedonism and romance as the facts of our own lives do against the fast pleasures of rock 'n' roll. When the poor white was thrown back on himself, as he was in the daytime, when he worked his plot or looked for a job in the city, or at night, when he brooded and Hank Williams' whippoorwill told the truth all too plainly, those facts stood out clearly: powerlessness and vulnerability on all fronts. The humiliation of a class system that gave him his identity and then trivialized it.[92]

The hidden injuries of class that pervade American society framed the way in which rock 'n' roll culture developed as a working-class culture of resistance. Marcus has, perhaps better than any other critic of popular culture, captured the significance of Elvis and his generation, but the effort to make "Saturday night a way of life" predates Presley by at least a decade. As I have argued above, the rhythm and blues culture of the late 1940s—which included key figures like Wynonie Harris—had already figured out how to make the weekend into a way of life.

While Hank Williams influenced the development of rock-a-billy, Louis Jordan's music made its way into the 1950s generation through the key figure of Chuck Berry. Berry's path to a career in rock 'n' roll was somewhat serendipitous, because he was invited to join the Johnny Johnson trio one evening at the Cosmopolitan Club in East St. Louis when the saxophonist, Alvin Bennett, was too ill to play. Prior to that fortuitous event, Berry had been playing various local clubs as a means to supplement his income from other jobs, including two stints as an autoworker, and a job as a janitor while he was attending college studying to be a beautician. When Bennett was unable to rejoin the trio after a stroke, Berry stayed on as a permanent member. It was thanks to Johnson that Berry had the opportunity to become a star in his own right, because Johnson was already a major talent as both composer and pianist extraordinaire, while Berry was still an amateur. In fact, many of Berry's classic guitar licks and famous riffs were interpretations of combinations of notes played by Johnson on the piano. According to Keith Richards—who was a key figure in drawing attention to the contributions of Johnson to the history of rock 'n' roll—one can hear evidence of Johnson's influence on many of Berry's signature riffs including "School Days,"

> because of what key it's in, it's Johnny's key. It's in piano keys. On guitar, in rock 'n' roll, you play in keys of A and E and D because you've got open strings. . . . If it's a guitar band you play in those keys because they're guitar keys . . . on top of that [Berry] plays in piano keys, horn keys, jazz keys, Johnny Johnson's keys . . . he [Berry] adapted Johnny's riffs and put those great lyrics behind them. Without someone to give him those riffs . . . no songs, just a lot of words on paper.[93]

At a young age, Johnson was a child prodigy on the piano, playing Count Basie and Earl "Fatha" Hines compositions on the local radio station in Fairmont, West Virginia, at the tender age of nine! Before moving to St. Louis in the early 1950s, Johnson worked in Chicago playing with such blues greats as Muddy Waters and Albert King. He moved to St. Louis in 1952 after he landed a factory job there, when he put together his popular trio that found a home at the Cosmopolitan Club, a year before Berry joined them. Berry eventually took over the trio after Chess Records signed him to a record deal as a solo recording artist after the recording of the hit record "Maybellene" in 1955. Johnson, though, continued to contribute to arrangements for many of Berry's biggest hits including "School Days," "Roll Over Beethoven," and "Johnnie B. Goode." Johnson stayed on with Berry until 1973. In recent years, Johnson has finally received recognition for being both a pioneer of rock 'n' roll and an accomplished blues pianist, having been inducted into the Rock 'n' Roll Hall of Fame in 2001.

Berry's music intentionally signified the blurring of boundaries, both sideways in terms of crossing over between rhythm and blues and country music, but also vertically, by pointing at class distinction in order to deconstruct it. Berry had a superb sense of humor, and in the tradition of Louis Jordan, Chuck Berry used humor, irony, and sarcasm to deconstruct the binary opposition between high and low culture. The most famous instance is "Roll Over Beethoven," cut on Chess Records in 1957. By 1956–57, the cultural backlash against rock 'n' roll was well under way, but Chuck Berry's way of intervening in the controversy over rock 'n' roll was to mock and displace it through irony and humor in a smash hit record. The song opens with what is now perhaps one of the most famous guitar licks in rock 'n' roll history, and in the lyrics that have become iconic in rock 'n' roll culture, Berry playfully jokes about Beethoven rolling over in his grave in order to tell Tchaikovsky the news about the cultural changes happening in America with the emergence of rock 'n' roll music. Chuck Berry had studied the techniques of the great jazz guitarist Charlie Christian, and in addition to being a virtuoso on the guitar, he was a very skilled songwriter and creative lyricist. For these reasons, he was the perfect rock 'n' roll recording artist to playfully deconstruct the highbrow/lowbrow cultural divide that prevailed in the 1950s and help legitimate the culture of rock 'n' roll.

Berry's music also continued the working-class tradition of singing about the drudgery of work and the profound hollowness of the Protestant work ethic for working-class people. In "Too Much Monkey Business," also recorded on Chess Records in 1957, Berry sings about the meaninglessness of low-paying, degrading jobs and other aspects of working-class life that get in the way of the important things, like driving fast cars, listening to rock 'n' roll, dressing up in the sharpest threads, romancing your lover, and pursuing more leisure time in general. The practices inscribed within the major institutions in our society, including work, school, and marriage, are interpreted by Berry as "monkey business" for these reasons. "Monkey business" is something to escape. Chuck Berry's genius was to articulate these experiences of alienation in a way that appealed to large numbers of working people, making him a huge crossover success, much like Louis Jordan a generation earlier. The first lines of "Too Much Monkey Business" proclaim: "Runnin' to-and-fro hard workin' at the mill / Never fail in the mail, yeah, come a rotten bill!/Too much monkey business, too much monkey business for me to be involved in."

At the end of the song Berry sings: "Workin' fill' station—too many tasks / Wipe the windows, check the tires, check the oil dollar gas! / Don't want your botheration, get away leave me! / Too much monkey business for me.[94]

The lyrical content of "Monkey Business" was mirrored, to some extent, a year later in Eddie Cochran's 1958 hit record, "Summertime Blues," recorded on the Liberty label. "Summertime Blues" has had a lasting influence. It was famously covered by the Who in the late 1960s, the Stray Cats in the 1980s, as well as by the country music recording star Alan Jackson in 1994.[95] The first few lines of "Summertime Blues" read: "I'm gonna raise a fuss, I'm gonna raise a holler / About a workin' all summer just to try and earn a dollar / Every time I call my baby, and try and get a date / My boss says, 'No dice son, you gotta work late." Cochran's song expresses what most working-class youth experience. Summertime is supposed to be about relaxation and pleasure, but the need to work makes summertime "blue." Eddie Cochran's career was not as extensive or successful as that of Chuck Berry's (due to his death in a car crash at age twenty-one), but Cochran's popularity in 1958 did rival that of the more popular recording stars of the 1950s. Despite his short-lived career, Cochran recorded a handful of other rock 'n' roll gems that appealed to working-class desire and rebellion, including "Twenty Flight Rock," "C'mon Everybody," and "Something Else." The latter tune was covered by the punk band, the Sex Pistols, in the late 1970s and Paul McCartney impressed John Lennon at one of their first meetings when McCartney showed him how to play "Twenty Flight Rock." In addition to being a brilliant songwriter and a skilled and creative guitarist, Cochran could play bass, drums, and piano. On the guitar Cochran not only demonstrated a superb degree of facility with picking, but he also showed his creativity through tinkering around in recording sessions, especially the application of overdubbing certain guitar parts of the recording in a manner pioneered by guitar legend Les Paul.

Cochran also had a brief career on film, playing supporting roles in the movies *Untamed Youth* from 1957 and *The Girl Can't Help It* from 1956, which featured Jane Mansfield. His appearance in *The Girl Can't Help It* gave him the exposure he needed to boost his recording career, leading eventually to his signing with Liberty Records. Both films prominently featured rock 'n' roll music following on the heels of the hit film *Blackboard Jungle*, which blew up the recording of "Rock Around the Clock" by Bill Haley and the Comets. In *Untamed Youth*, Cochran plays a juvenile delinquent sentenced to hard labor picking cotton on a ranch in central California. The film portrays Cochran and the other teenage inmates as the victims of a corrupt judge who has an arrangement with a crooked ranch owner to send juvenile delinquents to the ranch in order to work off their jail time in return for cash kickbacks. Cotton picking serves as the backdrop for a classic rock 'n' roll song written by Cochran, "Cotton Picker." During a scene in the film where the prisoners are in the fields, the teen inmates interrupt their picking work in order to join Cochran in a song of defiance as he exclaims, "You ain't gonna make a cotton picker out of me," the line which serves as the refrain of the tune. The film ends when the crooked judge and ranch owner are exposed for running an illegal slave labor farm, and the youth are allowed to go free. As was the case with other rock 'n' roll recording stars like Tina Turner and Johnny Cash, cotton picking served as the context for working-class cultural resistance. "Cotton Picker" provided Cochran with a foundation to develop his most important recording, "Summertime Blues," the following year.

In the hands of a maestro like Chuck Berry or Eddie Cochran, the electric guitar was a key development in rock 'n' roll and a crucial expression of working-class pretension, because it is impossible to ignore its sound, which is often too noisy for those who don't have an ear for rock 'n' roll. Indeed, the electric guitar is the perfect instrument for expressing cultural resistance, primarily because it's loud, but also because it can be distorted to create a gritty noise that nicely expresses a worker's desire to fight back against the boss, in the sense expressed by Willie Dixon, who argued that blues music is partly about "getting back at the boss."[96] My interpretation of the social significance of the timbre of the electric guitar in early rock 'n' roll appropriates key concepts from Walser's analysis of the semiotics of guitar distortion.[97] Although his discussion focuses on heavy metal music within the social context of postindustrial economic decline, his argument that guitar distortion is "associated with social fantasies and experiences of power" overlaps to some extent with my argument that the sound of the electric guitar signified working-class pretensions in the context of postwar working-class subcultures.

Following recent vicissitudes in the study of epistemology, Walser grounds the meaning of music in socially guided bodily experiences as a means of confronting the explanatory weaknesses of structuralist-linguistic and transcendentalist interpretations of the significance of music.[98] By emphasizing the place of the body in music, Walser challenges the perspective that only words and sentences can have meaning or that meaning must be propositional, linguistic, or abstract.[99] Focusing on the practices of the body is an approach that examines how language is dependent upon "pre-linguistic schematic structures," which, in addition to language, organize our experience. Pre-linguistic schematic structures are, according to Walser, produced by patterns of activity at the level of "bodily movements through space" as well as "our manipulations of objects and our perceptual interactions." These "pre-linguistic schematic structures," according to Walser, are mechanisms of meaning production that "inform the more abstract operations of language and conceptual thinking."[100] Thus, while structuralist-linguists have demonstrated that the material world is mediated by language, it is also the case that language is embedded in material aspects of human experience. Walser appropriates the work of the philosopher Mark Johnson to emphasize the way in which language is "embodied." "Our reality," according to Johnson, "is shaped by the patterns of our bodily movement, the contours of our spatial and temporal orientation, and the forms of our interactions with objects."[101] For Walser, the issue is how to employ Johnson's critique to retheorize the link between acoustical phenomena and other realms of human experience.

Charlie Parker's famous quote that "if you don't live it, it won't come out of your horn" and Duke Ellington's statement that "it don't mean a thing if it ain't got that swing" are both good examples of how everyday life — the movement of bodies through space — creates certain historically determined patterns of activity that organize our experience in pre-linguistic ways.[102] Parker's statement is "quite different," according to Walser, "from European aesthetic mystifications, for they locate hard-to-define meanings not in some imaginary transcendent realm, but in social (lived) experience and in the human body (swing)."[103]

Walser's emphasis is upon the meaning of guitar distortion in a social context of "young men who lack status" in a postindustrial economic environment characterized by the rapid decline of relatively good-paying blue-collar jobs. In that context, guitar distortion is appropriated by heavy metal fans as a means of coping with status anxiety and loss of political-economic power. Guitar distortion among fans and performers of heavy metal music is, according to Walser, "perceived in terms of power rather than failure, intentional transgression rather than accidental overload—as music rather than noise."[104] As a sign, the timbre of the electric guitar is open to multiple meanings and potentially the site of class conflict.[105] The issue is how to situate the sign in a particular historical and cultural context in order to unpack the social meaning of the sonic qualities of the electric guitar. In short, the reason why we may perceive the timbre of the electric guitar as "powerful" is due to the "socially guided bodily experiences" that shape our perception in particular historical contexts. Following the theoretical logic of Walser's analysis of the sound of the electric guitar, it is reasonable to argue that Chuck Berry's use of the guitar intervened in, and was mediated by class and racial conflict. In the social context of the tumultuous 1950s, the timbre of his guitar can be read as a signifier of working-class pretension.

Chuck Berry was also a key figure in the transformation of the division of labor in the music industry that followed rock 'n' roll because not only did he record on and make famous an independent record label—thereby contributing to the shift in the relations between independent and major record labels—but also he wrote most of his own material, which was a significant change in the traditional way of doing business in the music industry. The traditional division of labor in the recording industry had separated label owners and songwriters from producers, arrangers, session musicians, and vocalists. After the Beatles, most rock 'n' roll bands wrote their own material.

In rock 'n' roll during the 1950s, the cultural significance of the electric guitar in the hands of Chuck Berry was matched by the appropriation and deconstruction of the piano by Little Richard, Fats Domino, and Jerry Lee Lewis. Just as the zoot suit can be read as a text that signified resistance and rebellion in the working-class culture of African Americans and Chicanos during and shortly after the war, the use, and abuse, of the piano in rock 'n' roll performance can be situated in a reading of the rock 'n' roll performance as a text. Reading the rock 'n' roll performance of Little Richard and Jerry Lee Lewis as text focuses on how the piano signifies beyond the technical and formal aspects of the music itself, including instrumental arrangement. The cultural context within which the piano is embedded gives the piano symbolic importance that is layered upon the function of the piano as an instrument in the musical arrangement. The virtual destruction of the piano in the performances of Little Richard, Fats Domino, and Jerry Lee Lewis can be interpreted as working-class rejection and inversion of bourgeois norms. Attacking the piano in their performances was as much a symbolic attack upon bourgeois norms as it was a gimmick or shtick for the particular stage persona. Indeed their performances can be read as a cultural deconstruction of bourgeois cultural hierarchies that were established during the Gilded Age.

The coding of the piano during the Victorian era overlapped with a larger cultural movement during the Gilded Age that was marked by what Levine describes as the formation of a hierarchy within American cultural institutions that divided culture into so-called highbrow and lowbrow aesthetic practices.[106] In fact, as Raymond Williams notes, the very term *culture* took on new meaning during the Gilded Age, when it became widely used as a noun to describe "intellectual and especially aesthetic activity."[107] Prior to the eighteenth century, the word primarily signified "cultivation," as in horticultural activity. It was also during the late nineteenth century that the industrial and financial elite in the United States became increasingly conscious of themselves as a distinct class that had shared political-economic interests in repressing the incipient labor movement under the leadership of Samuel Gompers and the American Federation of Labor. According to Beckert, the political consolidation of the capitalist class was made possible in part by cultural practices that provided the necessary conditions for the formation of a collective consciousness among the industrial and financial elite.[108] In turn, the development of class consciousness among capitalists led to geographic divisions within the city that created a new form of spatial relations that participated in the reproduction of social relations of production in a new social formation of capitalism, monopoly capitalism.[109] According to Levine, socioeconomic elites developed strategies to "retreat into their own private spaces whenever possible . . . transform public spaces by rules, systems of taste, and canons of behavior of their own choosing . . . and convert the strangers [immigrant workers] so that their modes of behavior and cultural predilections emulated those of elites."[110]

It was during this time that elite industrialists and financiers formed a "historic bloc" together with Protestant religious leaders and cultural elites that eventually created a political-economic and (relatively independent) cultural bulwark against the growing proletarian population of U.S. cities, which was viewed by ruling elites as a threat to political stability and Protestant cultural values. As Gramsci argues, the formation of a historic bloc is not the work of conspiracy among capitalists working secretly behind closed doors, but the result of intersections between relatively independent interests developed in distinct spheres of bourgeois society.[111] Religious and cultural elites sincerely believed in the value of the cultural objects (music, literature, etc.) they promoted, and for Gramsci this is the primary motivating factor of these groups. When they align with the interests of the ruling capitalist class, a historic bloc is formed. In short, the often independent, aesthetic motivations of the institutions of high culture can under certain conditions reinforce class domination.

In addition to creating the conditions for a shared sense of identity as a "class" among the various factions of the capitalist elite, culture was used as a moralizing force in the latter half of the nineteenth century. Music played a key role in the social movement that spread bourgeois morality across the American society, while repressing the "deviant" cultural practices of the working class. Borrowing Gramsci's concepts "hegemony" and "historic bloc" to describe the ways in which power is exercised by the ruling class through securing the "consent" of the dominated — as an alternative to using brute force — Baur examines the political appropriation of classical music by the capitalist class during the Gilded Age, an era of extraordinary political and cultural turmoil as 16 million immigrants entered the United States swelling American cities seven times over between 1860 and 1910.[112]

A crucial cultural phenomenon that achieved hegemony was the Protestant work ethic, which occupied two important places in bourgeois discourse. On the one hand, since waged work was increasingly less and less likely to provide material rewards for the industrial working class, work was portrayed by the representatives of bourgeois morality as an end-in-itself, which was said to show evidence of a "dignified" existence and loyalty to God. In this manner, the work ethic helped legitimate the growing inequality in the United States.[113] From the point of view of the industrial and financial elite — as well as the Protestant middle class — the extremely unequal distribution of wealth in the United States and the abject poverty that plagued urban areas was the result of individual behavior. It was believed that on both ends of the economic spectrum, individuals got what they deserved based on their own efforts and merit. Urban squalor and abject poverty were explained as a result of the moral decay of the working class, both immigrants and non-immigrants.

Music was viewed as an effective instrument in the effort to combat the perceived moral depravity among the growing proletarian population, because it was said to be capable of transforming the aggressive nature of the proletariat. According to Baur, "The Mendelssohn phenomenon in Gilded Age America suggests that during this period of change and contestation, dominant groups embraced and promoted cultural practices that confirmed values conducive to their continued dominance."[114] Bourgeois music critics were outspoken about their goals to achieve a transformation in the behavior of the working class through the application of certain forms of music. Baur cites a *Harper's Magazine* (1875) editorial titled, "The Mission of Music," which viewed music as an "acknowledged force in molding character and governing men." The view that music played a crucial role in legitimating the rule of the bourgeoisie was discussed in most of the music journals in the United States. "By claiming that musical practices exerted an influence of public morality," writes Baur, "Gilded Age music critics and patrons endorsed a fundamental tenet of Marxist cultural criticism—that culture has an ideological function . . . they forthrightly declared their intention to propagate specific values through music."[115] Felix Mendelssohn's popularity during the Gilded Age is particularly important in Baur's view, because the music of Mendelssohn "provided confirmation for the established order in late-nineteenth-century America by reinforcing a disciplined work ethic and by naturalizing relationships of authority and submission."[116] The piano and sheet music for the piano played a crucial role in the dissemination of bourgeois morality.

In the late nineteenth and early twentieth centuries, the piano signified the "cult of domesticity" in bourgeois society as Victorian culture developed and thrived in New England. As Craig H. Roell argues, the term *Victorian* "conjures up images of prudery, hypocrisy, middle-class stuffiness, domesticity, sentimentality, earnestness, industry, and pompous conservatism."[117] Roell demonstrates that all of the images came to be embodied in the piano during the reign of Victorian cultural values in the United States. The piano was a foundational element in the creation of Victorian middle-class cultural values because it was used (along with other cultural objects) by middle-class status seekers as a means to separate themselves from the unwashed masses who, in the bourgeois mind, symbolized the supposed cultural and moral failure of certain individuals during the long process of proletarianization in industrializing America. The instrument not only signified social respectability and upward mobility but was also viewed as a tool for cultural uplift among middle-class families seeking recognition for their status achievements. It was also used to signify *moral* refinement in Victorian culture. The role of the piano in signifying moral respectability was the responsibility of the middle-class housewife, who used the piano as part of her repertoire in teaching her children the "proper," reserved and "well-mannered" middle-class way of life.

The playing of the piano in the Victorian middle-class family signified two key moral elements in Victorian culture. The middle-class performance on the piano reinforced the centrality of the Protestant work ethic, since it was believed that learning to play the piano demanded much sacrifice in terms of toil and delayed gratification. Bourgeois Victorian culture made a fetish of what was viewed as the perseverance necessary to master the piano. The process of learning to use the instrument was situated in a middle-class cultural context that celebrated the so-called dignity of hard work and the moral worth of productivity for productivity's sake. Indeed, work was glorified as the supreme virtue in Victorian culture, and playing the piano in the middle-class home was interpreted in terms of this so-called virtue.[118] Pupils — mainly women — were expected to suffer during piano lessons. In a story on the place of the piano in American society, the *New York Times* quoted a piano teacher who stated that "taking lessons on the piano had no equal in the realm of torture."[119]

The other key features of Victorian culture that the piano signified were gendered: the sexual purity of the middle-class housewife and the separation of the public and private spheres in social life, where the private sphere was the exclusive realm of the middle-class homemaker.[120] She was charged with the creation of a household that would protect the modern nuclear family from the social ills of the industrializing society. The home was thus seen as a shelter to protect the family from the moral "sickness" in industrial society, a safe haven created to foster moral and spiritual values that were said to be under siege by the emergence of "mass" culture. Women's magazines at the time emphasized four tenets of the so-called cult of domesticity that characterized the ideal mode of life for the middle-class housewife: piety, purity, submissiveness, and domesticity. Women were expected to be pillars of virtue, transmitting the culture of Christianity to their children, while practicing severe asceticism in the realm of sexual relations and practices. The tenet of domesticity followed from the separation of home and work, as the family in middle-class society ceased to function as an economic unit. Instead, the man of the house left home to work and engage in public activities, including politics, while the woman was expected to restrict her activities to the private sphere. The performance on the piano in middle-class homes signified these Victorian values, as articulated in the words of Calvin Coolidge, who said, "We cannot imagine a model New England home without the family Bible on the table and the family piano in the corner."[121] In short, the piano anchored, both physically and symbolically, the nuclear family in the Victorian, middle-class home.

A rock 'n' roll music performance, however, radically subverted the meaning of the piano. In opposition to the piano as coded by bourgeois culture, in the hands of Fats Domino, Little Richard, and Jerry Lee Lewis, the piano signified immediate pleasure over delayed gratification and the virtues of leisure and pleasure over the virtue of work and suffering. The piano took on new meaning in the general context of rock 'n' roll culture when used by all of the rock 'n' roll performers—which, as I have been arguing, challenged middle-class norms about the value of work and delayed gratification—but also the *particular* way in which Fats Domino, Little Richard, and Jerry Lee Lewis *abused* the piano in their performances can be read as a violation of bourgeois sensibilities about the proper place and signification of the body. Fats Domino did not attack the piano with the same ferocity as Jerry Lee Lewis or Little Richard, but he was known for pushing it across the stage with his belly during live performances that became legendary for their length and intensity.[122] In fact, his band members came to respect his strength and prowess on the keys due in part to his ability to manhandle a baby grand piano. During a performance in Evansville, Indiana, while playing the finale of his show, Domino pushed the piano so far across the stage with his large belly that it actually fell off the stage! Audience members promptly gave Domino a standing ovation as Domino was helped back onstage. According to Domino's biographer, Rick Coleman, they assumed that was part of Domino's stage act, due to the extraordinary energy and enthusiasm displayed by the band prior to the crash of the piano into the audience.[123] His performances not only violated bourgeois norms associated with the placement of the body next to the piano; his large size also signified a form of transgression as his relative corpulence signified "excess" and pleasure in opposition to bourgeois norms of moderation and asceticism fetishized in representations of the petite, delicate female body typically associated with the piano in bourgeois culture.

Little Richard would typically place one of his feet up on the piano as he played it while standing upright in a manner that inverted the vertical cultural hierarchy of high and low in the bourgeois cultural formation. The placement of the foot—the lowest area of the body—upon the piano, violated bourgeois codes that strictly regulated the place and appearance of the body in public. In the history of bourgeois culture in general, the body has been associated with filth and sin, and beginning with Cartesian epistemology, the body was seen as separate, in terms of existential substance, from the mind. The subordination and restriction of the appearance of the body in terms of vertical hierarchy mirrors the class hierarchy between the classes and the segregation of space in the city. As Stallybrass and White argue, "Thinking the body is thinking social topography and vice versa. . . . The high/low opposition in each of our symbolic domains—the psychic forms, the human body, geographical space, and social order—is a fundamental basis to mechanisms of ordering and sense-making in European cultures."[124] In capitalist modernity, the middle class depends upon certain types of boundaries to maintain its cultural identity as a distinct class. "The bourgeois subject," write Stallybrass and White, "continuously defined and re-defined itself through the exclusion of what it marked out as 'low'—as dirty, repulsive, noisy, contaminating . . . that very act of exclusion was constitutive of its identity. The low was internalized under the sign of negation and disgust."[125] In the Victorian era, some women covered the legs of their pianos so as to prevent the possibility that the "legs" of the piano might somehow be associated with the flesh of the woman's leg sitting at the piano, thereby suggesting sexuality, something severely repressed in the Victorian mind.

In rock 'n' roll performances on the piano, we can see the return of the repressed as the public display of the sexualized body attacked the piano. Both Little Richard and Jerry Lee Lewis would pound the keyboard relentlessly during the bridge of songs that they often extended significantly during their performances so as to continue the pounding. Both performers were prone to leap up off of the piano bench—thereby sending the bench flying backwards in the air—in order to get more leverage so they could pound the keyboard as hard as possible. Lewis would sometimes stomp the keyboard with his right foot as he pounded the keys with his hands. In one infamous performance that was captured on film, Lewis climbed on top of his piano and invited his fans to join him and dance atop of the instrument for the climactic end to his concert.[126] In short, attacking the piano during a rock 'n' roll performance was also an attack on the bourgeois images of prudery, earnestness, domesticity, industry, and pompous conservatism. Little Richard's performances also scrambled gendered and racial norms in addition to the norms structured by class hierarchy. Little Richard's gen-dered ambiguity added more controversy to the already charged sexual atmosphere of a rock 'n' roll concert, and his display of the black body also deconstructed the image of the black performer coded by the minstrel tra-dition in American popular culture.

In addition to carrying on the anti-work theme of 1940s rhythm and blues culture, Chuck Berry, Elvis Presley, and their generation also em-phasized the reality of, and desire for, an improving lifestyle that accom-panies greater access to material goods in an expanding economy. Just as workers demanded a bigger piece of the pie during and after World War II, working-class rock 'n' roll musicians and their fans in the 1950s affirmed their entitlement to their share of the good life, which increasingly involved fast cars as suburbanization spread across the United States. The theme of fast cars is a main feature of Chuck Berry's repertoire, starting with his first hit in 1955, "Maybellene," which is about a car race between a Ford and a Cadillac, where Berry's virtuoso guitar work and creative use of words like *motorvatin'* brilliantly captures the feeling of driving fast. Berry is the poor man driving the Ford chasing the object of his desire, Maybellene, who is a passenger in the rich man's Cadillac Coup de Ville. We never find out who is driving the Cadillac, just that Berry randomly spots Maybellene as he is motorvatin' around in his beat-up Ford. On the one hand, the song is about class revenge, for the cheaper Ford eventually catches the fancier Cadillac. But Berry's music has another layer having to do with the intersec-tions of class with race. As W. T. Lhamon Jr. suggests, the song begins as a song about "class in a race," poor man's Ford versus fancy Cadillac, but the end of the song is about "race in a race."[127] According to Lhamon: "Berry's apparent desire was to ignore race somehow and grab the same American promise of Fords and proms, jukeboxes and guitars offered every adoles-cent. But his quiet conviction, ever deepening from "Maybellene" on, was that the ways of his people claimed him."[128]

In short, "Maybellene" casts Berry's protagonist as more than working-class hero, because he must also negotiate race relations that overdeter-mine his class situation. Lhamon argues that Berry draws upon the trick-ster figure in the history of African American folklore when he describes how the protagonist in the car race uses the forces of nature to help him overcome the handicap of driving the weaker car.[129] Just as he is about to lose the car race because his Ford's motor is overheating, it begins to rain, cooling the engine enough to allow the Ford to catch the Cadillac. "When his Ford loses ground to the Cadillac's power," argues Lhamon, "he relies on trickster wiles to pull him out. When it started to rain he tooted for the passing lane; all that water under the hood surely did his motor good."[130] Lhamon uses the term *mobileman* to describe Berry's trickster figure. "Mobileman masters his own technology, but remains in league with sun, cloud, and rain."[131]

After "Maybellene," Berry deployed the trickster figure brilliantly in "Brown Eyed Handsome Man" recorded in 1956. The very title of the song points to race, as it is intended to be read as brown *skinned* handsome man. Berry's genius in this song is to articulate race and class together in a tale about the trickster who is able to outsmart "the man." The humorous beginning of the song opens with our main character in court after having been "arrested for charges of unemployment." The second line reads, "The judge's wife called up the district attorney and said if you want to keep your job you better free that brown eyed handsome man." Berry uses humor in a delightful way to weave together two particularly explosive cultural issues in these two opening lines, one having to do with the labor question and the other with the race question. On the one hand, the figures of authority are outraged that Berry's protagonist blows off the work ethic and throw him in jail for refusing to work. The second explosive issue having to do with racial miscegenation turns out ironically to favor our protagonist, since his lover is the judge's wife, and she has the power to have him set free. Our trickster hero is able to get the best of his oppressor in a double sense: violating racial norms allows him to violate class norms. A brown eyed handsome man who uses his jobless freedom as an irresistible lover in order to imprison his nemesis in a job! Chuck Berry as mobileman is once again able to overcome the odds against him as he weaves his way through the complicated intersections of race and class in American culture. According to Lhamon, Chuck Berry's music "smuggled black reality and black anxieties into the smiling heart of America, grafting them there so artfully that most listeners never dreamed Berry's incubus had visited them."[132] "Brown Eyed Handsome Man" has been covered numerous times since its release, including notable recordings of interesting arrangements by Wanda Jackson and Nina Simone.

Many of Berry's songs are also about upward mobility that was made possible by an insurgent labor movement. His songs reflect the climate of the rising standard of living among workers during the 1950s, as well as the emergence of a new class of working-class teenage consumers. Rising incomes for workers during the 1950s meant that their children had more money to spend on the jukebox and their gas tanks. Chuck Berry's songs are also grounded in an older tradition of African Americans using the entertainment industry as a vehicle to escape poverty. "Johnny B. Goode," Berry's anthem for every young, working-class, aspiring rock 'n' roll guitar player, is about a talented working-class kid beating the odds and becoming a famous rock star. The song is about him, of course, but millions of working-class kids (black and white) found inspiration in Berry's story of becoming a rich and famous rock star.

Unlike alienated subcultures from the middle class who rejected "materialism," working-class rock 'n' roll musicians and their aficionados embraced materialism and the good life. Indeed, they *demanded* it. "My father saw we never went hungry, but well, you know I never had a lot," Elvis once said. "When I first began to get some money, I bought a lot of things I had always wanted, like cars. I did some things I never could do before—and believe me, it was fun."[133] The same can be said about Elvis's peer group of rock 'n' roll stars as well as the generations that came before, including Howlin' Wolf and the other electric bluesmen of his era. Materialism was not viewed as a problem, because as Wolf says, when you don't have anything, you have the blues, you think you're a nobody. On another occasion, Presley spoke for all workers who appeal to music both as an escape from work and as a means to make some money when he said, "I wanted to be a singer because I didn't want to sweat. Had a job drivin' a truck when I got out of high school. After that I got a job at a dollar an hour in a defense plant. About a year and a half ago, when I first started singing, I figured it'd be easy. . . . I like making lots of money."[134]

Another key figure in the mid-1950s generation of rock 'n' roll recording artists is the incomparable Wanda Jackson, one of the few women who performed, wrote, and recorded rockabilly music. Jackson's work challenges the dominant view that women did not significantly contribute to the development of rock 'n' roll, the guitar is simply an extension of the penis/phallus, or that rock 'n' roll is inherently misogynistic.[135] As rock 'n' roll historian David Sanjek has argued, it was not only the case that young women were fans of Elvis and rockabilly more generally, but they also wanted to *be* Elvis, thereby scrambling gender codes and class sensibilities all at once. "Many young women wanted not simply to fuck Elvis," writes Sanjek, "but, instead, wanted to assimilate a portion of his authority and cultural power and assert that they too were ready, ready, ready to rock and roll, rip it up."[136] Women's place in rockabilly proves that the desire for pleasure expressed by rock 'n' roll is not always misogynistic. Wanda Jackson legitimated the working-class quest for pleasure in rock 'n' roll by fighting to carve out a space for women on equal terms with men.

Jackson was born in 1937, in Maud, Oklahoma. Her father scratched together a living working at odd jobs, including pumping gas, working in a bakery, and playing guitar in the local bars. In 1942, he moved the family to Los Angeles, where he landed a job in a munitions factory like thousands of other Oklahomans seeking to escape the Dust Bowl tragedy. After the war, the Jackson family moved back to Oklahoma City when Wanda's dad got a job driving a taxi cab and another one selling cars.

Jackson made her first inroads into the music industry when she won an amateur singing contest that was broadcast over the radio. Hank Thompson, a country music star from Oklahoma City, heard her and helped get her signed to a record deal on Decca in 1954 to cut mainstream country songs. When she performed at a show that featured both country and rockabilly bands, she met Elvis Presley. He recognized her talent instantly and encouraged her to pursue a recording career in rockabilly instead of country, since he believed that the future of music was in rock 'n' roll. "He kept saying, 'You can do this, I can tell. You've got the kind of voice for it, and you've got the feel,'" said Jackson in an interview. "He took me to his home in Memphis, and we went through his record collection of black blues."

Wanda Jackson went on to become one of the biggest rockabilly stars in the mid-1950s. She regularly toured with Carl Perkins and Presley, and her act always got equal billing. "I was really a maverick," she said. "I was trying to put some glamour and sex appeal into country music when it wasn't the done thing." Eventually Wanda gave up country music, in part because of the repressive culture. Jackson recalls an episode in 1955 where she was not allowed to wear a spaghetti strap dress onstage at the Grand Ole Opry in Nashville. "I had a brand-new dress and was about to go on stage," recalled Jackson, "when Ernest Tubb said, 'You're not wearing that dress on stage, are you?' I said, 'Yes, sir.' He said, 'You can't show your shoulders.' I said, 'What do you mean?' He insisted, so I had to get an old fringed jacket . . . and cover my dress. I was so mad I could hardly sing. That's the only time I did the Opry. I said, 'Never again.'"[137]

Jackson's decision to leave mainstream country music for rockabilly paid off when in 1956 she signed a recording contract with Capitol Records, where she scored a series of hits including "Fujiyama Mama," "Hot Dog! That Made Him Mad," "Mean, Mean Man," and "Rock Your Baby." Her backup band in the recording studio included Joe Maphis, Buck Owens, and guitarist Speedy West. Jackson wrote about half of all the music she recorded, which was more control than even Elvis had over his own work. She sang about things that were forbidden topics for the women of her day. While popular recording artists like Patti Page were singing about innocuous topics like cute little doggies for sale in the window — "How Much Is That Doggie in the Window" was an adaptation of a well-known Victorian music hall song — Jackson was singing about dating her boyfriend's best friend in order to take control over her relationship and get her man to behave. In "Hot Dog! That Made Him Mad," Jackson sings, "I've got a guy; I like him fine / But he takes me for granted all the time / To teach him a lesson and make him mad / I went on a date with the best friend he had / That made him mad, boy / Hot dog, that made him mad."[138] She also sang about the need for women to demand their rights to pleasure, including sexual pleasure. A decade before mainstream feminism articulated a position on a woman's right to control her body and her sexuality, Wanda Jackson was putting those demands on records, on *hit* records no less! In "Rock Your Baby," Jackson sings about a woman demanding that her man learn how to please her and please her well. More incredible is Jackson's signature tune, "Fujiyama Mama," a tune about Wanda enjoying the ecstasy of an orgasm. "I'm a 'Fujiyama Mama' and I'm just about to blow my top," sings Jackson. "And when I start erupting, there ain't nobody that can make me stop." "Blowing one's top" was a metaphor for having an orgasm, an expression that goes back to urban slang from the 1940s. The expression was very popular in jump blues records from the late 1940s. In "Fujiyama Mama," Jackson also brags that she can "drink a quart of sake, smoke a giant pipe / and blew your head off with nitroglycerine / and cause destruction like an atom bomb!" Jackson's songs were every bit as controversial as any written and performed by the men of her generation. Perhaps, not surprisingly, a recent video documentary about Wanda Jackson's career has been titled, "Every Night Is Saturday Night," demonstrating that working-class women were a crucial component to the project of making Saturday night a way of life in rock 'n' roll culture.[139] Jerry Lee Lewis may have had "great balls of fire," but Wanda Jackson was dropping atomic bombs. Jackson also cut a superb cover version of Jerry Lee's "Whole Lotta Shakin' Goin' On" to prove that she wasn't afraid to go toe to toe with the boys. The fact that in

1957 a pretty white woman was singing about killing people who dared to get in the way of her having an orgasm speaks volumes about how important Jackson is to both feminism and rock 'n' roll. Many of her hit records appeared after 1958, when supposedly the "dangerous" early generation of rockers were all gone, including Chuck Berry (in jail for allegedly violating the Mann Act), Jerry Lee Lewis (ostracized for marrying his thirteen-year-old cousin), Buddy Holly (killed in a plane crash), and Elvis (drafted into the army). She had a trilogy of hits in 1960 — "Let's Have a Party," "There's a Party Going On," and "Man We Had a Party" — that led to covers of older hit tunes, including Berry's "Brown Eyed Handsome Man," the Robins' "Riot in Cell Block No. 9," and Little Richard's "Rip It Up." It was not just the content of her lyrics that made Jackson controversial; it was the *way* she sang and the energy that explodes out of her records. She had a very aggressive style that used a slight growl to distort her voice, and she combined the growl with sudden pitch changes up and down that produced a feeling that was both tough and sexy.

Another interesting aspect about Jackson's career is that she recorded and performed with a mixed race rock 'n' roll band called Bobby Poe and the Kats from Arkansas. The pianist and lead singer, Big Al Downing was black. The guitarists, Bobby Poe and Vern Saundasky, and the drummer Joe Brawley were white. Jackson cut some of her best records with them, including "Rock Your Baby" and "Let's Have a Party." More importantly, they went on tour with Wanda in 1958 under the pseudonym "Party Timers." Perhaps it wasn't enough for Wanda Jackson to be in your face with her unapologetic, aggressive feminism in the midst of the conservative 1950s. Rather, she found it appropriate to challenge segregation, too, as she sang about her erupting orgasm while fronting an interracial rock 'n' roll band.

While one should be careful not to give rock 'n' roll too much credit for either challenging racial segregation or for furthering the cause of equal rights for women, it nonetheless did have a serious impact on race and gender relations. While it's true that most rock 'n' roll musicians at the time were men, and a majority of the tunes about sexuality were from a man's point of view, Wanda Jackson proved that she was able to seriously challenge gender norms and sexism in her music, since many of her records were relatively successful in terms of sales. Three of her records cracked the top 40 in the charts. Her recording of "Let's Have a Party," in 1958 reached number 37, and she had two more Top Forty hits in 1961, with "Right or Wrong," at number 29, and "Middle of a Heartache," which reached number 27.[140] In terms of race, many rhythm and blues and rock 'n' roll musicians believed they were contributing to the effort of ending Jim Crow. Carl Perkins, for instance, recalled a conversation with Chuck Berry, where the two agreed that they were "doing as much with [their] music as our leaders are in Washington to break down the barriers [of segregation.]"[141] What allowed rock 'n' roll musicians to break down the barriers was a shared class position. Their common experiences as workers provided a bridge between black and white cultures. More generally, as David Sanjek argues about rock-and-roll in the 1950s:

> In short order, the music produced by heretofore marginalized individuals in the music business — African Americans, working-class whites, women, Chicanos and others — occupied if not the center of the national culture then certainly prompted many of those in the majority to reconsider their behavior and point of view, some even further to constitute what Michel Foucault has called a "counterdiscourse" and what W. T. Lhamon Jr. designates "an alternative pest consciousness."[142]

Working-class blacks and whites have a long tradition of developing subcultures to deal with exploitation and oppression that goes back to the days of indentured servitude as well as the dangerous and exhausting work in the nineteenth-century coal mines that were filled almost exclusively with Scotch-Irish people of the Appalachia, the hillbilly "white trash." Of course, those experiences do not compare with the horrors of slavery, but one reason why the Celtic folk music of the Appalachian region began to cross over with the blues as early as the mid-nineteenth century was the shared experience in the social relations of production in the rural South.[143] But class position is not something automatic. On the contrary, class is, to borrow a phrase from E. P. Thompson, something that has to be made. To say class is not simply a subject position in a socioeconomic formation is to say that the cultural dimension matters as much as the structural dimension because there is no class without an awareness or consciousness of class. Culture matters, because it has material effects in the world, and in America, rock 'n' roll music played a key role in the social formation of the working class in the 1940s and 1950s. Working-class whites from the South were able to identify with the content of blues music, which developed out of the experiences of laboring in the cotton fields, because poor whites themselves were no strangers to backbreaking, meaningless work, especially cotton picking. That identification, which was also based on the failure of the sharecropping system in the 1930s, allowed working-class whites and blacks to create a crossover culture of rock 'n' roll. Of course, racism poisoned the music industry, especially during the early years of rock 'n' roll. Black recording artists were routinely exploited and ripped off by the unscrupulous white owners of the independent labels that recorded their music, and many white musicians made a living covering songs written by black musicians.

While most historians of rock 'n' roll peg the youth culture of the 1950s as the origin of rock 'n' roll, it is my contention that the substance of rock 'n' roll in the 1950s, including the bravado of the performers, the rough and tumble content and form of the music, and the spirit of pleasure and the rejection of delayed gratification developed out of the working-class culture that prevailed a decade earlier. In short, when rock 'n' roll went mainstream at the end of the 1950s, it seemed like a creation of youth culture exclusively, but an examination of its roots reveals that it was an extension of 1940s working-class pretensions.[144] The 1950s rock 'n' rollers themselves were well aware that they were continuing the tradition of class-based resistance inherited from the 1940s. While pretensions were high among the rock 'n' roll musicians, the promoters working at the independent labels were more cautious, because they foresaw the conservative backlash against rock 'n' roll that was just around the corner. As early as 1951, when Wynonie Harris cut several hits for King Records, the label's A&R man, Henry Glover, was worried about marketing rock 'n' roll music, because the middle-class audience considered it "filthy," particularly the term *rock* and other double entendres that signified sexual activity. According to Henry, "We were restricted with our possibilities of promoting [Wynonie's music] because it was considered filth."[145]

The impending cultural backlash against rock 'n' roll included, ironically, the musicians' union. The same working-class pretensions of the 1940s that made their way into rock 'n' roll music were partly created by the musicians' union, especially their great victory over the recording industry in 1942–43, but paradoxically, the union turned against those very pretensions when many representatives of the leadership and key figures in the rank-and-file attacked rock 'n' roll on aesthetic and cultural grounds as well as on the grounds that rock 'n' roll was a fad. It's to that topic that we now turn.

FIGURE 1. Wurlitzer company ad from 1943 showing servicemen and friends around jukebox. Victor Keppler/George Eastman House/Getty Images.

FIGURE 2. James C. Petrillo in studio with other musicians/singers making first recording to lift recording ban. FPG/Getty Images.

FIGURE 3. Workers on strike in Detroit in 1946. Keystone-France/Gamma-Keystone via Getty Images.

FIGURE 4. Louis Jordan with his band performing in Caldonia in 1944. John D. Kisch/Separate Cinema Archive/Getty Images.

FIGURE 5. T-Bone Walker doing the splits with guitar behind his head. Michael Ochs Archives/Getty Images.

FIGURE 6. Hank Williams in radio studio with the Drifting Cowboys in 1944. Michael Ochs Archives/Getty Images.

FIGURE 7. Little Richard performing with band, foot on piano, in 1956. Michael Ochs Archives/Getty Images.

FIGURE 8. Wanda Jackson performing with Roy Clark in 1960. Michael Ochs Archives/Getty Images.

FIGURE 9. Beatles fans restrained by police at the JFK Airport in February 1964. Hal Mathewson/New York Daily News Archive via Getty Images.

THREE. **If I Had a Hammer**

Union Musicians "Bop" Rock 'n' Roll

I ain't common, I know that cuz I got class I ain't never used.
— LOUIS JORDAN

In an interview from 1982, the recording artist Claude Trenier recalled, "When we used to jam at Billy Berg's club in Hollywood, all those bebop musicians would shy away from us. They thought we weren't cool because we jumped around and shouted and all that."[1]

Trenier, who had sung with the Charles Mingus Orchestra, formed a jump blues group with his twin brother, Cliff, Don Hill, and the Gene Gilbeaux Quartet in 1947. Like Louis Jordan's band, they played mostly jump blues music, and together with Louis Jordan and the blues shouters like Wynonie Harris and Big Joe Turner, they were influential in the development of rock 'n' roll and helped give the genre its new name through use of the expression "rock 'n' roll" in their songs. In 1949, the Blue Note jazz club in Chicago billed them as "the Rockin,' Rollin' Trenier Twins." One of their biggest hits was "Rockin' Is Our Bizness." The Trenier Twins had a background in jazz music, and like Louis Jordan, they stopped recording and performing jazz in the late 1940s to focus exclusively on jump blues. The musicians who left jazz referred to their music as jump blues because they appropriated the chord structure of the blues, but they sped up the rhythms and added more complicated harmonic structures and instrumental arrangements. The music industry, however, paid no attention to these changes and continued to market their records as "race" music until 1949 when *Billboard* finally changed the name of the category—at the urging of Jerry Wexler, who eventually became a producer for Atlantic Records—to rhythm and blues. Jump blues or R&B had the melodic structure of traditional blues music, but the musicians played it on top of a driving rhythm appropriated from Count Basie's style of swing jazz. A typical jump blues band had six or seven members: a drummer, a bassist, a pianist, a guitarist (electric), one or two saxophonists, one or two trumpeters, and a vocalist (or two in the case of the Trenier Twins), usually a blues shouter. This kind of band eventually became the template for rock 'n' roll bands in the 1950s, except that the electric guitar eventually displaced the saxophone as the featured lead instrument. The age of the big band ended after the war as jazz split into bebop and R&B. The only thing in common between jump blues groups and bebop groups was their size. Both preferred a small combo of no more than six musicians, rather than the big band ensembles from the 1930s that could have more than twenty musicians. Bebop musicians, however, preferred to create complex melodies and harmonic structures that led to surprising twists and turns in their performances, rather than orient the music around the driving rhythms and heavy backbeats that characterized jump blues and made jump blues—unlike bebop—more accessible for those who wanted to dance.

The cultural divergence in musical styles was also often accompanied by a political divergence between the worldviews of R&B and bebop musicians. The pianist Art Farmer has argued that for some beboppers, R&B musicians were considered "the enemy."[2] Jump blues/R&B groups were interested in "playing music for the working man," as Louis Jordan was fond of saying. The substance of the early R&B music scene placed an emphasis on the body and pleasure, particularly the sexual kind, as well as on an escape from the alienating experience of factory work and the relative boredom of the everyday. For beboppers, on the other hand, the musical emphasis was on educating the masses, "advancing" music by creating something new in jazz, playing music for the musicians rather than solely for the audience, and most important, fighting against racism in the music industry.

The pursuit of advancement in music and the self-conscious break from tradition — often times portrayed as "revolutionary" changes in music — represented a worldview that DeVeaux refers to as "modernism" in jazz music.[3] Beboppers considered themselves "serious" musicians, and some of them looked down on jump blues musicians like the Treneirs and Louis Jordan as clowns who were mere "entertainers," *not* musicians. Bebop musicians appropriated a modernist perspective not only because they looked to break from the past to create something new in jazz and contribute to the "progress" of music more generally, but also because they sought to create art in opposition to the commodification or commercialism of music, which had been imposed upon jazz by the music industry. Beboppers also frequently took a political stance, especially on the issue of racism in the music industry and in society as part of including political advocacy within their modernist viewpoint. The beboppers created a movement in jazz after the war that grew significantly, and eventually the movement became known as "modern" jazz. The term encompassed many directions in the movement including bebop, hard bop, cool jazz, West Coast jazz, and free jazz.

In some cases, the bebop musicians merely stated the obvious when they complained about the "vulgarity" of jump blues musicians, including the Treniers, who earned notoriety for their raunchy tunes. One of the most notorious songs written and performed by the Trenier Twins and despised by many jazz musicians was "Poontang." Many radio stations banned the song for its risqué lyrics, but it was a hit in working-class jukebox joints. In spite of controversial songs, however, the Treniers were invited to perform on television shows, including a performance on the *Colgate Comedy Hour* hosted by Dean Martin and Jerry Lewis in May 1954, where they performed "Rockin' Is Our Bizness." In fact, that performance is a good example of what Claude Trenier describes in his quote above: jumping around and shouting was the highlight of that performance, where toward the end of the show they invited Dean Martin and Jerry Lewis to join them for some improvisational dancing and shouting. Lewis, of course, was not reserved in his spastic, wild gyrations. Dean Martin was so pleased with the Treniers and enjoyed performing with them so much that he invited them to perform again when he had his own variety show years later.

For the bebop musicians, the sight of black musicians jumping around onstage, making silly faces, shouting and singing about things like drinking, fighting with the police, and pursuing casual sex perpetuated racist stereotypes that white audiences had come to expect from black performers. Be-boppers didn't see the irony of these representations because their modernist discursive field framed music in terms that often excluded irony and satiric humor. Beboppers thought that the jump blues musicians were conforming to the racist media representations of black people as dumb, silly, sex-crazed, drunk, happy-go-lucky buffoons. It was these representations that Gillespie referred to as "shameful." The sense of shame regarding blues music was prevalent among the political and cultural leadership of the middle- and upper-class African American community in the 1940s. Danny Baker, a jazz guitarist from Harlem, described an incident that took place in Harlem in 1938 when Eleanor Roosevelt appeared at a political rally hosted by the black leadership of Harlem. According to Baker, when Mrs. Roosevelt was onstage with Walter White (executive secretary of the NAACP), Bill Robinson, Mary McLeod Bethune (founder of the National Council of Negro Women), Marian Anderson (the famous opera singer), and other black leaders, somebody had hijacked a truck from the Savoy Ballroom that was outfitted with a loudspeaker system and then drove by the platform at a deliberately slow speed so that everybody, including the First Lady, could hear a song over the loud speakers attached to the truck. The song was the infamous "Don't You Feel My Legs," by Blue Lu Barker, the sultry blues singer who was popular in the working-class community. Other controversial and popular recordings by Blue Lu included, "You've Got to Show It To Me, Baby," "I'll Give You Some Tomorrow," "Loan Me Your Husband," and "I Feel Like Laying in Another Woman's Husband's Arms." According to Baker's account of the incident, the truck driver "slowed down the truck and he passed by mischievously, and finally went by. And you could hear, 'Listen to that filthy record . . .' 'It's filthy!' 'Get that record!' Somebody shouted, 'Stop the truck and get that record!' Some people were laughing; some of them were embarrassed: a song like this showed the vulgarity of the black mind. It was a disgrace. Yet at their houses, probably half of them had that record and played it at their parties. But they said, 'Get that record!'"[4] Baker's account reveals the complexity of the situation faced by bebop musicians and the cultural and political leadership of the black community in America during the 1940s. The black bourgeoisie felt a responsibility for lifting up the black working class, at least culturally, if not also economically. Bebop musicians had, by their professional middle-class status, proven the lie to the racist stereotype of the "un-educate-able Negro."

Bebop became somewhat "controversial" in the eyes of some because of the fact that very few white jazz musicians were playing bebop in the early years of its development, which followed from what was perceived to be a black nationalist perspective on music and society. Dizzy Gillespie once said, "We didn't go out and make speeches or say, 'Let's play eight bars of protest.'"[5] Nevertheless, the creators of bebop—Gillespie, Thelonius Monk, Charlie Parker, Charles Mingus, and others—intentionally developed a very complicated jazz music so white musicians would not be able to play it or, rather, *steal* it. Monk was reported to have said, "We're going to create something they can't steal because they can't play it."[6] Gillespie also referred to the issue of racism in the American music industry when he commented on the difference between the European and American reception of jazz. He observed, "They don't make a moral issue out of it as we sometimes do. It's of no moment to them that jazz was first played in the whore houses of New Orleans, that it was heard in Prohibition speakeasies. Nor do they make a racial issue out of jazz. There is no significant amount of anti-Negro prejudice in their countries for them to hold out against this music. They are interested in jazz for jazz's sake."[7] Gillespie recognized the complexity of jazz's history in terms of the complex intersection of class distinction—the fact that jazz was coded as lowbrow—and racial prejudice. The goal of the beboppers was to break down racial barriers by lifting up jazz to equal status with "classical" music. Class distinctions and hierarchy, however, were to remain as Gillespie told *Esquire* magazine in June 1957, "Jazz is too good for Americans."

Bebop emerged in New York City at Minton's Playhouse located uptown on 118th street in Harlem. Minton's place became famous as a spot where jazz musicians gathered for impromptu jam sessions. These typically consisted of small combos of musicians, as the big band era was in decline by the early 1940s, and out of these jam sessions emerged bebop. Henry Minton, who was the first African American delegate from Local 802 of the American Federation of Musicians in New York City, owned Minton's Playhouse, and although all the famous bebop musicians were members of the AFM, their music was—initially—not widely understood by their white rank-and-file colleagues in the union. In spite of the relative unfamiliarity with the new form, all the rank-and-file members of the musicians' union local in New York respected bebop because of the virtuosity displayed by those who composed and performed it. While bebop musicians maintained a critical stance toward a music industry that they considered to be racist, their white colleagues supported their musical movement, especially the white members in the AFM locals in New York, Los Angeles, and Chicago. At the time, New York was one of only two locals in the AFM that was racially integrated. The highbrow sensibilities of the bebop musicians ensured that they would enjoy relatively strong support inside the musicians' union. In places like New York, white and black jazz musicians were united by cultural elitism and a craft-conscious unionism, which was a labor union perspective that emphasized the difference between skilled workers who were members of the craft unions in the American Federation of Labor and unskilled workers who were largely dismissed and neglected by the AFL leadership. Unskilled workers were not organized by the labor movement in large numbers until the 1930s when the Congress of Industrial Organizations was created by dissidents within the labor movement who were critical of the AFL leadership. As stated in chapter 1, the "craft" of musicianship was based upon the ability to read music and perform an instrumental interpretation of a piece of music upon the first reading. For decades, the AFM excluded potential members on the basis of skill level in reading music and instrumental interpretation. Many musicians were barred membership because they failed a sight reading test.

The politics of bebop developed in the social context of changing expectations in the African American community during World War II. Many blacks had migrated to the North and West during the war to take advantage of the increased demand for labor during the war, as well as to escape the entrenched racism of the South. In the booming manufacturing areas in the North, and in the newly created defense industries in the West, blacks enjoyed a rising standard of living, and their influence as consumers gave them new power in the economy. Blacks had also successfully fought their way through the racial discrimination in some of the major labor unions in America, becoming activists in several industrial unions including important figures like A. Phillip Randolph, who built up the Brotherhood of Sleeping Car Porters into the first successful black labor union. At first the BSCP members were affiliated with the AFL, but Randolph moved the BSCP out of the AFL and into the Congress of Industrial Organizations after the AFL leadership refused to fight against racial segregation that prevailed in their numerous locals. During the war, Randolph proposed a march on Washington, D.C., to protest racial discrimination that prevailed in the defense industries and the federal government bureaucracy, forcing FDR to issue executive order 8802 in 1941, which later became the Fair Employment Act. Randolph had also proposed desegregating the troops, but that would not happen until Truman took office.

Racially motivated violence was a serious problem in the armed services. Earl Palmer, the famous session musician who played drums on many key recordings of early rock 'n' roll hits, has been given credit for cementing the heavy backbeat in rock 'n' roll music. After being drafted, Palmer was shot at by southern white soldiers while on a military base in California! In the South, there were several cases of lynching of black soldiers.[8] In discussing why he enlisted to fight in the war, Palmer recalls that "most people who enlisted were young and thought this would be a salvation. They were sorely disappointed. Any black person with his eyes open, the feeling was the same: 'what am I here for?' You was always running into stuff you didn't like. At first you took it. After two years you ready to hurt somebody." Palmer also revealed that many African Americans looked for opportunities to resist and rebel against the army, including going AWOL, misappropriating supplies and in many cases physically beating racist soldiers even if it meant risk of disciplinary action including court-martial. "We were dissidents . . . [and if we] got the opportunity to fuck the army, we took it. I'd never been very obedient."[9] In response to the abuse of black soldiers and the stark hypocrisy of the position of the U.S. government regarding the race question during the war, a renewed culture of resistance to racism and discrimination took hold in black communities. As a result of the economic growth driven by the military industrial complex, African Americans had accumulated significant amounts of economic and cultural capital, and these new sources of capital created the conditions for a growing black militancy.

Bebop musicians, for their part, challenged the entrenched racism of the music industry. Gillespie said that bebop musicians "refused to accept racism, poverty, or economic exploitation, nor would [they] live out uncreative humdrum lives merely for the sake of survival."[10] Fighting against racism involved cultural as well as economic strategies. On the cultural front, the strategy was to give jazz equal status with European classical music, as "highbrow" culture. This strategy included an educational component, especially for the black working class, who it was thought needed to learn an appreciation for modern jazz. In terms of the education of the masses, Gillespie made a formal request in 1957 that jazz "be taught to school children at all levels of their education. Let them from the very first day in their very first Music Appreciation class, let the children be made aware that no class distinction should exist between jazz and the classics."[11] Putting jazz music on equal footing with classical music was a very important issue, if not *the* issue for Gillespie and Mingus.

Bebop musicians were frustrated with what they thought was the simple and crude music of the southern black community. Beboppers struggled against the racist political economy of the culture industry that forced them to play in a particular style that perpetuated racist stereotypes of the "primitive" black entertainer, images that the racist white audience in the South came to expect from black musicians. Musicians like Gillespie, Charlie Parker, and Monk developed bebop as a way to break out of the race market created by the music industry. In addition to challenging racist stereotypes, bebop musicians struggled against the two-tiered wage scale that paid black musicians less than white musicians for the same work in both recording studios and live performances. Perhaps the worst injustice that plagued black musicians was the widespread thievery of unscrupulous record label owners who refused to pay mechanical royalties to their black recording artists.[12] Racist white record label owners were also known to take the credit as authors of songs that were written by their black artists, thereby stealing their royalty rights as composers.[13] Another issue for the bebop musicians and other black musicians who did not record jazz was the problematic practice of "covering" music, where one group of musicians performs or records music written by a different group of musicians. In the music industry, there is a long history of white musicians covering black music, thereby generating significant income in the process, while many black musicians were systematically cheated out of mechanical royalties and song writing credit. The practice was particularly widespread in the 1950s with rock 'n' roll.

Bebop musicians figured that if they could develop a revolutionary music that white-owned record labels would not be able to understand, let alone record, then they could protect their music and their culture. What made bebop unique was the fast tempo, complex harmonies, extraordinarily intricate melodies, and the way in which the drummers laid down the beat almost exclusively on the ride cymbal. These characteristics made bebop difficult to perform for musicians accustomed to the popular standards and the older forms of jazz, the musicians who were referred to as "traditionalists" by the beboppers. Eventually, many white musicians did begin playing bebop. One of the first was Woody Herman, who learned how to perform the new style from Dizzy Gillespie, and Herman's work opened the doors for more white musicians to play bebop. The vigorous adherence to highbrow aesthetic ideals together with a craft-conscious unionism was a means of creating interracial solidarity among union musicians, a solidarity that would eventually contribute to the integration of all the AFM locals by the mid-1960s. Mingus, for example, was very active in the integration of the Los Angeles locals. As white musicians began to participate more in the jam sessions in the after-hours clubs, black and white musicians in the AFM began to challenge racial segregation, especially in Los Angeles, where beboppers from local 767 were jamming with young white musicians from local 47 in the clubs on or near Central Avenue, a hub of activity for both bebop and jump blues. In many ways, Central Avenue in Los Angeles was the counterpart to Harlem in New York, especially in places like Minton's that became famous for the incredible late night jam sessions. According to the drummer William Douglass, who was a member of local 767:

> There were a number of us like Buddy Collette, Charlie Mingus, Chico Hamilton, and myself, who are moving around and working with some of the white guys from local 47. Musicians, when they start digging one another, well then it happened . . . you know Central Avenue was the place. Everybody came to Central Avenue. That's where the black and white folks meet. They talk about Basin Street. Well, hell, you've got Central Avenue again. The people when they'd leave those clubs [Basin Street] they'd come down here, and all the after-hours activity was all up and down the streets of Central. And, of course, the musicians are going to get to know one another.[14]

While the bebop musicians were carving out an oppositional culture of their own against the racist establishment that controlled the music industry, many also joined in with white jazz musicians in the public attack against rhythm and blues and rock 'n' roll music. Rock 'n' roll's roots in the working-class culture of resistance to work and exploitation were never articulated by bebop musicians, who spoke out against R&B and rock 'n' roll. Rather, they focused upon the formal aspects of the music, separated from social context. If social context were considered in their criticisms, it was within a framework that assumed an ignorant listening audience. Dizzy Gillespie told *Esquire* that the "people of the United States, the people who gave birth to this wonderful music [jazz], have never fully acknowledged it as an important part of culture."[15] Instead, according to Gillespie, the American music listening audience preferred "bad" music, like rhythm and blues, country, and rock 'n' roll. When reflecting on the development of jazz in the 1940s, Gillespie said, "I had the feeling in those days that jazz was well on its way to becoming the real folk music of America. But now [1957] almost all of that's gone. The folk music of today is a mongrel of made up strains of Presley . . . Tennessee Ernie Ford, Lombardo, and Sh-Boom!"[16] Gillespie's mention of Tennessee Ernie Ford as part of the "mongrel" music—as opposed to the "pureness" or authenticity of jazz—demonstrates that jazz musicians in the union looked down their noses at country music much in the same way they dismissed the perceived vulgarity of jump blues. Country musicians were still considered "hillbillies" by the active, successful rank-and-file members of the AFM based in New York, Chicago, and Los Angeles. Tennessee Ernie Ford was one of the most successful recording artists in country music at that time, and his biggest selling record was "Sixteen Tons," a song about the sorrows and suffering of coal miners. Ford's cover of the tune in 1955 sold over 200 million copies.[17] It is a classic working-class anthem. The song was written in the 1930s by ex–coal miner George S. Davis, although it is sometimes mistakenly attributed to Merle Travis, who recorded it in 1946. "Sixteen Tons" is part of an oeuvre of songs Davis wrote about the issues faced by mine workers and their union. The chorus of the song reads, "You load sixteen tons, what do you get? Another day older and deeper in debt. Saint Peter, don't you call me 'cause I can't go. I owe my soul to the company store."[18] Since Travis's recording, the song has been covered and recorded by Big Bill Broonzy, Bo Diddley, Johnny Cash, Stevie Wonder, the Platters, the Statler Bros., and the Weavers. Gillespie's dismissal of Ernie Ford as a "mongrel" revealed how out of touch many jazz musicians in the AFM were with working-class culture.

Hank Williams was also dismissed by jazz musicians and classical musicians as an unskilled vulgar entertainer. In fact, Williams was brushed off by the highbrows from his own local! In December 1952, he performed at the eighth annual party of local 479 of the AFM in Montgomery, Alabama. The president of the local, Tom Hewlett, explained that he "enjoyed" Williams's performance in spite of the fact that Williams was an unsophisticated, "un-modern" artist. The trick to enjoying the performance, according to Hewlett, was to forget that he and the other union musicians were skilled and sophisticated and listen to the performance without bias. According to Hewlett:

> To the average modern musician, frequently called "jazzmen," and also the serious musician, often called "squares" or "long-hair," folk music or *hillbilly* music is not of their taste. When Hank Williams played and sang to us at the Musicians Party . . . all of us, including the above two groups, were there. We listened attentively *as if* attending a concert by Benny Goodman or hearing the *cultivated* voice of some operatic star. *We forgot our talent, our technical skill, and musical training* [in order to] truly enjoy every note.[19]

The fact that Hewlett made a point of clearly marking out a distinction between the jazzmen/long-hairs on one side and hillbillies on the other revealed that country musicians were culturally marginal in the minds of "serious" musicians in the union. Also, the fact that he was still referring to country music as "hillbilly" music as late as 1952 signified his contempt for the genre in general.

It would be a mistake, however, to claim that all beboppers were mounting a full-scale attack on working-class culture per se. Rather, most jazz musicians were primarily concerned with performing music that stimulated their interests. Part of the issue for bebop musicians was how to perform standard pop tunes—in order to make a living—without succumbing to boredom. Bebop musicians who traveled with groups like the Cab Calloway Orchestra and Billy Eckstine's band resented touring in the South because they were forced to play "down" to a rural audience that expected to hear the blues. Charlie Parker disparagingly referred to the blues as "rice and beans" music. When they were on tour playing in one of the big bands, Gillespie and Parker would make changes to standard arrangements of popular tunes during live performances to amuse themselves and make the music more "sophisticated," but they were careful not to change things too much because they had to keep it "simple" enough for audiences to be able to dance to it. Gillespie claimed, "They're not particular about whether you're playing a flatted fifth or a ruptured 129th as long as they can dance."[20] Earl Palmer also recalls smuggling bebop phrases into live performances when he was traveling with Dave Bartholomew's band from New Orleans. "Dave kept that band very commercial," recalled Palmer. "He didn't want no bebop rhythm section, the drummer dropping bombs—people were dancing out there. . . . I'd sneak in a bomb and Dave would flash me a dirty look and say, 'Uh-uh Chief.' . . . Tyler and McLean and I always snuck in a little bebop."[21]

Bebop musicians signified their upward mobility and sophistication in part by using the abstract language of music theory, which was central to their modernist discursive field. Talk of smuggling "flatted fifths" and "ruptured 129ths" past an unsuspecting and uneducated audience was a way to demonstrate their highbrow sensibilities, their "craft" as skilled musicians, and signify their social *distance* from working-class culture as well as their rejection of what they viewed as degrading media representations conditioned by the culture industry. Gillespie admitted that "the bebop musicians didn't like to play the blues. They were ashamed. The media had made it shameful."[22] In another discussion about bebop musicians begrudgingly performing popular dance music in public in order to fulfill contract obligations to club owners, Dizzy Gillespie argued: "Bebop is a highly sophisticated form of music; the blues is very simple in form. The bebop musicians wanted to show their virtuosity. They'd play the twelve bar outline of the blues, but they wouldn't blues it up like the older guys they considered unsophisticated. They busied themselves making changes, a thousand changes in one bar."[23] While the bebop musicians were doing their best to distance themselves from the blues by appropriating a bourgeois, modernist aesthetic, working-class kids growing up in the United States and the United Kingdom were getting turned on to the blues.

Ironically, blues music was an avenue for *upward* mobility for working-class youth seeking to accumulate cultural capital and become potential recording stars. The "older guys," that Gillespie refers to, including blues musicians like Robert Johnson, Muddy Waters, Howlin' Wolf, Lead Belly, and the R&B shouters like Wynonie Harris and Big Joe Turner may have been dismissed by the jazz musicians in the union as lowbrow and unskilled, but they were icons for young rock 'n' roll musicians. The Rolling Stones, for example, took their name from a Muddy Waters tune, and Keith Richards, their rhythm guitarist, was a huge fan and self-studied pupil of Robert Johnson, the guitar virtuoso known as the "king of the Delta blues." Johnson's techniques were carefully studied by guitarists like Richards and Eric Clapton. Many rock musicians from the British Invasion era, including the Rolling Stones, the Beatles, and Clapton, often attempted to endow the blues with cultural prestige by using the bombast of musical intricacy. Sometimes they would compare the great blues musicians with classical composers. Richards said of Johnson, "When you listen to him . . . the cat's got Bach going down low and Mozart going up high. He was counterpointing and using incredible stuff."[24]

Ironically, Richards used virtually the same vocabulary to give praise to the blues that jazz musicians used to *dismiss* the blues and rock 'n' roll. Richards himself was academically trained in music, having attended Sidcup Art College in England, and he was well versed in the rhetoric of musical complexity. Richards points out above that Robert Johnson was a master of counterpoint techniques in his music, and he compares Johnson's accomplishments to those of a Bach or a Mozart, two central figures in the canon of "highbrow" European music. Richards's appeal to the classical tradition in some ways mirrored Mingus's, although for very different ends. Each made an appeal toward the classical tradition, but Mingus and his colleagues made the appeal to distance themselves from the blues, while Richards and his generation made the appeal to legitimize the blues and therefore rock 'n' roll.

The construction of the discursive field in bebop involved moving jazz music in the direction of the modernist movement in twentieth-century European music, which is characterized by composers like Schoenberg, Ravel, Stravinsky, and Debussy.[25] Some beboppers like Miles Davis were trained in the classical idiom by the academy. Other bebop jazz musicians like Charles Mingus composed musical works that combined jazz and classical music.[26] Mingus sometimes referred to jazz as "black classical music" because he was ambivalent about the term *jazz*. He was concerned that usage of the term would marginalize African Americans both in the business of music and in the art world. "Don't call me a jazz musician," Mingus once berated a journalist. "To me the word *jazz* means nigger, discrimination, second-class citizenship, the whole back-of-the-bus bit."[27] In a similar vein, Nina Simone once said, "Jazz is a white term to define black people. My music is black classical music."[28] To be successful in the endeavor of articulating jazz and classical music, Mingus believed that he had to break down racial barriers between the two genres, in particular racial discrimination that prevented black musicians from working in the classical arena. Thus the beboppers' discursive field contained a contradiction that revealed the complexity of their interventions in the development of American music. Racial inequality and discrimination were being challenged by the bebop generation, while they simultaneously maintained a *class* separation between themselves and their contemporaries performing and recording blues and jump blues. Bebop musicians were breaking down racial barriers in the industry and in the union, while also creating *more distance* between themselves and working-class culture. Mingus, for example, was an activist in the effort to desegregate the musicians' union during the period when he was experimenting with compositions that combined elements of classical and jazz music. As an influential member in the black local in Los Angeles, Mingus spearheaded the successful movement to merge Local 767 with the white Local 47 in 1952.[29] Mingus's and the other black musicians' success in the integration drive was due in part to the construction of an elitist aesthetic discourse that united white and black musicians in the union under a shared identity that was part "skilled" musician and part "artist."

The Los Angeles musicians were the first segregated musicians to amalgamate a black and white local in the AFM. The strategy to integrate the union was grounded in developing solidarity by way of interracial participation in the performance of classical music. The other key figure in the drive to integrate the black and white locals in Los Angeles was the saxophonist, composer, arranger, and lifelong friend of Mingus, Buddy Collette. It was Collette's idea to form an interracial Community Symphony Orchestra as a way to develop support for the amalgamation movement among rank-and-file musicians in both locals. In his recollections of that time, Collette recalled that "our main goal was to make sure more blacks were placed in different circuits because at that time they only worked clubs. . . . We were on the phones talking to people and many of them just wanted to be there: 'Interracial symphony? Let's do that!' . . . A lot of enthusiasm. . . . We had a board to set policy and to let people know about the orchestra. The main aim was to bring about one musicians' union in Los Angeles, black and white under the same roof."[30]

Mingus was also active in breaking down racial barriers in musical education. He argued that although black musicians could receive extensive training in the black musical community, there remained serious obstacles in the development of musical training for black musicians because of institutionalized racial discrimination in academia. One area in particular that demonstrated the continued problem of discrimination in music academies in the 1950s was the lack of black musicians working in America's symphonies. Mingus argued that too much potential talent was going to waste, and he situated the issue in the language or context of classical music. Mingus asked, "Can we send a potential Ravel, Debussy, or Stravinsky to his grave without affording him the chance to prove that music has advanced many steps and that many composers as great as any of the old are being forced to write background music for slipping off Mabel's girdle, rather than the *true* emotions of the inner self?"[31]

It is interesting that Mingus coded "talented" black musicians as potential "Ravels" or "Stravinskys," while he used the term *girdle* to signify "low" music. As Scott DeVeaux has demonstrated, Stravinsky was a particularly influential figure.[32] In some cases, modern jazz musicians would borrow phrases from Stravinsky and incorporate them into their performances. Unlike in previous cases where bandleaders like Billy Eckstine would incorporate bars of classical music in a sly manner so as to poke fun at classical music, for modern jazz musicians, "the butt of the joke [was] not the 'classical' repertory, but the squares who (obviously) wouldn't know Stravinsky if they heard it. . . . Stravinsky returned the favor by writing the *Ebony Concerto*."[33]

Mingus's words demonstrate that the appropriation of highbrow bourgeois values by jazz musicians was a way to dismiss jump blues and blues on *moral* grounds as well as aesthetic grounds. Morality was often coded in the rhetoric of musical erudition. Rhythm and blues and rock 'n' roll are largely oriented toward sexual pleasure, which is embedded in the music by the use of double entendres and bawdy humor. But for highbrow aesthetes, sexual pleasure was coded as "savage" and thus lacking in value. Moral disgust with double entendres and references to sexuality undergirded the elitist and sometimes academic critique of jump blues and rock 'n' roll. Mingus and other beboppers like Gillespie often used technical academic language in their dismissal of rock 'n' roll. But what it boiled down to was that for them, singing about girdles was morally offensive and simply vulgar. There was relatively little room for irony or bawdy humor in the "serious" modernist discourse of the beboppers. Ironically, the language of musical sophistication sometimes employed by jazz musicians in the trade magazines to signify the supposed "simplicity" of the structure of rock 'n' roll songs and the general "backwardness" of R&B was code for bourgeois moral disgust with working-class culture. Moral disgust with the working-class, in short, was *displaced* through the rhetoric of music complexity that signified the jazz musicians' facility with academic music theory.

Because Mingus, like Gillespie before him, appealed to highbrow sensibilities to break down racism in music, *class* distinction and discrimination became (by default) a *goal to be achieved*. Mingus felt that he had to break down the conventional separation of jazz and classical music because he thought—rightly so—that the two genres were unjustly kept separate by racism, which stifled the potential talent in the African American musical community. But *class* distinction was never posed as a problem by Mingus or the other key modern jazz recording artists who voiced concerns about racism in the music industry and in society at large. Mingus was searching for the "true" emotions of the inner self and the "true" essence of music, and he felt the racial coding of "good" music as either jazz or classical got in the way of pursuing the advancement of music beyond racialized categories. For Mingus, the way to get beyond racialized categories was to appropriate the bourgeois aesthetic form, then expand and change it to include black musicians.

Central to what I refer to as a bourgeois aesthetic appropriated by the modern jazz musicians is the marginalization of the body and the belief in progress. The search for "true emotions of inner self" required dismissing the body or bodily pleasure as merely transient pleasure, an activity understood to be for unlearned and uncultured individuals, below the sensibilities of legitimate, mature artists. Mingus's aesthetic modernism that valued mind over body framed his point of view about pursuing the "universal" characteristics of music, and he thought he was finding parallels in jazz and classical music as a way to get to a place free of racial markers and restrictions. "Today," Mingus said, "musicians in all races are proving that no race is endowed with special abilities for any profession and that every musician has an equal chance if given the proper start and study needed for playing correctly. . . . One day it will no longer be necessary for a musician to jump up and down on a drum or dance on a bandstand to receive recognition of his talent."[34] "One day" implies that the history of music is linear, and it is the task of enlightened musicians to push music forward and upward. "Progress," however, contains a contradiction because the movement for breaking down racial discrimination carried within it the *maintenance* of class distinction and discrimination. There was no reflection upon this contradiction among Mingus, Gillespie, and their cluster of jazz musicians because distancing themselves from working-class culture signified "progress" in the steady march of musical history. Like Mingus, Gillespie framed progress in terms of the bourgeois binary between mind and body, where the body represents backwardness and the mind represents progress through sublimation and cultured sophistication. Complaining about what he believed to be the perceived "lowbrow" cultural status of jazz music in *Esquire* in 1957, Gillespie said, "I believe the mass of the American people still consider jazz as lowbrow music. They believe, as John Philip Sousa said, that 'people hear jazz through their feet, not their brains.' To them jazz is for kids . . . music to rub bodies to. Not 'serious' music. Not concert-hall material."[35]

Of course, it would be disingenuous to argue that Gillespie and Mingus lacked any sense of irony and humor in their repertoire. Indeed, I do not intend to overplay the extent to which Mingus and Gillespie displayed a dour and serious attitude toward jazz music. There are many examples of play-fulness, satire, and mimicry in their bodies of work. It is perhaps a cliché to say so, but Mingus and Gillespie occupied contradictory locations in the political economy of American music. Scott DeVeaux's book on bebop has adequately captured the complexity of Gillespie's place in the history of American music. According to DeVeaux:

> Gillespie may have disliked what he perceived as the obsequious tone of older forms of black entertainment, including Louis Armstrong's "grinning in the face of white racism," but in reaching beyond the circumscribed world of the jazz virtuoso to the broader sphere of commercial entertainment he discovered his own accommodation with audience expectation—what he later called "my own way of Tomming." . . . In short, Gillespie became a "personality," within the bounds allowable to African Americans at midcentury. This strategy put a public face on bebop and undoubtedly helped to neutralize the impression of racial antagonism that many audiences may have drawn from the sight of black instrumentalists determined not to entertain.[36]

Elected officials in the AFM echoed the aesthetic elitism of the beboppers and jazz musicians in general, although the highbrow attitude was over-determined by the discourse of "skill" as part of craft-conscious union-ism. For example, William Everett Samuels, who was secretary treasurer of Local 208 (the black Chicago local that existed before the merger with the white Local 10) from 1931 to 1955, referred to rock 'n' roll music as "crap."[37] Just as in the case of Mingus, Samuels used the metaphorical language of high and low regions on the body to map out the regions of sophisticated and uncultured music. Unworthy music was associated with bodily plea-sure. Words that emphasized the lower regions of the human body like *girdles* or *shit* were used as a way to create class distance between good musicians and bad musicians. It was an appropriation of the classic bourgeois dualism between the mind and the body, but it was articulated within a discourse on "skill" or "craft." In bourgeois dualism, the body is understood as an obstacle to be overcome. In the discourse of skill and craft, skilled labor is labor that has been sublimated into a craft and rigorously separated from unskilled labor, which is unsublimated, the raw expression of the body. Samuels went so far as to argue that rock 'n' roll music belonged in the toilet.

Like Mingus, Samuels was active in the effort to break down racial segregation in the AFM, and his efforts were part of the successful drive to integrate the black and white locals in Chicago. In this case, too, bourgeois aesthetic sensibilities articulated within the perspective of "skilled" labor provided the necessary if not sufficient conditions for a movement toward integration of black and white locals. For Samuels, the crucial aspect of being a "good" musician is the ability to read music, and since most rock 'n' roll musicians of his era in large part did not read music, they were considered second-class musicians. Speaking about his experience working in Chicago, Samuels discussed what he considered to be a straightforward and uncontroversial separation of musicians into "good" and "bad." "I never had to search hard for good musicians," claimed Samuels:

> I knew where all the good ones were. Musicians always know one another. They're cliquey. They got their little cliques. I was looking for musicians who could read and play anything I wanted them to play. I was very lucky in that respect. Most of the musicians in my era could read music. Most of the pop artists today don't read music. See, it was a different era. We didn't have that *rock-and-roll crap*. You had to play; you had to be able to play, to read. If you didn't you just got you a job as a porter or something and got by the best way you could. They [rock-and-roll musicians] would work, but they would work in second-class places. We've always had *cheaper* places like taverns. We called 'em toilets. . . . The city doesn't have a *cultural* life anymore. Fewer and fewer places every year. The main places are from North Michigan Avenue from the river back on down to the Drake Hotel, down Michigan Ave., they've got all those big fine hotels; they all got good music in 'em. . . . They have that *rock-and-roll crap* over there on Wells Street in Old Town. But back over on this side they have some pretty good music; and you don't have any trouble.[38]

The movement toward racial integration and solidarity within the AFM carried within it the institutionalization of first- and second-class musicians within the union. In some ways, the AFM was following in the tradition of exclusion that marks the history of craft unions in the American labor movement.[39] The problem for the AFM was that the demand for jazz and classical music was in sharp decline by the late 1950s, and their adherence to an exclusionist craft mentality prevented them from aggressively organizing so-called unskilled rock 'n' roll musicians and including them as equals in the everyday organizational maintenance and culture of the union. In short, their craft union strategy of exclusion, combined with their cultural elitism, which legitimated their practice of exclusion, cost them dearly, because rock 'n' roll and the structural changes in the music industry that followed the shift toward rock 'n' roll eventually displaced the union from its position of power and influence in the music industry.[40]

Of course, there were musicians in the union—including some within the leadership structure—who criticized the dominant point of view that adhered to a rigid distinction between good and bad music. Some individuals within the AFM leadership argued against constructing a culture of separation between skilled and unskilled musicians that institutionalized a structure of first- and second-class musicians. George Cooper Jr., who took over as president of the Nashville Local 257 of the AFM in 1937, was a visible and outspoken leader of one of the largest and most influential locals. Cooper warned against separating the culture of music within the union. One of his key issues was the fight against the use of auditions—which were based upon the ability to perform an interpretation of a written score upon one sitting—as a basis for determining membership in the union. Cooper's fight against music exams made it possible for country, blues, jump blues, and rock 'n' roll musicians who couldn't read music to gain access to Local 257. Reading music was one of the main, if not *the* main, way in which musicians in the AFM created an identity of "skilled" musician, and the ability to read was a central element in the bifurcation of musical culture between highbrow and lowbrow musicians. Cooper's musical training was on the bass and horns. He joined the AFM in 1918 when he was playing in a band that was accompanying a traveling circus. Cooper came to Nashville to play in vaudeville theaters in addition to a movie house ensemble that accompanied silent movies. When Cooper assumed leadership of Local 257 in 1937, it had just seventy-three members, having been decimated by the Depression. Cooper went on to be one of the most successful local presidents, turning around the fortunes of Local 257, which is today one of the largest locals operating in one of the major hubs of the American music industry. Among his accomplishments, Cooper was able to raise the scale (rate of pay) for musicians working on the Grand Ole Opry.

Appropriating bourgeois norms was not, according to leaders in the union like Cooper, a sustainable strategy for creating solidarity within the union. Nor was it a viable strategy to promote solidarity within the black community. Jazz musicians striving to attain highbrow status ultimately gave up on their quest to educate the "uncultured" masses. Comments by jazz bassist Milt Hinton revealed this problematic strategy and fatalistic perspective, when he said it was a "lost cause" trying to educate the black working class. The working-class preference for the blues was simply too strong to overcome, Hinton said. The best they could hope for was that the "best and brightest" among African Americans could become upwardly mobile. According to Hinton:

> Trying to educate the southern black people . . . [was like fighting a losing battle]. . . . All they wanted was dirty records . . . old dirty blues. . . . So they didn't dig [our music]. . . . I guess I got the idea [of educating the black working class] from Cab [Calloway] that this kind of thing [blues music] kept the black mind in the South down. . . . The music we played was completely different from what blacks usually heard. In most southern towns there'd be a small radio station catering to a black audience. The music they'd play was real trash-blues, with lyrics that had sexual messages. "You got bad blood, mama, I think you need a shot," "Now my needle's in you, honey," those kinds of lines. . . . Southern black people seemed to be kept ignorant, poor, and fighting among themselves.[41]

Louis Jordan was frequently attacked by bebop musicians for these reasons. Among his repertoire of performance practices, Jordan had developed a character he dubbed "Deacon Jones." Jordan's character was a very popular component in the live performance of his tunes. Deacon Jones was also the name of one of his hit records. In fact, Deacon Jones is also mentioned in both Roy Brown's and Wynonie Harris's historical recordings of "Good Rockin' Tonite," which was their way of tipping their hats to Louis Jordan as a key influence in their music. As part of the character, Jordan wore gigantic white plastic glasses, a top hat, and a silly tie and suit. Jordan also made lots of silly faces while playing the Deacon Jones character. Be-boppers were ashamed of these kinds of performances, due in part to Jordan's background in minstrelsy.[42] Jordan learned his stagecraft when he was a performer for W. C. Handy's traveling minstrel show in the South before coming to work for Chick Webb's orchestra in New York City in the late 1930s. Jordan's southern background and his background in minstrelsy led many of the members in Webb's band to accuse Jordan of being an "Uncle Tom," and many musicians working in New York referred to him behind his back as "Stepin Fetchit."[43]

In self-defense, Jordan said that the people in his audience who laughed the loudest at his stage frolics were blacks, not whites. Jordan also was not ashamed of being an "entertainer" as well as a musician. Jordan said, "See, before I got a band, I knew what I wanted to do with it. I wanted to give my whole life to making people enjoy my music. Make them laugh and smile. So I didn't stick to what you'd call jazz. I have always stuck to entertainment."[44] In another interview he talked about how he didn't take part in the perceived aloofness of the beboppers. "I really wanted to be an entertainer," said Jordan. "I wanted to play for millions, not just a few hepcats. . . . Those guys [beboppers] really wanted to play mostly for themselves, and I still wanted to play for the people. I just like to sing my blues and swing."[45] Jordan, the Treniers, and other jump blues musicians agreed, in part, with how the beboppers and modern jazz musicians separated music between entertainment and serious music, but the jump blues musicians did not create a hierarchy out of that difference, unlike the modern jazz musicians who were struggling for increased cultural status. While Jordan made a distinction between his music and bebop, he never spoke disparagingly about the bebop musicians. On the contrary, he liked and respected bebop. "Like bebop?" Jordan asked during an interview in 1948. "Man, I love it. . . . You know Dizzy Gillespie's my boy. I worked with him back when I was with Chick Webb."[46] Jordan was a fan of bebop, but his band did not perform much of it during his live gigs, preferring not to interrupt the shuffle rhythms that made him famous. Some of the bebop musicians who played with his band, however, resented him for those very reasons. The tenor saxophonist Paul Quinichette, who played a few gigs with Jordan, referred to him as a "dictator with 'Uncle Tom' qualities." In an interview, he recounted, "I hated all the time I was with him. I didn't like the kind of thing he was doing, it wasn't jazz. I think Louis was a prelude to this rock thing. I didn't like those tunes."[47] Quinichette eventually left Jordan's band to join Count Basie's band as the replacement for Lester Young. Quinichette also performed and recorded with John Coltrane, but found success mainly with Duke Ellington.

Jordan's comedy and stage performance practices were always full of irony and humor. According to Jordan his audience was usually "too damn busy laughing at me, and at themselves, to make any complaints." Jordan was aware of how middle-class urban dwellers felt about rural working-class folk, and he knew how to make them laugh at caricatures of country people. But he also knew how to make fun of "sophisticated" urbanites and poke fun at them when he played for working-class rural audiences. Jordan always pointed at class distinctions with irony, signifying in ways that took sides with the working-class against the snobbery of highbrow elitists. Jordan used irony as a form of covert resistance, a tradition going way back in black culture to the trickster tales, stories about slaves fooling their unsuspecting masters by deploying irony, exaggeration, and deception.[48] Aaron Izenhall, who played trumpet for Louis Jordan, described the controversy between Quinichette and Jordan in an interview. According to Izenhall, "Paul Quinichette and those bebop disciples didn't like the idea of wearing really bright, wild-colored clothing and moving around while they played or putting on a show."[49] Quinichette didn't see any irony in Jordan's outrageous stage antics or in his bawdy lyrics, but other musicians and performers did understand. Years later, Sammy Davis Jr., who performed with Louis Jordan, said, "Louis Jordan was the first recording artist to project the life and situations of the black community on records with humor and dignity. I and many others like me have dropped nickel after nickel in the jukebox to enjoy his messages in song and monologue. Mr. Louis Jordan is the original soul brother."[50]

Indeed, many of Jordan's tunes make you laugh. The content of the lyrics and the call-and-response storytelling technique are irresistibly funny. In a hilarious tune called "Open the Door, Richard," Jordan sings about the "embarrassing" predicament of a "well respected man" being seen with his drunk friends out on the streets late at night. In one of the spoken verses, Jordan says:

> But I hate to be caught out on the street like this because it makes
>   you seem so common, and I know I ain't common cause I got class
>   I ain't never used. But I guess I better get on in the house cause I
>   don't want my pastor to catch me out on the street like this.

Open the door, Richard!

Now look at that old woman across the street, stuck her head out the
window.

'Tis everybody's business in the neighborhood.

Done stuck her head outta the window callin her sister.

Look at her callin' her sister and her sister sayin, 'Ain't that him, ain't
that him?'

Yes, it's me, and I'm drunk again!!

Hey, Richard, open the door![51]

In "Open the Door, Richard" Jordan was using humor to reveal the relative absurdity of morally uptight people who might be appalled at the thought of people staying out late, getting drunk, perhaps also having sex and getting into fights. Jordan was the master of ironic humor. In the lyrics to "Open the Door, Richard," Jordan points to class as a marker of distinction through irony as a way to signify an awareness of class subordination while resisting it through the deployment of humor. Jordan was well aware of the possibility that elitists looked down their noses at his music when he makes a reference to the issue in the lyrics to "Open the Door": "I know I ain't common, cuz I got class I ain't never used." Jordan humorously and ironically claims to have "class" while using the word "ain't," which is usually understood to be incorrect English. Similarly, in "Inflation Blues," he sings, "I'm not one of those highbrows, I'm average Joe to you," as a way to draw attention to and deconstruct the binary of high and low culture.[52]

In the late 1940s, it was not uncommon for jump blues groups to perform at the same venues where bebop musicians played. But as Claude Trenier describes in the passage that opens this chapter, there wasn't much camaraderie between the two groups of musicians. It was even relatively common for session musicians who were members of the union to record both kinds of music. Many of the key recordings in the history of rock 'n' roll — recordings we now consider "essentials" — involved session musicians well-traveled in the jazz world, including the incomparable drummer Earl Palmer. Palmer, who is widely recognized as one of the innovators of the rock 'n' roll beat, was inducted into the Rock and Roll Hall of Fame in 2000. He played drums on recordings by Fats Domino, Richie Valens, Tina Turner, the Beach Boys, and Little Richard.

Nevertheless, rhythm and blues and rock 'n' roll remained a topic of controversy among professional musicians. While there was virtually universal agreement among bebop musicians and the older generation of swing jazz musicians that rhythm and blues was inferior to jazz in technical terms (especially to bebop), most musicians did not attack rhythm and blues and rock 'n' roll publicly, especially those who were making a good living as session musicians recording rock 'n' roll. Palmer, for example, was very active in recording sessions for rock 'n' roll recording stars, while also very active in the union, believing that the successful recording stars like himself had a duty to take care of less successful musicians in the union, the kind of musicians he referred to as the "little guys." In fact, Palmer was critical of the successful session musicians who were looking out only for their own interests and who did not see any need to sacrifice anything for their colleagues in the union who were struggling to get by, either in recording studios or onstage performing for live venues. The successful session musicians in the AFM who resented having any of their earnings—which were accumulated through mechanical royalties—used to contribute to the growth of the Musicians' Performance Trust Fund (MTPF) formed a dissident organization called the Recording Musicians Association (RMA) to fight against the AFM policy of supporting less successful musicians with the earnings of session musicians who were enjoying a good living. The MTPF was set up as the main vehicle through which successful musicians could assist their union brothers and sisters who were less fortunate. Although Palmer was one of the most successful session musicians in the AFM, he was very critical of the RMA: "We are all union men. The RMA is just for itself. They don't give a damn about regular guys in the union."[53]

Musicians like Palmer represented an interesting contradiction among those AFM musicians who believed in the importance of solidarity within the union, even if it meant that financially successful musicians like himself had to sacrifice for the well-being of their union as a whole, because while the emphasis on solidarity—"we are *all* union men"—implied a sense of *sameness* among the members, Palmer and musicians like him also articulated a point of view that emphasized distinction and hierarchy among musicians in the union, which was explained in terms of "sophisticated" and "simple" music. Jump blues and rock 'n' roll musicians were never truly equal in the eyes of jazz musicians like Palmer, because their music was of "low" quality. Palmer said of Little Richard that his music was as "exciting as a sumbitch. *I'm not talking about the quality of it. It wasn't quality music.* It wasn't no chords, it was just the blues. . . . It was exciting because he was exciting."[54] Palmer and other jazz musicians like him worked in the recording studio on rock 'n' roll sessions to get a paycheck, not because they had any connection to or appreciation of the music. "I enjoyed going to the studio," recalled Palmer. "I knew I'd make more money in six hours than in a week of gigs. But we didn't realize how popular that stuff [rock-and-roll] was getting. What was rock-and-roll to me? I lived in a jazz world. I was not interested in Fats Domino or Little Richard. . . . 'Tutti Fruitti' was fun, but [it wasn't] music. . . . Disliking the music was not a problem for me. Like it or not, I took pride in playing. . . . I was a finished musician."[55] Thus, while Palmer disliked rock 'n' roll, he took pride in being a professional musician in the recording studio, no matter what it was that he was recording. His identity as a "finished" or professional musician meant for him that he was able to record all kinds of music and make a good living. When he wanted to play for himself, not for the money, then Palmer preferred bebop over all other music. The culture that created first- and second-class citizens in the union, however, meant that the AFM leadership would not take rock 'n' roll seriously, and that attitude would end up compromising the power of the union in the music industry.

Although Palmer did not dislike rock 'n' roll enough to go on the attack against it publicly in the trade magazines — since he was making a living off of the music — many other union musicians with jazz backgrounds did, including Billy Taylor and Les Elgert.[56] Taylor criticized the structure of jump blues songs for being simple and stupid, and in what would become a major refrain within the AFM, he referred to jump blues musicians as entertainers, *not* musicians. As stated above, the "entertaining" aspect of jump blues was not only a class issue, because "entertainment" was thought by the jazz musicians who criticized it to be particularly degrading for black Americans, since it seemed to borrow elements that signified performance aspects from the minstrel shows of the past. Consequently, the Trenier Twins and Louis Jordan frequently experienced a lack of respect and collegiality from jazz musicians who shared their venues in the 1940s. The tension in the nightclubs eventually became public. As rhythm and blues continued to grow in popularity and as R&B musicians continued to separate themselves from the culture of jazz music and bebop in particular, jazz musicians began to publicly criticize rhythm and blues in the trade magazines. The criticisms intensified with rock 'n' roll music in the mid-1950s, when rock 'n' roll dominated the music charts.

In 1955 and 1956, *DownBeat* magazine published a series of articles on the "problem" of rock 'n' roll music in America. Jazz instrumentalists and bandleaders, most of whom were members of the AFM, used the magazine to hold a forum on the various issues associated with rock 'n' roll music. By 1955, rock 'n' roll music had taken over the *Billboard* charts. Jump blues hits had been on the charts since 1946, but rock 'n' roll didn't appear on the charts until Bill Haley's single "Crazy, Man, Crazy" broke the *Billboard* "hot 100" charts in 1953. It was basically the same music in 1953 as it was in 1946, but the electric guitar had replaced the saxophone and white musicians were performing it more frequently, which was one of the main reasons for the name change to "rock 'n' roll."[57] In 1953, the market for rhythm and blues (formerly race music) was only 6 percent of the market, and country music (formerly hillbilly music) was just 9 percent of the market. All that would change in a few short years, however, as the two genres collided to produce rock 'n' roll. In 1955, Haley's single "Rock Around the Clock" occupied the charts for twenty-four weeks. Chuck Berry's "Maybellene" went to number one on the R&B charts and number five on the "hot 100" singles (the pop charts). By 1956, Elvis had the first, second, sixth, fourteenth, and fifteenth spots on *Billboard's* top 50 singles. Also in the top 50 for 1955 and 1956 were Little Richard, Fats Domino, Jerry Lee Lewis, Carl Perkins, and Gene Vincent.

The issue for the union musicians involved in the discussions in *DownBeat* was nothing less than the future of music in America. What would become of bebop jazz and big band music? Would rock 'n' roll last? Or was it just a fad, and if so, how was it possible that it could be so popular? While there were many disagreements about what was "wrong" with music in America, the union musicians involved in the discussion agreed that rhythm and blues/rock 'n' roll music was seriously lacking in cultural value. No matter what specific explanations were used for why rock 'n' roll had become so popular, there was universal agreement that rock 'n' roll was *not* good music. The question for the musicians featured in *DownBeat* was how jazz musicians in America should respond to rock 'n' roll and how they would figure out who was to blame for its popularity.

One of the first jazz musicians in the *DownBeat* forum was Les Elgart, a longtime member of the AFM. Elgart made a name for himself as a trumpet player in the Woody Herman orchestra in the 1940s, and in the 1950s he became a bandleader in his own right. Elgart's big band was among the last of the bands in the United States that played in the style of the swing era. When interviewed for the March 23, 1955, issue of *DownBeat*, Elgart referred to rock 'n' roll as "something that will just have to run its course, like an epidemic." The labeling of rock 'n' roll as an "epidemic," "disease," or "social pathology" would become a widespread mantra among the conservative establishment in America during the 1950s. A headline in the May 28, 1956, edition of the *New York Times* read: "Rock-and-Roll Called Communicable Disease." The article referred to a "noted" psychiatrist who had argued that rock 'n' roll could be considered a bona-fide disease! But the union musicians' criticisms of rock 'n' roll went beyond dismissing it on the grounds that it was popular among "undesirable" elements in society because musicians coded their moral attacks on rock 'n' roll by basing them on technical grounds as well, through arguments that were based in music theory and modernism. Musicians agreed with conservative critics that rock 'n' roll attracted delinquents and deadbeats, but they also attacked the structural elements of the songs themselves. According to Elgart, rock 'n' roll was an extremely simple music that, for him, led inevitably to boredom, and he predicted that rock 'n' roll would be a passing fad. "The rhythm and blues," argued Elgart, "is so limited that they [kids] get over it in a hurry. It ceases to be exciting to them in no time at all." [58] By the time *DownBeat* took the jazz musicians' criticisms of rock 'n' roll public, the issue was as much a class issue as an issue having to do with race, since by the mid-1950s rock 'n' roll had crossed the color line for both musicians and audience. While the racial integration of the audience for rock 'n' roll was still controversial, especially in the South, from the point of view of jazz musicians, rock 'n' roll was simply second-class music, just plain trash. As was the case with the beboppers' attitude toward the southern black audience, union musicians on the attack against rock 'n' roll in *DownBeat* were hoping to convince American consumers of music that rock 'n' roll was worthless, and to do so required that union musicians "educate" the masses and expose them to "good" music that was played with proper technique.

In 1956, Chuck Berry, Little Richard, Fats Domino, Elvis, Jerry Lee Lewis, and Bill Haley were still firmly in charge of the music charts. That year *DownBeat* ran an article titled, "Musicians Argue the Value of Rock-and-Roll," and several famous AFM members seized the opportunity to criticize rock 'n' roll. The list of union musicians who participated included Benny Goodman, the famous bandleader from the swing era, Thad Jones from the brass section of the Count Basie orchestra, bassist Milt Hinton, and pianist Billy Taylor (who played with Ben Webster). Taylor was the harshest: "It's musically trite. It's obviously gimmicked up with old boogie-woogie phrases, pseudo-Spanish rhythms, recurring triplets *ad nauseum*.

The melodies are repetitious. . . . Harmonically, a lot of it is incorrectly written, and worse than that, incorrectly played." Taylor was among those who believed that rock 'n' roll was a fake, a music that was "invented" by suspect "independent" record label owners looking to exploit impressionable teenagers who weren't aware they were being duped, because, unlike himself, they were not trained in music theory and therefore were unable to recognize bad music. Teenagers were framed as victims who were not aware they were being exploited by record labels that specialized in rock 'n' roll recordings. "Let me repeat," said Taylor, "that this R&B [rock-and-roll] taste was created; it didn't come spontaneously from the teenagers. It grew out of the race records and since then has been getting progressively worse musically. They took the worst parts of that music . . . and capitalized on them."[59] In the case of Taylor's dismissal of rock 'n' roll, class was displaced through race. In other words, his assault on "race" music was grounded in class distinction: he was distancing himself and "good" musicians in general from what he saw as the garbage of rock 'n' roll music, regardless of whether or not it was being performed by white or black musicians. Perhaps Taylor thought there were some redeeming aspects to the older "race" music, but they didn't find their way into rock 'n' roll. Taylor himself was formally trained in academic music departments. He earned a PhD in music from the University of Massachusetts, and for a few years he was the house pianist at Birdland in New York City. Taylor's attack on rock 'n' roll was influenced by his academic training in music theory, and that particular theoretical paradigm structured his point of view on popular music.

Dizzy Gillespie made a similar argument about how the mass audience for popular music was unable to identify "good" music, but he argued that if young people had the proper education in music, then they would choose not to buy rock 'n' roll records. "Let them [the masses] be taught jazz traditions and what elements to listen for when they come into contact with jazz in their daily lives," argued Gillespie:

> Then, as adults with the power of selection, they will be less likely to accept bad music and reject the good, which is largely the present state of affairs. Let organizations such as the National Congress of Parents and Teachers and the National Education Association give serious consideration to such a jazz-education program and I am sure that in the long run they will do considerably less worrying about periodic flare-ups like the rock-and-roll craze.[60]

For union musicians like those who voiced their opinions in the national media outlets, rock 'n' roll didn't really count as music because it didn't measure up to the formal standards taught in music schools. Since it was not considered music, the widespread perspective among union musicians was that not only was rock 'n' roll mere "entertainment," but it was also considered a youth culture fad, or a "craze" to use Gillespie's description.[61] The onstage practices of Little Richard pounding on his piano and Elvis's infamous gyrating pelvis involved "nonmusical" elements in their performances, and it was for these reasons — the dancing and "crazy" behavior — that union musicians claimed that rock 'n' roll performers were not "serious" musicians; they were merely entertainers. An officer from Local 47 revealed to me in an interview that when he was a young man in the late 1950s, he formed a rock 'n' roll band that became very successful and popular in Vancouver, Canada, but his band was initially shunned by the AFM in that city, Local 145. After gaining success in the venues of Vancouver, his band was asked to join the Vancouver local. He recalled that each year, the local presented an award to the most successful local band in the area, which was determined by the number of appearances in local venues that charged patrons for live music. When it became clear that his band should win the award, they were snubbed by the union leadership. "The traditional musicians in the union were disgusted by us," he said. "They tried to give the award to someone else. The AFM at the time wanted nothing to do with rock-and-roll." Local 47 has been on the forefront of reaching out to rock musicians as of late, but they too resisted adding rock 'n' roll bands to their ranks in the 1950s. Most notoriously, Local 47 refused membership to the Beach Boys when Brian Wilson first applied for membership because the band failed a music reading test.[62]

When Elvis traveled to New York to appear on the *Ed Sullivan Show*, the *Steve Allen Show*, and *Saturday Night Bandstand*, union musicians in New York, including Tommy Dorsey, greeted him with extraordinary hostility. Dorsey thought the excitement around Elvis and rock 'n' roll would be a temporary phenomenon. When it came time to rehearse for the show, Dorsey complained that Elvis was unable to perform his tunes "properly." Music producer Quincy Jones told one account of the episode:

> I remember writing arrangements for the Tommy Dorsey band for his television show, *Saturday Night Bandstand*. And one night this little kid from Memphis came and sang on the show and the band

was pissed off. They [Dorsey's band and Elvis] couldn't play with each other or get into a groove with Elvis or whatever. Sam Phillips [the owner of Sun Records, the label that first broke Elvis] said we'll send for the band in Memphis [guitarist Scotty Moore and bassist Bill Black, Elvis' own band mates] and they came back up and played on the show. Tommy was upset and he said this guy [Elvis] won't last. He'll be out of here tomorrow. Then 8,000 letters from Elvis's fans came in and Elvis played on the show til it closed.[63]

In retrospect, of course, we know that rock 'n' roll was not a fad, but in the mid-1950s the mind-set among jazz musicians was to keep a holding pattern and wait for rock 'n' roll to pass away. Tommy Dorsey had enormous success as a big bandleader for more than two decades, and it was perhaps inconceivable to him that a "country hick" from Memphis could ever become more successful than he was, let alone upstage him on his own show. Elvis's trip to New York by himself to sing in front of Dorsey's band was similar to the experience Jimmy Rodgers had a generation earlier, when Rodgers was asked to leave his band at home in Tennessee to record with professional union musicians in New York. In both cases union musicians in New York were frustrated by singers/guitar players who came from the South because they couldn't find a way to play in the style of the southern musicians. As was the case with Rodgers, the professional union musicians blamed Elvis for the incompatibility between the styles of music. After all, it couldn't be the fault of "trained" musicians in the union. If the northern union musicians couldn't play Elvis's music, it was because southern music was "incorrect" in its structure or form. The Tommy Dorsey band was used to playing behind singers like Frank Sinatra, who stuck to mainstream conventions. Elvis's unusual, offbeat style was foreign to Dorsey and his band, which demonstrated an incommensurability of sorts between the two genres. Elvis's infamous gyrating hips added to the controversy by drawing attention away from the music itself.

In spite of Elvis's popularity, famous jazz musicians in the rank-and-file of the musicians' union continued to believe that rock 'n' roll was a fad. When the writers of DownBeat asked Benny Goodman to comment on rock 'n' roll, he gave them a dirty look, described as "raised-eyebrows and mouth turned down." The writers did make a point, however, of conveying Goodman's negative opinions through their own paraphrasing. Of course, not all members of the AFM were against rock 'n' roll music, but there wasn't a single AFM member who came to its defense in the trade magazines in the 1950s. This phenomenon represented a break from previous generations of professional musicians who argued that popular music, while inferior to "good" music—which was usually coded in terms of elements that were found in the European traditions—had potential for improvement.

As H. Wiley Hitchcock has demonstrated, the professional musician in the United States has always been enmeshed in a tension between "cultivated" and "vernacular" music. According to Hitchcock, the cultivated tradition was "a music exclusively based on continental European models, looked to rather self-consciously; an essentially transatlantic music of the pretenders to gentility." Vernacular music, according to Hitchcock, was "a music based upon . . . newly diffused American raw materials; a 'popular' music in the largest sense . . . whose 'success' was measured not by abstract aesthetic standards but by those of the marketplace."[64] At the end of the nineteenth century, professional musicians understood their task to be one of presenting the American public with the best music, which for them was European. On the other hand, since they were professionals, they had to also play vernacular music, since the audience demanded that from them. As a way to cope with the tension between preferring to play European classical music and having to make a living performing popular music, professional musicians developed a way to find "good" qualities in popular music and accentuate those as a means of "improving" it until popular music could be considered close to or equal to the cultural status of European music. In short, professional musicians bifurcated popular music into music with potential for improvement and music that would remain merely vernacular.

Just as when union musicians attacked ragtime music, most union musicians who publicly criticized rock 'n' roll knew relatively little about it. They made extraordinary attempts to take the high road and display their "superior" skills and knowledge through the deployment of the jargon of music theory and the ideology of modernism, but there was rarely any particular referent that corresponded to their criticisms. The criticisms were usually blanket attacks, with no specific case mentioned to demonstrate their criticisms. John Lewis, the music director of the Modern Jazz Quartet, admitted he didn't know anything about rock 'n' roll, but he was still eager to pass a negative judgment. "Most of what I've heard," claims Lewis, "has been of very poor quality. *I haven't heard very much of it because I don't care to*" (emphasis is mine).[65]

Ironically, many rock 'n' roll recording stars were students and aficionados of jazz music. Chuck Berry, who is by many accounts the true king of rock 'n' roll, was himself a student of jazz and quite comfortable and talented enough to play in the jazz, blues, country, and rock 'n' roll idioms. Carl Perkins said that Chuck Berry was the most versatile musician he had ever seen and that many people who heard Berry, but had never seen him, thought he was white because he recorded many songs that crossed over into the country genre. Berry also played in recording sessions for jazz arrangers and producers, having learned to play guitar from studying the style of Charlie Christian. Christian, of course, was a member of Benny Goodman's swing band, the same Benny Goodman who dismissed rock 'n' roll in the pages of *DownBeat* magazine.

It could be argued, in retrospect, that there was some irony in conversations between the jazz musicians in *DownBeat* about the merits of rock 'n' roll, because their own idiom, jazz, was continuous in many ways with rock 'n' roll, especially the sophisticated and technical improvisational guitar solos that are the heart and soul of rock 'n' roll. Charlie Christian legitimated the electric guitar as a lead instrument through his unique skills and innovations, and it can be argued that his elevation of the electric guitar as a lead instrument was a cornerstone in the foundation of rock 'n' roll.[66] How ironic, then, that it was Goodman himself who suggested that Christian be featured for guitar solos, including the famous arrangement for "solo flight." In an indirect way Goodman can be given some credit for the development of music he claimed to despise. We know in hindsight that Chuck Berry is both a skilled composer and arranger of music and a virtuoso on the guitar, but it seems that those connections were lost on jazz musicians like Benny Goodman, who never made the connection between what individuals from his own band were doing and rock 'n' roll. After Charlie Christian, the other electric guitarist who most influenced the advancement of rock 'n' roll was "Tiny" Grimes, who played with Coleman Hawkins and Charlie Parker. In 1946, Grimes cut "Tiny's Boogie" at the WOR studios in New York City, a record that many music historians consider one of the first rock 'n' roll records. These examples reveal that the jazz musicians' critique of rock 'n' roll was largely misplaced and misinformed because many of the rock 'n' roll recording stars of the 1950s possessed "serious" skills, which they learned from playing guitar in the jazz style. The issue that was displaced in these conversations was a moral issue as morality was as much the problem as simply musicianship per se.

The other area of continuity between jazz and rock 'n' roll is the language used by musicians to refer to themselves and their culture. As much as jazz musicians tried to distance themselves from the rock 'n' roll culture, the rock 'n' roll musicians borrowed much of the language of jazz musicians, especially the bebop musicians, including terms like *cat, cool cat, hepcat*, and various versions of *bop*. Elvis, for example, referred to himself and other rockabilly musicians playfully as "Hillbilly Cats," and Carl Perkins used the term *cat* in his lyrics in "Blue Suede Shoes": "Go, cat, go!" Perkins also wrote a tune called "Boppin' the Blues." Buddy Holly, who was influenced by Western Swing music and Bob Wills, referred to his own music as "western bop." The continuity between jazz and rock 'n' roll — in terms of improvisational technique on the electric guitar — was overdetermined by contradictions rooted in opposing class aesthetics. There was incommensurability between the bourgeois, formalist "paradigm" of academic or symphonic jazz musicians, on the one hand, and the "paradigm" of rock 'n' roll, which developed outside of the conventions of the formally trained musicians. Rock 'n' roll grew from the leisure spaces of the working-class.

Formalism, as a method of analysis, divorces a composition from the conditions of its production or from its context. It reifies a particular genre of music (namely, western classical music), derives principles from that particular genre and treats them as *universal* principles for all music, and attempts to measure all compositions by standards derived from the particulars of classical music. The attack on rock 'n' roll was virtually the same attack that was waged against ragtime music fifty years earlier. The form of rock 'n' roll compositions strays from the rules of "good" music in similar ways that ragtime did at the turn of the century. Rock 'n' roll pushed the envelope a little further by reappropriating the techniques of bending or "blueing" notes, and together with the unorthodox use of poly-rhythms, syncopation, and atypical falsetto singing, created a style of music that is in some sense incompatible with traditional European music that is reified in formalism.[67] It was precisely these techniques that Taylor refers to as "incorrectly written, and worse, incorrectly performed."

The features of working-class life that made their way into rock 'n' roll and made rock 'n' roll an unconventional form from the point of view of formally trained musicians include a resistance to alienated labor that dominated life in the factory and an affirmation of leisure time, or life *outside* the factory. It's most obvious in the playful lyrics that emphasize pleasure and hedonism in leisure activities, including sexual pleasure, but you can also find working-class sensibilities in the structure of the songs themselves, including poly-rhythms, syncopation, guitar distortion, and the bending of notes. In certain contexts, the unique poly-rhythms and unorthodox beats and points of emphasis on blue notes in rock 'n' roll can become a form of resistance to the strict regulation of everyday life based upon adherence to the clock, which was used to habituate workers to a life dominated by factory work. According to George Lipsitz, the rationalization of activity in the factory based upon obedience to the clock was turned upside down in the working-class leisure spaces of the city. The poly-rhythms and the unorthodox placement of beats in rock 'n' roll provided a playful sense of timing that rejected the regime of the clock in the factory.[68] The use of beats in rock 'n' roll emphasized that time was something created by the musicians, as something they could mold to their desires, whereas time in the factory was an alien phenomenon imposed by the system from the outside.

The attack on rock 'n' roll by union musicians took place mostly in the trade magazines, which meant that the audience for their assault on rock 'n' roll was rather narrow. Their attack on the structural elements of rock 'n' roll, however, coincided with the social backlash against rock 'n' roll in society at large, and while much of the criticism of rock 'n' roll by union musicians was focused on the structure of the music, those criticisms were often code for the same things that mainstream society was claiming was wrong with rock 'n' roll. Musicians in the union might have used the grandiloquence of musical intricacy, but it remained the case that the working-class cultural content of rock 'n' roll was the core of the "problem."

There were roughly five reasons why rock 'n' roll was controversial in American society during the 1950s. First, it undermined sexual mores in society by emphasizing sexual activities through the use of double entendres in the lyrics of rock 'n' roll songs. Second, rock 'n' roll was seen to promote "juvenile delinquency," which is another way of saying that it encouraged working-class kids to resist authority, especially the kind of authority that preached the moral value of the work ethic, obedience to your employer, and delayed gratification. The issue of juvenile delinquency contained both a class dimension and a generational dimension that cannot be entirely reduced to the category of class. A new generational identity, the "teenager," emerged with rock 'n' roll in the 1950s, and even in cases where teenagers were not delinquent per se, the emergence of teenage identity represented another dimension of conflict as parents felt as if they could no longer understand and in some cases control their kids. Third, and perhaps most ridiculous of all, rock 'n' roll was seen as part of a communist plot. Although few critics of rock 'n' roll actually believed this, it was a fairly widespread belief among the Far Right in America. Fourth, because rock 'n' roll emerged primarily on independent record labels, it threatened the traditional business model in the music industry, shifting power away from the major labels and the established powers in the industry.[69] Lastly, rock 'n' roll was controversial because it encouraged a mixing of the races in public places at live venues. Again it was the Far Right wing in America that attacked rock 'n' roll on this basis, but miscegenation made "middle" America uncomfortable as well.[70]

The "public" concern over rock 'n' roll became hysteria in the mid- to late 1950s. At first the concern was with the "dirty" lyrics of R&B songs. In the 1940s, R&B was raunchy, but by the 1950s R&B had crossed over to the "white" market. Working-class white teems in the South were the first to get turned on by rhythm and blues, since they had access to some of the first radio stations that specialized in an all-black broadcasting format, but as long as rock 'n' roll remained exclusive to working-class "juvenile delinquents," it was not seen as a widespread threat to the moral order. When rock 'n' roll went prime time all across the country, middle America took issue because by then middle-class white teens were getting turned on to the new music. *Variety* magazine (which took the side of the American Society of Composers, Authors and Publishers against rock 'n' roll) embarked on a campaign in the mid-1950s against so-called leerics in rock 'n' roll music. According to the writers in *Variety*, the double entendres betrayed a vulgarity not to be tolerated in American society, and the magazine called on radio stations to ban "filthy" records and for record labels to censor their controversial artists. Many radio stations did, in fact, ban rock 'n' roll records, while record companies cleaned up the main acts on their rosters out of fear that they might face declining sales for their wares.

The most controversial aspects, however, were the race and class mixing of teenagers at rock 'n' roll concerts. The sight of white middle-class youth attending concerts and interacting with black youth and with "white trash" delinquents helped spark a backlash against rock 'n' roll culture. Working-class musicians like Chuck Berry and Elvis Presley were aware that they were promoting racial integration. Carl Perkins, in an interview from the 1990s, recalled a conversation that he had with Chuck Berry, where the two stars agreed that their music was indirectly promoting the cause of racial equality and the end of Jim Crow. New technologies and the changing structure of the entertainment industry provided structural opportunities that accelerated these changes. Radio played a key role. At times the listening audience could not tell whether the recording artists were black or white. When Presley's cover version of "That's All Right Mama," which was originally recorded by Arthur Big Boy Crudup, was first heard on WHBQ, it created a stir because after an interview that Elvis gave on the air, people were trying to find out if he was white or black. When Elvis told Dewey Phillips that he drove a delivery truck for the Crown Electric Company in Memphis, it created confusion among his listeners because many of them knew that there were just two drivers for Crown Electric, one white and one black. Gladys Tipler, who worked for Crown Electric, said, "A lot of people were calling us up asking if he was white or 'colored,' because they knew our other driver was 'colored.'"[71] Even many disc jockeys that regularly played Elvis's records in 1956 were unaware that he was white. A black DJ from Clarksdale, Mississippi, named Early Wright admitted he was shocked to find that Elvis was white when Elvis made an appearance on Wright's radio show. On the other hand, many white disc jockeys could not make sense of Elvis when they first heard him, assuming he was a black musician playing in the hillbilly style. Young working-class fans embraced the confusion, because they found excitement in the new culture, whereas for older generations of conservative whites, the racial confusion was a serious threat to their worldview and way of life.

Even before he was signed to the major record label RCA Victor and became a famous recording artist, Elvis Presley was very popular among southern blacks. The blues singer/songwriter Rufus Thomas had a radio show on WDIA, also in Memphis, and he recalled that Elvis was well liked among his mostly African American audience, in spite of the fact that most program directors at radio stations in the South assumed that a black audience would not go for Presley's music. According to Thomas:

When I played his records on the air, my eyes had really been opened to his impact on people. Our station's program editor, David James, had in fact told the disc jockeys at WDIA not to play Elvis's recordings. He didn't think the station's black audience would go for a white singer. I didn't agree. I had always been able to feel music and I knew our listeners wanted songs like Elvis's songs. So I started playing them. They were electrifying, and my phone didn't stop with requests for more.[72]

Unfortunately, when it became widely known that white rockabilly musicians over at Sun records were recording their hybrid version of R&B /hillbilly music and "acting like blacks" while playing for live audiences, racist white southerners threatened Elvis and his Sun Records peers, including Jerry Lee Lewis and Carl Perkins. For white racists, rockabilly music represented racial mixing and the potential end to Jim Crow segregation, which at that time was seen by white racists as a transgression punishable by extreme measures. Carl Perkins admitted that he feared for his life when he played live shows in the South during the mid-1950s. On one occasion, when he was on tour with his good friend Chuck Berry, a ticket that included the Coasters, the Drifters, and Little Richard, Perkins recalled that because he was the only white performer on the tour, he would become a target for the Ku Klux Klan. "They were all blacks, Perkins recalled in an interview, "and I was nervous about it, being the only white boy on the tour. I told my brother: We could get killed. . . . We're gonna be the next Nat King Cole. Somebody's gonna kill us."[73] In 1954, Nat King Cole was attacked during a live performance in Birmingham, Alabama, by members of the Ku Klux Klan, who in public were known as the Alabama Citizens' Council led by the notorious Asa Earl Carter, who spearheaded the racist backlash against rock 'n' roll music in the South. Elvis also took great risks, appearing in public at all black concerts even after he became famous. B. B. King recalled that "for a white boy to show up at an all-black function took guts."[74]

If Presley took any risks by performing at an all-black function, then it took Chuck Berry and Little Richard much more courage to appear in public for an all-white audience, because Berry and Richard were challenging the embedded racist institution of minstrelsy that had shaped the expectations of racist white audiences in the South. During the early twentieth century, black musicians who performed for white audiences in the South were expected to conform to the "Sambo" image of the happy-go-lucky, ignorant, deferential black performer. Little Richard and Chuck Berry — buoyed by the culture of working-class pretension that preceded them a decade earlier — appropriated and changed the appearance and performance of the "black body" by wresting control over the representation of blackness away from the racist white audience. Berry displayed himself and his music on his own terms, which included original moves like the duck walk. Berry also put his racial pride on record for white America to hear loud and clear over the radio. His hit tune "Brown Eyed Handsome Man" is a not so subtle message of black pride. Astute listeners knew the song was really about a brown *skinned* handsome man. While not as explicitly militant as James Brown's refrain, "Say It Loud, I'm Black I'm Proud!," "Brown Eyed Handsome Man" was still a bit of a risk for Berry, since he had much more cross-over popularity with white audiences than did James Brown, and also because "Brown Eyed Handsome Man" was recorded years before "Say It Loud," which was recorded after the civil rights movement had made significant strides toward political equality for African Americans.

In the early 1950s, before he became a star, Berry was surprised to find that some of the most energetic fans to attend his live performances in the South were white teenagers. In most of the live venues where rock 'n' roll musicians performed, the audiences were assigned separate sections for blacks and whites, but there were many cases where enthusiastic white audience members, who were eager to see their favorite rock 'n' roll star, would rush the stage and inadvertently integrate the audience. A typical advertisement for a live rock 'n' roll show from that era would list the names of all the bands, the time and place, of course, and usually near the bottom, the advertisement would read "gallery reserved for white spectators."

In those cases working-class kids challenged the tradition of segregation, and it started with white youth listening to black programming on the radio and jump blues records in the jukebox, and vice versa. Carl Perkins once said, "There was no segregation on the jukebox. Kids danced to it all."[75] Many of Berry's singles after "Maybellene" also crossed over to the country charts, and his musical repertoire didn't stop at hillbilly and rhythm and blues. Chuck Berry's extraordinary talent is undeniable. He was comfortable and fluent in many genres of music, spanning and mastering the playing styles of jazz, rhythm and blues, and hillbilly.

Class mixing also created a relative hysteria in the United States at that time. Ironically, while Asa Carter argued that rock 'n' roll was a conspiracy devised by the NAACP, civil rights leaders also attacked it. Martin Luther King Jr. joined in, although for very different reasons than the Klan. "Rock-and-roll," argued MLK, "plunges men's minds into degrading immoral depths."[76] Many established black Americans in the music industry agreed with King. Nat D. Williams, a black disc jockey, betrayed his middle-class disposition when he referred to rock 'n' roll as "cacophonic trash . . . no one should mistake rock-and-roll for Negro music." Ideological membership in the middle-class united blacks and whites against rock 'n' roll. A letter to the editor of the *Pittsburgh Courier* by an African American read, "As for

Elvis and Little Richard, they are two filthy performers. . . . I hate to see the Negro race associated with such musical junk and vulgarity."[77] Here it's interesting that a white teenage rockabilly musician like Elvis Presley is viewed as helping drag down the Negro race. The letter to the editor of the *Courier* is the inverse argument to that of Asa Carter. It demonstrates the complexity of how race and class are inextricable in American culture.

Middle-class liberals who were hoping to improve race relations in America accused rock 'n' roll of damaging the cause of civil rights because of its working-class roots, which were viewed as "degrading." In other words, middle-class, liberal whites and blacks argued that equal rights between blacks and whites involved disassociation from the working class. An anonymous disc jockey wrote an editorial where he said: "On my show . . . I feature only the records of talented performers like Nat Cole, Lena Horne, and Count Basie. Fats Domino has done much to harm race relations."[78] Much in the same way that Charles Mingus worked to create interracial solidarity among union musicians, here the disc jockey seeks to create racial equality among whites and blacks by creating class separation between filthy working-class people and respectable middle-class people. According to Amiri Baraka, "Rhythm and blues was hated by the middle-class Negro."[79] The attack went national when *Time Magazine* ran a feature story that warned America about the serious threat posed by rock 'n' roll. The article was titled "Combat the Menace," and the writers warned Middle America that they were under assault from greasy dishwashers and truck drivers who were broadcasting their vulgarity across the airwaves and undermining basic moral principles of good citizens. The heathen beasts were crashing the gates of middle-class Eden. In 1956, *America Magazine* exclaimed, "Beware Elvis Presley!" In the *New York Daily News*, Ben Gross wrote a review of Presley's television appearance on Milton Berle's show arguing that "Elvis, who rotates his pelvis, was appalling musically. Also he gave an exhibition that was suggestive and vulgar, tinged with the kind of animalism that should be confined to dives and bordellos."[80]

The musicians' union entered the broader public attack on rock 'n' roll when their members appeared before Congress during the payola hearings in 1958 and again in 1963, during congressional hearings on the "cultural front" of the Cold War. Although the musicians' union did not send its officers to the payola hearings to take a specific position on behalf of the union itself, many of their members did attend, since there was much at stake for rank-and-file members in the AFM who had additional interests as songwriters, composers, and publishers, interests that were represented by the American Society of Composers, Authors and Publishers (ASCAP), which lobbied extensively for Congress to hold the hearings in the first place. Also, the AFM was loyal to ASCAP because ASCAP had supported the AFM's strike against radio and the National Association of Broadcasters (NAB) in 1940. While the congressional hearings in 1958 and 1963 focused on different issues, the AFM, like ASCAP, used both sets of hearings to position itself as a public leader in the shaping of taste in America. As part of an attempt to legitimate the union's role in shaping taste during the 1963 hearings, the AFM appealed to anticommunist hysteria in America.

The "payola scandal," as it came to be known, reached its zenith in 1958 when Congress investigated the practice of payola as part of an amendment to the Communications Act of 1934. At issue was the practice of bribing disc jockeys to play certain records. Payola has always been a part of the music industry, going back to the days of song plugging by Tin Pan Alley writers seeking to sell their sheet music. Record label owners realized in the early years of radio that if they could get their record on the air, it was almost guaranteed to stimulate an increase in demand. Under the Communications Act of 1934, however, it became illegal for record companies to pay disc jockeys at radio stations for playing their label's records. According to the language of the act, "a license for a radio or television broadcasting station shall not be granted to, or held by, any person or corporation engaged directly or indirectly in the business of publishing or manufacturing or selling of musical recordings." Payola became controversial when it was associated with rock 'n' roll, in part because rock 'n' roll was perceived as a cultural threat to mainstream American values, but another reason behind the investigation was ASCAP's attempt to push back against the growing power of Broadcast Music Inc. (BMI), which was created by NAB to challenge the power of ASCAP. BMI represented the majority of rock 'n' roll writers, composers, and publishers. ASCAP instigated the congressional investigation into payola in an effort to make the case that the demand for rock 'n' roll music was *created* by payola. The argument by ASCAP — as well as many of the major record labels — was that independent labels had manufactured this demand by bribing disc jockeys. If the independent record companies were prevented from bribing disc jockeys, so it was argued, then rock 'n' roll would fall off of the charts. To help bolster their case before Congress that disc jockeys were spreading filth through their broadcasting to vulnerable youth, ASCAP representatives referred to "research" conducted on rock 'n' roll by "experts" like Dr. Francis J. Braceland, a noted psychiatrist who was quoted by the *New York Times* as saying that rock 'n' roll music was a "communicable disease," a "cannibalistic" form of music.[81]

Historically, ASCAP excluded authors, composers, and publishers of rhythm and blues and rock 'n' roll tunes as a matter of cultural preference based on bourgeois values and ethnocentrism: ASCAP, like the rest of the major players in the music industry, considered rock 'n' roll as low-class garbage, so they took it upon themselves to keep it out of the public arena. Until the 1940s, ASCAP had a virtual monopoly on copyrighted music, and if radio stations wanted to play music on the air, they had to go through ASCAP and share revenues based on public performance of ASCAP-owned music.[82] In turn, the organization was responsible for distributing the fees among its membership, which was dominated by the major publishing houses on Tin Pan Alley. Prior to the creation of BMI, ASCAP was able to use its monopoly on copyrighted songs to control the majority of content in the industry, since they refused to extend membership to composers, writers, and publishers in the genres of hillbilly (country music) and race (blues and R&B) music.

Like the AFM, ASCAP severely limited the participation of African Americans in the early years of its existence, and only gradually and begrudgingly accepted black members, but only after jazz music was "sanitized," to borrow a term from Neil Leonard used in his book, *Jazz and the White Americans: The Acceptance of a New Art Form.* The sanitation process involved removing lyrical content that addressed the problems associated with the daily life of working-class people, which often included descriptions of sex and violence. Of course, most of the lyrical content portrayed the travails of working-class life in a humorous and ironic manner, but for bourgeois-minded listeners and producers from the Tin Pan Alley era, the exposure of working-class life in the culture industry was unacceptable. Leonard provides analysis of lyrics used by Louis Armstrong before and after the Communication Act of 1934 to make his case. Many of the members of ASCAP were behind the nationwide effort to "clean up" jazz in the 1920s that culminated in the 1934 legislation designed, in part, to censor content on radio. Leonard found that after 1934, Armstrong's lyrics were less sexual, less humorous, and much less rooted in the content of daily life. After 1934, "the words of these songs constituted a collection of clichés which resemble parodies of bad nineteenth-century romantic poetry. Their elevated sentiments seem empty and sometimes ridiculous because the inflated diction, trite imagery, and sugary tone communicate little conviction or depth of emotion."[83]

Among the 192 founding members of ASCAP, only 2 were black. Twelve years later, the number of black members stood at 10. Eventually, most of the better-known black composers in jazz music were admitted to ASCAP, but they remained marginal members relative to the composers and publishers from Tin Pan Alley, who continued to dominate the governing structure of the organization. The exclusion of lyrical descriptions of the struggles of working-class life in popular music was also made possible by the exclusion of white working-class genres like country music. According to John Ryan, "ASCAP treated country-music songwriters in much the same way as black writers. A survey of the over 2,000 entries in the ASCAP *Biographical Dictionary* (1948) reveals that only 22 writers were even remotely connected to the 'hillbilly' genre."[84] Exclusion continued into the genre of rock 'n' roll. For instance, May Axton, who co-wrote "Heartbreak Hotel" for Elvis Presley, was denied membership to ASCAP despite repeated requests.[85] Through BMI, the NAB found its chance to challenge the dominance of ASCAP beginning in the late 1940s by taking advantage of the demand for hillbilly and race music among working-class blacks and whites. In roughly a decade, BMI had a catalog large enough to challenge the power of ASCAP.

While the AFM did not take as strong a stand as ASCAP during the payola hearings, many of the union's members had a stake in the outcome because they were also members of ASCAP. During the course of the congressional hearings it became known that Paul Whiteman (formerly and ironically known as the king of jazz) was a major player in both the musicians' union and ASCAP, which partially explains why he was an outspoken critic of rock 'n' roll. Some AFM members also had an interest in BMI, which is why the AFM did not take an official public stand before Congress during the hearings. Still, major rank-and-file star recording artists like Whiteman overpowered any AFM members who might have been aligned with BMI because both the leadership of the AFM and famous rank-and-file members were interested in helping ASCAP marginalize rock 'n' roll. Leonard Bernstein, who more than once graced the cover of the AFM's newspaper, *International Musician*, was among those who wished to see the end of rock 'n' roll, and he gladly took the opportunity to make his point of view part of the public record. He wrote to Senator John O. Pastore, the lead investigator into the payola scandal and chair of the congressional hearings, "Best wishes on this newest phase of your good fight and congratulations on all your efforts hitherto."[86] Some of the other famous musicians (including vocalists, instrumentalists, and songwriters) who testified before Congress on the "depravity" of rock 'n' roll were Frank Sinatra, Bing Crosby, Steve Allen, Ira Gershwin, and Oscar Hammerstein. The strategy was to take the high road on taste and morality. In March 1958, Dr. Louis Pichierri, director of music for public schools in Providence, Rhode Island, testified before Congress during the payola hearings:

> I am gravely concerned over the questionable character of a signifi-
> cant portion of the music, which is being broadcast today via radio
> and television. It is evident that the airwaves are being exploited and
> tastes are being manipulated. Second-rate tunes, and there are too
> many of them, are being promoted at the expense of more imagina-
> tive music. . . . Recently, the people of the United States were shaken
> out of their complacency by *Russia's successful launching of the first
> earth satellite*. The incident, which caused both indignation and fear,
> also provoked some serious soul searching. It brought about an
> increasing awareness of the importance of the Nation's intellectual
> resources and has already precipitated various movements osten-
> sibly to upgrade the entire educational structure of the country.
> Does it not follow, then, that the entertainment world in sympathy
> with this projected twentieth-century revival of learning, has an obli-
> gation to society, namely, that of providing entertainment which is
> artistically inspired, uplifting, and above reproach. . . . This is a very
> serious problem for us, because we are competing with the radio,
> and it is very difficult for us to be trying to teach Mozart and Beetho-
> ven, on the one hand, and have the radio blasting away with some of
> the [objectionable] materials we have to put up with. . . . When the
> broadcasting interests dominate the airwaves with music of ques-
> tionable character, music which lacks substance or ideas, the *moral
> and cultural health of our youth is in jeopardy* [emphasis mine].[87]

Here we see, without elaborate coding in the rhetoric of musical complexity, that the problem with rock 'n' roll music, in the end, is not about technique, or harmonic structure, or any other criteria taken separately from social context. As much as musicians appealed to formalism and modernism and as much as they pointed to the structure of rock tunes *in themselves*, the real issue with rock 'n' roll went well beyond the music itself. Ultimately, what was at issue was moral health and ultimately moral discipline. In the midst of the Cold War, moral outrage against rock 'n' roll usually included a reference to communism, as Pichierri mentioned in his testimony before Congress. The most infamous testimony during the payola hearings came from Frank Sinatra, who said that rock 'n' roll was the music of "cretinous goons" . . . [and] rock-and-roll was "the most brutal, ugly, desperate, vicious form of expression it has been my misfortune to hear." Sinatra's caricature of rock 'n' roll fans and musicians as "cretinous goons" reflected the widespread hysteria over juvenile delinquency during the 1950s.

Rock 'n' roll was generally associated with juvenile delinquency, and it was the hysteria around the perceived crisis that provided so much traction for the foes of rock 'n' roll. The American obsession with juvenile delinquency produced the classic movies *Rebel without a Cause*, *The Wild One*, and *Blackboard Jungle*. But unlike *Rebel* and the *Wild One*, which both had musical scores written by jazz arrangers for big bands, *Blackboard Jungle* prominently featured Bill Haley's hit record, "Rock Around the Clock," which helped cement the relationship between rock 'n' roll and juvenile delinquency. The outcry over juvenile delinquency did, however, have some basis in the statistics that measured numbers of crimes committed by young people. Between 1950 and 1959, arrests of people under the age of eighteen roughly doubled.[88] Nevertheless, the obsession with juvenile delinquency was also conditioned by the media. In 1954, Benjamin Fine had a best-selling book with *1,000,000 Delinquents*, and in 1955, the *Saturday Evening Post* declared juvenile delinquency "the shame of the nation."

Congress was concerned enough with the perceived problems of juvenile delinquency to hold hearings in 1954. These were organized by New York Republican senator Robert Hendrickson and held by the Senate Judiciary Committee. One issue that the committee focused on was the impact of the graphic images found in crime and horror comics on juvenile delinquency. On April 22, the *New York Times* published an infamous exchange between Senator Estes Kefauver and the publisher William Gaines: "He [Gaines] was asked by Senator Kefauver . . . if he considered in 'good taste' the cover of his Shock Suspense Stories, which depicted an axe-wielding man holding the head of a blonde woman. Mr. Gaines replied: 'Yes, I do — for the cover of a horror comic.'" The payola hearings four years later were significantly influenced by the 1954 hearings on juvenile delinquency, insofar as the attack on rock 'n' roll in 1958 was similar to the way the issues were framed in 1954; in both cases, there was an attempt to show a cause-and-effect relationship between the media and juvenile delinquency.

Hollywood soon jumped on the bandwagon of hysteria regarding juvenile delinquency, producing movies like *Crime in the Streets* (1956), *The Delinquents* (1957), *Juvenile Jungle* (1958), and *High School Hell Cats* (1958). It was *Blackboard Jungle*, however, that had the most significant effect. "It was unfortunate," said the disc jockey Alan Freed, that "that hoodlum-infested movie . . . seemed to associate rock 'n' rollers with delinquents."[89]

The musicians' union was also concerned. Local 802 of the AFM went so far as to prescribe a "cure" for juvenile delinquency: namely, "decent" music. The musicians' union argued that juvenile delinquency could be abolished if teenagers listened to good or "decent" music rather than the troublesome rock 'n' roll "noise," which was understood to be, at the very least, "indecent." According to the leaders at local 802, the "cause of juvenile delinquency is that young people from low income families lack the means and opportunity for decent entertainment in their leisure time."[90] The musicians' union decided steps had to be taken to confront the problem, so in 1955, President Manuti of Local 802 in New York City met with Mark McClusky, chairman of the New York State Youth Commission, to hammer out the details. Manuti proposed that the AFM pay half of the costs associated with an annual state music conference, which including busing low-income teenagers to agreed-upon locations within the jurisdiction of Local 802 where they could listen to "decent" music, performed for free by union members.

Although many famous musicians publicly denounced rock 'n' roll during the congressional hearings on payola in 1958, the rank-and-file of the AFM was split, especially over the issue of juvenile delinquency. While nobody in the musicians' union openly defended rock 'n' roll music, some did speak out against the logic that music is to blame for "delinquent" behavior. Count Basie was one. While hardly an advocate of rock 'n' roll—he referred to it as "gimmick" music—Basie still insisted that music is never a cause of antisocial behavior. In a letter to Senator John Pastore, Basie wrote, "I'm pretty surprised at the people who attempt to couple rock-and-roll with juvenile delinquency. . . . I always thought it was the failure of parents or schools or the lack of a good influence at home that caused most of the trouble kids and adults have. It's too easy for people who fail where it counts to try to pin the blame for the failures on some other factors. And today, a lot of them are using rock-and-roll as a whipping boy."[91] Basie went on to discuss his experience as a leading musician in the swing music craze that swept across the country in the 1930s, describing how much of what conservatives were saying about rock 'n' roll in the 1950s was also said about swing music in the 1930s, namely, that music causes "pathological" behavior. Basie insisted that it was ridiculous to say such things in the 1930s, and it was still ridiculous to make those claims in the 1950s. Unfortunately, many of his fellow union members who also lived through the backlash against swing music failed to develop Basie's understanding of the issue in the 1950s.

While there were some major fall-outs and shakedowns in the music industry as a result of the payola hearings, rock 'n' roll survived the backlash, although the structure of the music industry was profoundly altered. If there was any perception that rock 'n' roll might go the way of most fads, it would have accompanied the destruction of Alan Freed. Freed, who copyrighted the phrase "rock-and-roll," was a main target of the payola hearings because he, perhaps more than any other disc jockey in America, was responsible for bringing rhythm and blues music to a white teenage audience. After success as a disc jockey in Cleveland with his show "Moondog House," Freed established himself as a major player in the music industry when he found a much bigger market in New York City on WINS. ASCAP's strategy was to link him to the illegal practice of payola as a way to get rock 'n' roll music off the air.

While the figure of the disc jockey was a key target of conservative groups—due to the perception that disc jockeys created the demand for rock 'n' roll—the disc jockey had also been perceived as a foe of the musicians' union for decades, since he personified the drastic loss of jobs for professional musicians who worked on radio in the studio bands. Prior to the rise of the disc jockey and the rise of television in the American culture industry, many radio stations maintained orchestras on their staff, and these orchestras were a main source of income for union members. In the early years of radio, it was universally agreed among the industry insiders that live music over the airwaves was preferable to the use of records, due to the relatively poor quality of records at the time. The U.S. Department of Commerce granted licenses more frequently to radio stations that didn't use records, because the feeling was that the use of records did not serve the interests of the public. But as the Depression forced smaller radio stations to tighten their belts, the use of records became more and more prevalent. For decades, the musicians' union continued their campaign to raise the public's awareness about the superiority of live music over recorded. From the union's point of view, the disc jockey represented a debasement of culture, since he was the main vehicle through which the public gained a taste for "canned" music while losing the ability to recognize the superiority of the live performance. Rock 'n' roll emerged with and through the disc jockey, as he helped to create and spread a record culture. Rock 'n' roll was, and is, in large part a record culture. This is one of the main reasons the musicians' union stood opposed to rock 'n' roll, in addition to the fact that many rock 'n' roll musicians did not read music and lacked formal training.

After Freed was accused of accepting payola, he was subsequently forced to quit his job at WABC in New York, which led ASCAP president Paul Cunningham to claim that "we can expect a revival of good music in the style of the Gershwins, the Kerns, and the Rombergs."[92] While Cunningham's prediction did not come to pass, it is interesting to compare the fate of Alan Freed with that of Dick Clark, who emerged virtually unscathed from the congressional hearings and went on to create a virtual empire of businesses in the music industry. Dick Clark's image was much closer to what Cunningham had in mind about "good music" than was Alan Freed's. Clark, who possessed a white, bourgeois, and clean-cut persona was not persecuted with the same fervor as the gruffer and more ethnic (Jewish) Alan Freed, in spite of the fact that it was later revealed that Clark's extensive business dealings may have been more crooked than Freed's involvement with payola. Clark reigned over three record companies, six music publishing companies, a record pressing plant, a distribution firm, and a company that managed singers. Clark made a point of promoting his own records, songs, and recording artists on his television show while excluding much more popular recording stars. An article published by *Life* revealed that over a period of twenty-seven months, Clark gave much more air time to one of his own singers, Duane Eddy, a newcomer, than the top star of the time, Elvis Presley. In spite of the fact that Clark was a recipient of payola and was able to exploit his position on television and radio to promote songs and records that were owned by his companies, he was virtually exonerated by Congress when Congressman Oren Harris, chairman of the committee investigating payola in 1960, told Clark, "Obviously you're a fine young man."[93]

Freed had found success spinning rhythm and blues records by African American artists on his radio shows, while Clark's television show, *Ameri-*

can Bandstand, featured a virtually all-white audience, a contrast which was recognized in an article published in the *New York Age*, an African American newspaper. "If there's one shining star in the constellation of Alan Freed's career," wrote the editors of the *New York Age*, "it has been his determined, quiet, but effective war on racial bigotry in the music business. Have you ever seen Negro kids on Dick Clark's program? Perhaps a few times. . . . Somebody should raise the question as to whether there was ever any payola to keep Negro kids off of Dick Clark's *American Bandstand* program."[94]

After the payola hearings, it did seem to some as if the most controversial aspects of rock 'n' roll culture had passed. Presley went into the army, then on to Hollywood. Chuck Berry was convicted under the Mann Act for transporting a minor across state lines for "immoral" purposes. Buddy Holly died in a plane crash, and the public shunned Jerry Lee Lewis after he married his thirteen-year-old cousin. "Whether it was payola or radio stations were afraid of it, rock 'n' roll went into a coma almost, with very few exceptions," argued Joe Smith, a record executive at Warner Bros. "All those hit records that stars like Little Richard made, and Jerry Lee Lewis made . . . all happened within two or three years. That's it. And it was over." In his analysis of the fall-out from the payola scandal Tom Petty argued that "an entertainer is a force to be reckoned with socially. So let's put him [Elvis] in the army. Calm this boy down. Chuck's in jail, little trouble with the border, you know. Conveniently, Buddy went down. Jerry Lee, oops she's 14. They're all gone. That is my theory on that early period. It [rock-and-roll] just suddenly got too wild, so they had to calm it down and it got taken over by businessmen."[95] While Petty's account may seem like a stretch because it leans on conspiracy theory, it remains the case that the payola hearings had a profound cultural effect at the end of the 1950s. According to Trent Hill, "Such was the power of the hearings as a theatre of guilt that they succeeded in their cultural goal — the general containment of rock-and-roll."[96]

What Petty describes as the process where "businessmen" took over rock 'n' roll refers to the corporate creation of the teen idol in the late 1950s and the dominance of the collection of songwriters working in the now famous Brill Building in New York, also during the late 1950s. Reebee Garofalo describes this era in rock 'n' roll history in terms of the "empire" [the major record labels and Tin Pan Alley] striking back at rock 'n' roll.[97] The threat of rock 'n' roll was mainly an economic issue for the major record labels, because between 1955 and 1959, the percentage of rock 'n' roll hit records represented largely by the top ten selling records jumped from 15.7

percent of the market to 42.7 percent in popular music. The structural shift in the industry posed a serious problem for the majors, since the majority of rock 'n' roll records were produced on independent record labels. The market share commanded by the indies rose from 21.6 percent in 1955 to 66.3 percent in 1959, eventually forcing the major record labels to respond. The rise of the indies was led by labels like Atlantic, Chess, Dot, Imperial, Monument, and Sun.[98] The cultural result of the intervention by the majors into rock 'n' roll—combined with the sudden departure of Little Richard, Chuck Berry, Elvis Presley, and Jerry Lee Lewis—was that rock 'n' roll took on a more middle-class white image and form. In what has become somewhat of a controversy among popular music scholars, Garofalo refers to this era of teen idols and Brill Building-produced songs as "schlock rock," as a way to describe how the excitement of early rock 'n' roll had ended, taken over by a less dangerous music created and produced by record executives and the major record labels rather than by working-class black and white musicians, the group Jerry Wexler referred to as "southern proletarians." "This new reality," argues Garofalo, "brought forth a new generation of white, middle-class teen idols, whose roots barely scratched the surface of pop. Performers like Paul Anka . . . Frankie Avalon . . . Annette . . . Fabian . . . Connie Francis . . . and Neil Sedaka . . . as well as many others ushered in a style of music that can only be referred to as 'schlock' rock."[99]

Of course, it would be misleading to represent the years of rock 'n' roll from 1958 to 1963 as completely devoid of social significance or musical value. Many scholars have taken issue with Garofalo's description of these years as the era of "schlock" rock, not only because it can be argued that the music of the Brill Building has legitimate aesthetic value, but also because if one were to focus on gender relations in society, then one cannot so easily dismiss this era of rock 'n' roll as not containing as much social significance as the early and middle 1950s. Jacqueline Warwick has made the case that girl groups from the late 1950s and early 1960s, such as the Chantels, the Shirelles, the Marvellettes, and the Bobbettes, developed a kind of girl-speak through the use of "nonsense syllables of doo wop" that should be seen as the creation of a "proto-feminist forum."[100] While rock 'n' roll challenged American norms having to do with race relations, in the late 1950s feminism was mediated by rock 'n' roll music as young women developed new practices for challenging sexism and established norms governing gender relations in American society. Work by scholars like Warwick has helped to more adequately represent the complexity of the history of rock 'n' roll, by focusing on the issue of gender to supplement previous historical works that have focused primarily on race. In short, Garofalo's perspective is not incorrect, just incomplete.

I find Garofalo's account to remain very useful, however, because it remains the case that in the early 1960s, the major labels were able to regain control of the recording business, and there was a marketing strategy developed by the majors to clean up rock 'n' roll in order to make it safe for middle-class white society. It is these particular aspects of Garofalo's work that I'd like to emphasize, rather than the argument that the music can be best understood as "schlock" or that music created by the major labels is not somehow "authentic" from the point of view of consumers. In short, there are good reasons to challenge the received wisdom that these years represent a long stretch of mediocrity. Rather, for the purposes of my argument, the significance of this era has to do with how it fits into the history of the structural transformation of the music industry. As Trent Hill has argued, "Economically, the hearings worked to force a consolidation of power and hierarchy in the music business; conflicts of interest that had resulted from the limited number of qualified people performing a variety of institutional and economic functions disappeared by force. The hearings worked, as it were, to bring the music industry from the age of liberal competitive capitalism into the age of monopoly capitalism."[101]

As a result, it became harder and harder for small labels to compete for talent; indeed, by the mid-1960s, they would no longer be factors in the marketplace. Payola had been a force that increased competition in the record business; without payola, the small record labels lost the means by which they could compensate for the majors' promotional weight. Not coincidentally, the small labels were responsible for much of the music in the first place. The payola hearings also revealed the complexity of the relationship between the structural and cultural aspects at play in the pop culture industry. Sometimes the structural and the cultural right do not line up in American politics. During the payola hearings, organizations like ASCAP and the AFM were structurally on the left, because those organizations are, for the most part, the representatives of labor that negotiate with and struggle against capital over the control of the music industry. The interests of capital were represented by the record labels, BMI, and NAB. In terms of culture, however, it was the organizations on the *structural* right, the representatives of capital like BMI, NAB, and the record companies that were on the cultural left, which in the 1950s was the side of rock 'n' roll. In short, the structural right helped to open up a space for rock 'n' roll in the music industry. At other times, however, the structural and cultural right line up like social scientists might expect them to, as in the era following the payola hearings.

Between 1958 and 1963, the focus of the music industry had shifted back to New York City. In fact, Reebee Garofalo refers to this as the return of Tin Pan Alley. "As rock-and-roll became too popular for the established music industry to ignore, it also attracted a new breed of professional to its ranks — songwriters with a respect for the Tin Pan Alley tradition who could write (and sometimes sing) in the teenage idiom," writes Garofalo. "They put another nail in the coffin of early rock-and-roll . . . as they tried to professionalize the genre."[102] The emergence of the Brill Building sound and the domination of the record charts by the Brill Building collective of songwriters signaled a return to Tin Pan Alley, not only because of the white, middle-class sound of the music but also because the division of labor at the Brill Building resembled the older way of doing business.

The traditional division of labor separated songwriters from singers and instrumentalists. The artist and repertoire agent working for the major record label had the task of bringing together these separate forms of labor as a means of ensuring the record executives that the appropriate performers would be matched with the appropriate song. Everything was controlled in-house, from the top down. The early years of rock 'n' roll threatened to break apart this traditional division of labor, not only because it was produced with very small budgets on small independent labels, but also because many of the early rock 'n' roll stars wrote, arranged, performed, and sometimes produced their own music. Rock 'n' roll musicians eventually broke down the traditional division of labor in the music industry. One of the reasons the Beatles admired Little Richard, Chuck Berry, and Buddy Holly is because they all wrote, recorded, and performed their own music.

Although it may have seemed to some that the more subversive aspects of the rock 'n' roll controversy was on the wane in the early 1960s, the musicians' union continued to seek out a public presence, as it pursued a role as arbiter of taste in American society. Five years after the payola hearings, Herman Kenin, president of the AFM, testified before the House Foreign Affairs Committee about the important role of culture in the prosecution of the Cold War with the Soviet Union. The committee was in charge of a $2.5 million budget for sending American musicians abroad for public performances to foreign audiences. The money was earmarked for the "cultural program." At issue was an increase in funding for the cultural program as part of an effort to stem the tide of communism around the world. For Kenin it was crucial that only the "best" American musicians be involved in the program set up by the House committee. According to Kenin:

> Any relaxation from the policy of "only the best" will eventually cause harm. . . . In stressing the value of the contributions made to the cultural program by the professional practitioner it is not my intention to belittle or denigrate the non-professional or amateur groups who also participate. It is my earnest conviction, however, that the professional, by the very nature of his experience and total immersion in his art, operates within a framework peculiarly suited to the needs of the program.[103]

During the same hearings, AFM member Rosario Mazzeo, the director of the Boston Symphony Orchestra, asked Congress:

> What are we doing today to see that foreign nations hear this supreme expression of our music? We are doing little, currently, almost nothing, even though these orchestras are acknowledged by experts to be the very finest in the world. We are a great nation; we believe the best. . . . I have been continually disturbed with the trend in the last years, watching the new stream of musical ambassadors we are sending forth. . . . It seems incomprehensible to me that we have been sending abroad the various musical forces almost to the exclusion of our great orchestras.

Although Mazzeo did not name rock 'n' roll specifically, it was clear that what he meant by "disturbed" was that the American music industry—the private sector—was exporting rock 'n' roll around the world rather than America's best orchestras. Mazzeo was requesting that Congress intervene in order to save America's orchestras as a way to defeat communism.

While Pichierri's testimony during the payola hearings and Kenin's before the House Foreign Affairs Committee were separated by five years, a common appeal to Cold War patriotism connects the two. Both testimonies argue that a decline in artistic integrity in the field of music was detrimental to the effort to defeat communism. If the United States were to succeed in its struggle against the communists, then it was imperative that the U.S. government fund the arts as a means to improve American music. The payola hearings were not specifically about the threat of communism, but there were those who believed the fight against rock 'n' roll was part of the fight against communism. Right-wing groups like the John Birch Society claimed, for example, that rock 'n' roll was conceived as a communist plot to take over the minds of American teenagers. They argued that rock 'n' roll seduced American teenagers with a relentless backbeat that had the power to take possession of their bodies and force them into a frenzy of irresistible and uncontrollable dancing. Once teenagers were in a trancelike state induced by the music, their minds could be taken over by communist propaganda and ideology.[104]

The cultural program sponsored by the House Foreign Affairs Committee was a success in the eyes of Dizzy Gillespie, who was one of the jazz musicians who participated in the program. Gillespie argued that the success of jazz musicians overseas had to do with the different attitude that Europeans have toward art. "The Europeans are far more attentive as audiences than the Americans," argued Gillespie. Gillespie also commented on the progress made within the countries inside the Communist bloc. "Even behind the Iron Curtain," said Gillespie, "where communists used to denounce it [jazz] as 'poison for the workingman's mind' and 'the wild wailing, hissing and moaning of madmen and sex maniacs,' it is now permitted on all satellite and radio networks, in Moscow night clubs and at an annual jazz festival in Poland. One American newsman even reported hearing it before the sacrosanct Stalin-Lenin mausoleum in Red Square."[105]

Between 1958 and 1963, it may have seemed to some like rock 'n' roll was on the wane, but that scenario was not to be, because the Beatles and the British Invasion of rock 'n' roll bands were about to upend virtually the entire music industry, in spite of the best efforts by the musicians' union to stop them. It is to that story that we now turn.

FOUR

**A Working-Class Hero
Is Something to Be**

The Union's Attempt to Block the British Invasion Rock Bands

Rock 'n' roll gives you a sort of feeling of freedom. It makes you relax
and want to jump. Youth's gotta have freedom today. You know?
— TEENAGE ROCK 'N' ROLL FAN

The way things are going, they're going to crucify me.
JOHN LENNON

On April 4, 1964, Bonnie Wilkins, a teenage rock 'n' roll enthusiast from
Scottsdale, Arizona, wrote a letter to Herman Kenin, then president of the
American Federation of Musicians. Attached to the letter was a petition
containing thousands of signatures from other teenagers in the Scottsdale
area. On behalf of her peers, she wrote:

Dear Mr. Kenin,

We have discovered that you are trying to keep those fabulous, wonderful, tremendous Beatles out of the United States. We have never
heard of anything so shocking in all our lives. We don't know much
about this cultural exchange bit, but since you don't think they are
culture, why don't you go mess up the affairs of someone else. You
really have a lot of nerve, trying to keep them out of the United

States, but if you can brainwash the authorities into doing it, you can just say goodbye to us teenagers — we're all moving to England. And to think that all this time we thought that America was a free country . . . sometimes we wonder.

Sincerely,
Bonnie Wilkins.[1]

The phenomenon called "Beatlemania" had, by the time Ms. Wilkins wrote her letter to the musicians' union, already swept across the United States following the extraordinarily popular and financially successful debut tour of the Beatles in January and February 1964. Shortly after that tour, a rumor began to spread that the American musicians' union was going to ban the Beatles from future tours, prompting Beatles fans like Ms. Wilkins to write letters to Kenin and the AFM in protest of any such ban. The "cultural exchange bit" that Ms. Wilkins refers to in her letter was an arrangement crafted between the AFM and the British Musicians' Union (BMU) in March 1964, which was designed to regulate the movement of professional musicians between the two countries. In that arrangement, the unions agreed to allow the free "exchange" of musicians who were considered "uniquely talented" or who were thought to possess, and be of, "culture." Any musician deemed to be highly valuable to the culture of society was allowed to move about freely between the United States and the United Kingdom. On the other hand, rock 'n' roll musicians, all of whom were deemed "culturally *non*-valuable" by the two unions, were restricted by the unions to very limited touring and commercial performances outside of their home country. According to the language of the agreement, rock 'n' roll bands were considered "uncultured" because the prevailing belief in both unions was that virtually anyone could play rock 'n' roll music because supposedly it did not require any special talent, whereas there were relatively few truly exceptional musicians and these musicians performed and composed music exclusively in the classical and jazz idioms. It was thought by the unions that performances by these musicians advanced the accumulation and progression of culture, and it would be a mistake to restrict their performances, since they had so much to offer the masses.[2] Unexceptional rock 'n' roll musicians like the Beatles, however, were thought to be in relatively high supply in both countries. Thus, according to the agreement, if a rock 'n' roll band like the Beatles were to come and play in the States, then

England would have to accept a rock band from the United States as a fair exchange: one job for one job.

The agreement was ostensibly about protecting jobs in both locations and not oversupplying the labor market with *un*exceptional musicians. While Kenin was working out the deal with the BMU, he was also lobbying the U.S. secretary of labor, Willard Wirtz, to place an embargo of sorts on rock 'n' roll musicians coming from the UK. Kenin requested that Wirtz support the arrangement between the AFM and the BMU by mobilizing the Department of Labor's resources to help enforce the rules of the musicians' unions' arrangement by closing the borders to foreign rock 'n' roll bands. Kenin insisted that any of the available musicians in America could perform the same music that the Beatles performed and that therefore the Beatles need not visit the States, since they might take jobs away from "mediocre" American musicians. He could not foresee that the Beatles would be dearly missed. Kenin also could not have predicted that anyone would disagree with the union's use of the term *culture* and the labeling of rock 'n' roll as a music that lacked culture. Unbeknownst to Kenin, the culture wars over rock 'n' roll that were supposed to have ended with the payola scandal were about to flare up again.

Young fans all over the United States like Bonnie Wilkins were very upset by the news of the agreement between the two musicians' unions, because it meant that the Beatles could be blocked from returning to America for a second tour in August. On April 7 Kenin received a rather feisty letter from three teenagers in Dayton, Ohio:

> Dear Mr. Kenin,
>
> In reference to a recent article in the *Dayton Daily News*, in which you state that the Beatles are not culture, we would like to know what you mean. In the opinion of many Dayton teenagers we get the idea that you are trying to culturize American teenagers. However, we would like to inform you that American teenagers have been keen on the idea of Pop music for the last thirty years and we don't think that you are going to change them. In the article it indicated that you intend to keep the Beatles out of America, unless there is a reciprocal exchange for the performance of American musicians in Britain. . . . In our opinion, we feel that if U.S. musicians, which you claim to be unemployed, were any good, they would not need

the government to help them. . . . In addition, we do not think adults have a right to stop the younger generation from enjoying what it loves and wants: the BEATLES!!!! Please give us a chance to enjoy something we love! Please don't ask us to Hold Your Hand in this action. . . . Sir, you have a big fight ahead of you: for we who have stood amongst the screamers, the twisters, and the jumpers know what a fight it will be. Hell hath no fury like a Beatle-nik spurned!

Respectfully,
Cindy Westendorf and Linda Hausfeld and Carol Herbert
Beatle fans, and—PROUD OF IT!!!!!!

P.S. We think the BEATLES are fabmost, really gear, and not swelling about the bounce like some groups. If you would like to acquire the meaning of this last sentence, go buy yourself a BEATLE book!!!!!![3]

By April 1964, a panic had spread among Beatle-niks who were agitated by the idea that the Beatles would never return to the United States after their triumphant debut tour. Some took a confrontational stance, threatening to fight the musicians' union by various means, including demonstrations, civil disobedience, and lobbying Congress if the ban were not lifted and the arrangement between the unions revised to make an exception for the Beatles.

Self-described "Beatle-niks" were also writing to Secretary Wirtz. Virtually all of the letters condemned the AFM policy and referred to Kenin by name as the object of their anger and frustration. Some rock 'n' roll fans referred to the musicians' union and Kenin collectively as "those stupid, jealous musicians."[4] Other letters were even more caustic, referring to Kenin and the musicians' union as "communists" and suggesting that labor unions like the AFM were akin to corrupt, power-hungry Communist Party bureaucrats because the union was lobbying for restrictions on both the freedom of movement among individuals and the freedom of consumers to choose what kind of music to consume. Bonnie Wilkins commented sarcastically that she was surprised to find out that the United States isn't really a "free" country.

Letters condemning the musicians' union came from every corner of the country. Patsy Johnson of Mississippi wrote, "I read an article in our paper that Herman Kenin, the president of the American Federation of Musicians, is complaining to you about the 'surprise' invasion of the Beatles. . . .

Mr. Kenin is going to do all he can to keep the Beatles out of America, while we are going to do all we can to get them back."

Janet Mitchell from San Diego wrote:

Dear Mr. Wirtz,

In the April 4 *San Diego Tribune* was an article stating that the Department of Labor "must approve the entry of aliens seeking work in the U.S." The paper also said 'such admission is refused if qualified Americans are available for the work sought by such foreigners." According to the newspaper this immigration clearance was issued because Mr. Kenin, president of the American Federation of Musicians, protested the February visit of the Beatles. . . . Please sir, what is the exact story on this? How will you determine whether there are qualified Americans when the Beatles request readmission? If you ask me or any other teen-age girl (and there's a lot of us) there is no one who even comes near to their [the Beatles] talent, and we mean it! Could you please tell us how this is going to affect the August visit of the Beatles? We're looking forward to it, so *please* don't disappoint us. Thank you for taking the time to read this letter.

Sincerely yours,
Janet Mitchell[5]

Nearly all of the letters from angry Beatle-niks took the musicians' union to task over the issues of culture and framed the controversy as an issue having to do with freedom of speech and freedom of movement. Beatles fans rejected the union's notion that rock 'n' roll music lacked culture, and many astute teens raised the issue on a philosophical level by questioning the very meaning of the word *culture*. This was the first time that the musicians' union had to face a serious public challenge to their self-appointed role as arbiters of good taste. It was not until the explosion of "Beatlemania" that they found themselves in a public dispute with the fans of popular music. By criticizing the union for restricting the freedom of expression and the freedom of movement, Beatles fans drew attention to the irony of the ban on the Beatles: namely, the United States was supposed to be the "good guy" in the Cold War, on the side that valued freedom of expression against the tyranny and repression of communism. Red-baiting was used on both sides of the rock 'n' roll controversy, as hard-core right-wing elements like the John Birch Society were convinced that the Beatles were themselves part of a communist plot to brainwash young people in the United States and the rest of the free world.

As a result of the brewing controversy over the Beatles, Kenin became a villain in the public imagination, fulfilling in many ways the stereotype of the corrupt and selfish union boss. It was also ironic that Beatles fans were accusing the musicians' union of acting like communists, because just a year earlier, the AFM had testified before Congress on the importance of the cultural dimension in the Cold War, claiming that the musicians' union could contribute to the American effort to defeat communism by exporting the best music in the world and by fighting against the dogmatic ideological definitions of "legitimate" music by the communists. One of the main points made by the AFM in those hearings was that it was crucial to fight against the Communist Party's supposed campaign to eliminate modern "bourgeois" music in favor of a so-called proletarian aesthetic, because, according to the AFM, democracy and freedom in society depend partly upon the freedom of expression in the arts.[6] From the point of view of Beatleniks, however, it may have seemed like a contradiction for the AFM to make a case for the importance of freedom of expression while simultaneously seeking to restrict the performances of certain musicians and degrade the value of certain kinds of music in the name of culture. After all, was that not what the communists were doing?

While conservative forces had led many of the attacks on labor unions since the war, they were not alone. The New Left, as well as the related youth and countercultures, took a critical stance against labor unions as well, beginning in the mid-1960s. Young people came to see labor unions as part of the establishment, part of what was wrong with America.[7] The controversy over the Beatles and the musicians' union has to be seen within this larger context of ideological conflict. Kenin and the musicians' union were framed by the pro-Beatles youth culture as "squares," part of the conservative older generation that didn't understand the cultural changes taking place.

Another aspect of the social environment of the 1960s that contributed to the framing of the Beatles controversy with the musicians' union was the growing political turmoil of the 1960s. Young Beatles fans felt empowered by the climate of social unrest that was produced by the civil rights movement and by increased student activism, including the free speech movement that caught fire on the campus of University of California at Berkeley in 1964. Dissent and civil disobedience were in the air, which had an impact on the way in which fans responded to the Beatles crisis. Pamela Moe, a teenager from Springfield, Massachusetts, predicted "boycotts, riots, and Beatles-Rights marches" if the AFM went through with the ban on the Beatles.[8] Priscilla H. Aspinwall from Skaneateles, New York, vowed, "WE WILL PROTEST!"

Other letters by concerned Beatles fans went straight to the top of the chain of command, to the president of the United States, Lyndon B. Johnson. Again they identified the musicians' union as the antagonist to the freedom of speech as they asked Johnson to intervene and overrule Kenin regarding the matter of the Fab Four. Debbie Carey of Philadelphia wrote:

URGENT!!
Dear Mr. President,

In a newspaper recently there was an article saying that if the Beatles come in August the Musicians' Union won't allow them to bring their instruments. It also stated that they needed government approval. Will you please give that approval? I know your daughters like them, although you may not, *please* do it for the teenagers of America! . . . *Please* tell the Union to disregard that statement! About 50 million teens will love you for it. Mr. Johnson you can't allow them [the musicians' union] to keep them [the Beatles] or their instruments out of America, please, please do something.

Love,
Debbie Carey

P.S. Do you like them? (answer quick).[9]

Ms. Carey's letter reveals that teenagers in the 1960s were aware of their power as a collective force in American politics. The political reality of "50 million teens" self-conscious of themselves as a distinct generation with a distinct culture made it prudent for Wirtz and the Johnson administration to respond to the controversy. While teenagers were responsible for most of the letters of protest against news of the impending ban on the Beatles, adults were writing, too. A parent from Dayton wrote:

I am not a teenage girl, but a responsible housewife and mother of three preschool children. The anti-Beatle fanatics cannot be half as bored with the Beatles as I am with their prejudiced views on what

constitutes good music and what is fit, in their opinion, for teenagers
to swoon over. . . . No wonder teenagers rebel when parents and
teachers are constantly criticizing their clothes, hairdos, and rock-
and-roll idols. Naturally, after a while they're bound to believe anything they do is wrong.

Mrs. Terry M. Lackey.[10]

This letter suggests that the controversy around Beatlemania included the
struggle over personal appearance, an important element in the construction of the identity of rock 'n' roll fans. As discussed in the previous chapter, through an application of the theoretical framework of semiotics, Dick
Hebdige argues that hairstyles, like articles of clothing, can be read as a text
containing signifiers that draw attention to how postwar youth subcultures
developed a means to criticize aspects of social life that they found alienating.[11] Just as the zoot suit had signified resistance to middle-class norms in
the 1940s, and the black leather jacket and dungarees had in the 1950s, the
"mop-top" hairstyle of Beatles fans posed a challenge on the part of teenagers against the "square" adult world.

Most of the letters coming into the offices of Kenin and Wirtz were
from Beatles fans who were against the ban. But there were also some from
people who were glad to hear the news, and they wrote to Kenin supporting his position on the Beatles and foreign "entertainers" in general. In
these letters, the issue was presented as a labor market problem, the idea
being that foreign workers took jobs away from American citizens. Barbara
Lea of Manhattan wrote: "I have read that a new rule placing an embargo
of sorts on foreign talent has just taken effect. This is good news to professional entertainers who are often out of work in their own country."
Wirtz responded, "We are hopeful that the arrangements which we have
made with the Immigration and Naturalization Service will result in improved employment opportunities for talented entertainers in this country."[12] Simone Tucker, also from Manhattan, wrote, "If it is true that one of
the major problems in the United States is unemployment, why can non-
American citizens come over here to seek and find employment? . . . If you
give a job, any job to a non-American, this means that an American similarly qualified is precluded from obtaining that job. . . . I believe that if you
are a citizen of this country you are entitled to seek and secure employment
in this country without having to compete with foreign imported help." In

1964, unemployment was a central issue in American politics, compelling Secretary Wirtz to respond:

> Dear Miss Tucker,
>
> This is in response to your letter of April 21, 1964, in which you request information concerning importation of aliens for entertainment positions. . . . We have assumed recently the task of reviewing visa applications for entertainers seeking temporary employment within the United States. As our participation in these occupations increases, we anticipate that the increased protection will accrue to citizen entertainers seeking employment. These actions are taken under responsibilities assigned to the Secretary of Labor by the Attorney General pursuant to authorization contained in the Immigration and Naturalization Act.
>
> We appreciate your interest in the welfare of the citizen labor force and in programs which are of major concern to us.
>
> Yours sincerely,
> W. Willard Wirtz
> Secretary of Labor

The controversy over the Beatles proved to be complicated because it involved two seemingly separate issues, one having to do with the meaning of culture, the other having to do with the distribution of jobs between Americans and "aliens" within the U.S. labor market. Supporters of the Beatles were addressing the issue of culture and particularly the labeling of the Beatles and rock 'n' roll performers generally as musicians who lacked talent and music that lacked culture. Those who argued in favor of banning the Beatles interpreted the issue as a problem of competition for scarce jobs. Those who framed the issue as primarily a labor market problem still included the issue of culture as an important subtext. The main issue may have been presented in terms of jobs, but in the eyes of the supporters of the Beatles ban, it was also a good idea to keep controversial British rock 'n' roll bands out of the United States. In 1964, cultural conservatives still viewed rock 'n' roll music as a menace and its fans as hooligans. In short, the Beatles were a double threat: job stealers *and* juvenile delinquents. Herman Kenin was himself positioned by Beatles fans as a cultural conservative, and in his own words he presented himself as such when he argued that the Beatles were not "culture." Regardless of the prevailing conditions in the labor market for musicians, foreign rock 'n' roll was not welcomed by the leadership of the musicians' union. In this way, culture mattered as much as perceived economic conditions. To understand the full complexity of the issue requires going back to the origin of the controversy over foreign entertainers.

In April 1963, the president of Actors' Equity, Angus Duncan, wrote to Secretary Wirtz to complain about the increasing number of British actors coming to the United States in search of work. According to Duncan, British actors were displacing American actors and exacerbating the problem of unemployment. Duncan requested that Wirtz and the Department of Labor help the Immigration and Naturalization Service enforce a particular subsection of the Immigration and Naturalization Act that was designed to govern the number of foreign workers coming to the United States. In Section 101(a) (15) H of the Act, foreign workers seeking work in the United States are supposed to be separated by the INS into two categories: "H (i)" and "H (ii)." The difference turns on the question of merit and talent. Workers of "distinguished merit and ability" fall under the category H (i), whereas workers who "have no unique talents" fall under the category H (ii). Aliens who seek work under category H (ii) face many more restrictions than those entering the states under H (i). The logic is that only under conditions of severe labor shortage will the United States allow the free flow of H (ii) workers into the United States. Workers with "distinguished merit," on the other hand, were understood to be in such short supply that their presence would not have a negative effect on American workers seeking employment. Thus H (i) aliens were allowed unrestricted entry into the U.S. labor market.

Until 1964, it had been the job of the INS to determine the status of foreign performers seeking temporary employment in the United States, and they decided whether or not an entertainer possessed "distinguished merit" and "unique talents." Foreign entertainers who qualified as H (i) aliens were allowed entry into, and freedom to move about, the United States. Those who didn't qualify would either be refused entry or allowed very limited commercial engagements. According to Actors' Equity, however, both the INS and the Department of Labor had been inconsistent and haphazard in their enforcement of the law. The main issue for Duncan and the actors' union was that too many entertainers were coming into the United States who should have been recorded under category H (ii), "no unique talents," and therefore they should have been restricted to very limited engagements. In short, the INS was not enforcing the rules. According to Duncan:

> The British actor is not required to receive certification from the United States Employment Service regarding the unavailability of like persons in the United States.... British immigration authorities have discouraged American actors from working in England.... Actor's Equity has no objection to the appearance on the American stage of truly distinguished performers, such as Laurence Olivier, John Gielgud, or Ralph Richardson. The presence of such people and others of similar stature enhances the American theatre and enriches the cultural fare available to American audiences. Equity strongly objects, however, to the importation of people under section 101 (a) (15) (H) who possess far less talent and fame. Equity also objects to the importation of undistinguished alien performers when American actors and actresses — fully capable of performing with competence — are unemployed and seeking work.
>
> I call your attention to this problem in the hope that the Department of Labor will exercise the authority given it by the Congress to correct what has become a matter of great concern to the working men and women of the American theatre.
>
> I shall be happy to discuss this matter further with you at your convenience. Meanwhile, I look forward to your reply.
>
> Sincerely yours,
> Angus Duncan.
> Actor's Equity Association[13]

Angus Duncan and the actors' union had set the precedent for President Kenin and the AFM, giving Kenin a firm ground from which to lobby the government for a ban on the Beatles the following year. The Beatles were, according to Kenin, a variation of the same problem faced by the actors' union: British entertainers entering the United States illegally as H (ii) workers. Almost a year after Duncan's first appeal, Wirtz finally wrote back to the actors' union, saying that he agreed with Duncan's assessment of the problem, and furthermore that the Department of Labor would indeed take a more active role in restricting the number of "non-talented," or H (ii) foreign performers seeking temporary employment in the United

States. The timing of Wirtz's statement was favorable for Kenin, because the change in the Department of Labor's policy, which was announced by Wirtz in March, came right on the heels of the Beatles' inaugural tour in February. Since the Beatles were allowed entry into the States illegally under category H (ii), Kenin asked that the INS and the Department of Labor keep them out the next time they applied for work in the States.

The Beatles' first tour in 1964 and the explosion of "Beatlemania" soon thereafter had taken the adult world by surprise, but it particularly disturbed Kenin and the musicians' union. In addition to the chaos created by thousands of screaming fans who greeted the Beatles at each concert—which for the conservative establishment seemed like a throwback to the chaos and riots that accompanied rock 'n' roll concerts in the 1950s—the Fab Four created some controversy in the AFM because of the enormous impact they had upon the political economy of the music industry.

Between 1957 and 1961, record sales in the United States were down 5 percent (down to about $600 million), thanks in part to the payola scandal and the backlash against rock 'n' roll music.[14] By 1963, there was a slight turnaround in the industry: sales went up by 1 percent. But with the arrival of the Beatles, record sales grew by double digits every year, eventually reaching $1.6 billion in sales in 1969. In the year 1964 alone, the Fab Four charted twenty-eight singles and commanded the top five slots in the first week of April.[15] The single "I Wanna Hold Your Hand" sold over 2.6 million copies in just one week, the week before the Beatles arrived in February. Also that month, they accounted for an astounding 60 percent of all singles sold worldwide. The Beatles also released six best-selling albums in 1964. All told, between 1963 and 1968, the Beatles sold more than $154 million worth of records worldwide.[16] Their success inspired other British rock bands to try their luck in the States, which led to the "British Invasion" by the Dave Clark Five, Herman's Hermits, the Rolling Stones, the Who, the Zombies, Them, the Searchers, Gerry and the Pacemakers, and the Kinks.

The issue for Kenin and the musicians' union was that the economic spoils of the American music industry were going to foreign-born musicians, especially in terms of public performances. More important, the British Invasion sealed the fate of the music industry: rock 'n' roll was number one again, dispelling the notion that the music was merely a fad. The very same music that was suppressed by the cultural backlash that fueled the payola hearings before Congress, namely, the "threatening" music of Chuck Berry, Little Richard, Jerry Lee Lewis, and Elvis Presley, was returned to America by the Beatles, indicating that the demand for rock 'n' roll was continuing to grow. "The British were going straight to the sources, Willie Dixon, you know, Chuck Berry," said producer Quincy Jones. "They were going straight where it came from, and they hit it hard because they knew the Delta blues and everything else, because they knew exactly what the sources were. They were students of American music, much more than American musicians."[17]

As a way to secure the AFM's role and stake in the new labor policy under Secretary Wirtz, Kenin wrote to him in March to reiterate some of the issues raised by Angus Duncan and to underline the AFM's specific concerns. Kenin was hoping to get a guarantee from Wirtz that the AFM would get the same deal as was given to Actors' Equity, a commitment from the Department of Labor to continue funding the program that screened foreign entertainers. Thus, just a few weeks after the Beatles left the United States, Kenin sent the following letter to Secretary Wirtz:

Dear Mr. Secretary:

If it be true, as I am informed, that the Department hopes shortly to extend its permit scrutiny of imported labor to include actors and other performing artists, we ask most urgently that its expertise extend to musicians coming to the United States to fill commercial engagements.

As you know, the American Federation of Musicians has not attempted restraints against those instrumental artists or combinations that qualify clearly as cultural exchanges. The other category — instrumentalists fulfilling stage, ballroom, and TV engagements for strictly mass audience commercial entrepreneurs — is cutting deeply into the employment opportunities for American musicians who, unhappily, constitute one of the most consistently unemployed groups in the entire labor spectrum. The influx from England recently . . . has grown out of all reasonable proportion. In too many instances we have not been able to obtain the protections we deserve and demand from the Immigration Service.

I most sincerely hope that the Department of Labor will indeed extend its expertise into the field of musicians. If this be the intention, please advise me what our procedures should be in communicating our recommendations to the Department for its determination.

Thanking you for your attention to this rather pressing matter, I am,

Sincerely,
Herman Kenin, President
American Federation of Musicians, AFL[18]

Following the strategy used by the actors' union, Kenin argued to Wirtz that because the Beatles and other rock bands entered the United States under category H (ii), they were essentially working in the United States as illegal aliens. Wirtz agreed, and the Department of Labor set up regional offices in New York, Los Angeles, Nashville, and a few other locations to deal specifically with the issue of foreign musicians. It was the task of the staff in these offices to determine whether or not musicians coming to perform in the states were "uniquely talented." In most cases, the staff consulted the local branch of the musicians' union to help determine whether or not foreign musicians had special talent.[19] Once the bureaucratic apparatus was set up, the Beatles and the rest of the British Invasion rock bands would not be able to enter again without serious restrictions.

While Actors' Equity was continuing its lobbying efforts with Secretary Wirtz, Kenin had been working on a separate deal with the British Musicians' Union (BMU) to limit the movement of rock 'n' roll musicians between the United States and the UK, which was the arrangement mentioned in the letter by Bonnie Wilkins. In March 1964, it seemed as if everything had fallen into place for Kenin and the AFM: he was able to broker a deal with the BMU to stem the flow of British rock bands coming into the United States, and the U.S. Department of Labor agreed to work with the INS and the AFM to restrict the flow of "non-talented" foreign entertainers coming to the states. But Kenin's problems were just beginning.

Outlined in Kenin's letter to Wirtz is a clear attempt to draw a distinction between a highbrow and lowbrow aesthetic, what he refers to as the difference between an "exchange of culture" and "mass entertainment." The problem of the "mass" and mass culture is imbedded in a context signifying issues having mainly to do with the labor market, but nonetheless mass entertainment is posed as a cultural problem. Popular culture was framed in Kenin's letter as a problem both because it lacks inherent value and because there was too much of it. Such a distinction between high art and popular culture was common sense to certain factions within the musicians' union and thus not controversial, but the AFM would soon find itself a main target in the resurgence of culture wars in the 1960s precisely because of its conservative, elitist point of view on rock 'n' roll. Kenin eventually did receive the same deal from Wirtz and the Department of Labor, but the Beatles issue did not go away, nor was Kenin able to stop the British invasion of rock bands. On the contrary, things were about to change drastically, but not in the direction that Kenin had hoped. Wirtz promised to protect the jobs of American musicians, but the relentless British Invasion of rock 'n' roll would continue.

In March, *Variety* published an article claiming that "Irate AFM Flips Lid over Invasion of 'Rocking Redcoats' *Sans* Culture."[20] The article had an alarming tone and portrayed the Beatles as a renewed threat to the U.S. music industry. *Variety* had waged an earlier campaign against rock 'n' roll in the 1950s because of its alleged "dirty lyrics," and with the Beatles, the trade magazine once again was eager to attack. The article reads: "There's a strong possibility that the AFM will make some moves with the U.S. State Department and the British MU to block unrestricted entry of the British rockers whose cultural stature is viewed very dubiously." It wasn't just the union that viewed the cultural stature of rock 'n' roll "dubiously." The editors at *Variety* were ready to start churning out articles on the moral depravity of rock 'n' roll again when the Beatles launched the British Invasion. The *Variety* article did not cause widespread controversy, however, because it appealed to a fairly small audience of readers in the entertainment industry. But things changed dramatically in the coming weeks.

On April 2, 1964, the same week that the Beatles held the top five slots on the *Billboard* charts, the U.S. Department of Labor issued a press release that described changes in its policy on foreign entertainers. After the successful lobbying efforts of the actors' and musicians' unions, the Department of Labor went public with its changes, to ensure American workers that the government had their best interests at heart. The press release read as follows: "Effective April 15, entertainers for whom entrance visas are requested under Section 101 (a) (15) H (ii) of the Immigration and Nationalization Act will no longer be exempt from clearance certification. Performers who come within this category are aliens who have *no unique talents* [emphasis mine]."[21] This press release probably would not have created widespread panic across the legions of Beatles fans if it were not for an article written by Victor Riesel, a syndicated columnist, who covered the press conference. His article, "Keeping Out the Beatles," was reproduced in newspapers all across the country, and it was his article that teenagers like

Bonnie Wilkins and others had read and responded to by the thousands. Riesel's piece reads like a tabloid article, with the opening lines exclaiming, "'Tis the final conflict! Let each stand in his place. At my side is a man of awesome courage.... This fellow is Herman Kenin, president of the American Federation of Musicians.... Kenin just doesn't believe the Beatles are culture. He is not much impressed by 'Yeah, Yeah, Yeah . . . I Wanna Hold Your Hand.'"[22] He reported that the AFM had virtually forced the Department of Labor into agreeing to ban all British rock groups, including the Beatles, making it seem like the musicians' union had more power than was actually the case. Riesel had Beatles fans believing that it was probable that the Fab Four would never return to the United States, and overnight letters began pouring into the offices of newspapers, Kenin, Wirtz, and President Johnson. While the *Variety* article and the article by Riesel certainly portrayed the Beatles and other British bands as a potential crisis for the musicians' union, it was Kenin himself, not the Beatles, who created a crisis, because his comments on the cultural status of the Beatles seriously damaged the AFM's image. Kenin had been following the union's policy, which was decades old: the policy of taking the "high road" on culture that positioned the union as a gatekeeper of American "values." This policy had provided the union with leverage during negotiations with government agencies in the past, and there seemed no reason for Kenin to change the course in 1964. Kenin also had no reason to believe that young rock 'n' roll fans would also lobby the secretary of labor and take him to task over the issue of culture, since nothing like that had ever happened.

Beatle-niks focused on two comments made by Kenin that were revealed in Riesel's article, comments that emphasized the issue of culture. In the first, Kenin argued, "The Beatles are not immortal to us. . . . *We don't consider them unique. They are musicians and only sing incidentally. We can go to Yonkers or Tennessee and pick up four kids who can do this kind of stuff.* Guitars are now on the ascendancy in this country [emphasis mine]." Kenin betrayed his age and "squareness" with the last comment on guitars, since guitars and rock 'n' roll were on the ascendancy long before 1964. His claim that anybody in the States could reproduce the energy and music of the Beatles was ridiculous. But many in the leadership structure knew very little about rock 'n' roll, thought for so many years that it was a fad, and assumed that rock 'n' roll was so easy to perform and the audiences so ignorant that teenagers would be unable to tell the difference between the performance of one band and the next. To fans, Kenin's reference to "guitar music" proved to them that the musicians' union was living in the past, with the rest of the square adult world. Kenin's comments on the Beatles and the union's position on mass culture and the masses was virtually the same in content as that of AFM president Joseph Weber's comments at the AFM's annual convention in 1901, where the union first made it a policy to intervene in American society on matters of musical taste among the masses. At that time, the problem was ragtime. In 1964 the problem was rock 'n' roll.

American teenagers sensed that Kenin was preaching to them about the supposed virtues of "high culture," and they resisted it as so much dogma from an ossified establishment. For instance, the letter from the three Dayton teenagers vows that teenagers would resist the AFM's attempt to "culturize" them. Most of the letters from Beatles fans questioned the union's legitimacy as gatekeepers of culture. Who gave the musicians' union the right to tell them what kind of music they should listen to? In the second controversial passage from Riesel's article, Kenin positions the union unequivocally as anti–rock 'n' roll.

> Of course we have a cultural exchange with other countries, *but this is not culture. They are no Rubinsteins or Heifetzes.* Artists are welcome. But as for the Beatles, if they do get back into the country, they're going to have to leave their instruments at home. . . . They were here before we realized what happened, but it won't happen again. [emphasis mine]

Kenin is confrontational in the way he states in no uncertain terms that the Beatles will not get back into the country. Perhaps more important, however, is the claim that the Beatles are *not* culture. Kenin employed the conservative definition of culture as something akin to refined aesthetic taste: a definition of culture that appealed to traditional conservative, formalist ideals that found the essence of enlightened mankind in the works of the great European composers like Bach, Beethoven, and Brahms: hence the comparison of the Beatles to Artur Rubinstein and Jascha Heifetz. On the other hand, teenagers were adopting a more relativistic notion of culture, similar to an anthropological or sociological definition. Paula Victor from Rochester, New York, wrote to Wirtz that the labor agreement regarding the Beatles was grounded on serious mistakes in reasoning about the content of the very concept of culture.

Sir:

The undersigned and I respectfully wish to disagree with Mr. Kenin's reasoning and should like to submit our own reasons for doing so. Because the decision seems to rest on the question of what is culture, we have tried to get an idea of what culture is. Briefly, we feel that culture consists of all those activities, which express the personality of an age. With this definition in mind, we feel that what the Beatles do is a cultural activity. Without any disrespect to musicians [AFM] and their cultural function, we think that the art form the Beatles perform is a combination of instrument playing and singing. We particularly feel that their performance is not interchangeable with any other group of its kind.

We should like to add that most of us consider ourselves moderately well rounded and are able to appreciate a wide variety of cultural expressions.

On the basis of our above remarks, we respectfully submit our request to readmit the Beatles without restriction.

Very Sincerely,
Paula Victor
(Age 14)[23]

The emphasis on "activities of an age" nicely sums up the impending cultural conflict between the labor movement and the counterculture during the 1960s, a conflict foreshadowed by the AFM's ban on the Beatles. Miss Victor, and young rock 'n' roll fans like her, made an important intervention in the culture wars over rock 'n' roll because they shifted the definition of culture from one grounded in the hierarchical divide between the "high" art of the elite and the popular art of the masses to a relativistic and inclusive concept of culture. Culture, as Beatles fans understood it, was not about ranking musical expression from high to low; nor was it about whether someone possessed refined taste. Rather, in a sociological manner, culture was understood to be a collection of activities that expressed "the personality of an age." Paula Victor also positioned herself and her generation as "well rounded" consumers of culture, insinuating that to be a cultured person, one must have an open mind to all sorts of music. The musicians' union, on the other hand, was positioned by young rock 'n' roll fans as a conservative institution, and therefore as culturally backward, because of their closed mindedness. In short, an open mind was seen as a necessary condition for the consumption and accumulation of culture that makes a well-rounded, cultured person.

The intervention into the struggle over the meaning of culture by teenagers is a good illustration of Raymond Williams's discussion in his book *Keywords*. The term *culture* is one of the two or three most complicated words in the English language, as it has undergone several permutations. According to Williams, the reason behind why the term is so intricate today is "because it has now come to be used for important concepts in several distinct intellectual disciplines and in several distinct and incompatible systems of thought." As Williams reveals, even the Latin root has several meanings, including, "cultivate," "protect," "honor with worship," and "inhabit." These differences led to distinct differences in the English language found in words like *cult*, which developed out of the meaning to worship, *colony*, which emerged from the meaning "to inhabit," and *cultivate*, which was embedded in agricultural activities, having to do with farming. In the earliest incarnations, according to Williams, the term "was a noun of process: the tending *of* something, basically crops or animals."[24] Eventually, the notion of developing, nurturing and growing crossed over from husbandry to describe intellectual cultivation in human development. The use of the word to signify the best in art, or someone who has a sophisticated facility with the cultural objects considered most valuable, is one of the more recent manifestations of the changing meanings. Williams notes that it was toward the end of the nineteenth century when the term *culture* came to signify fine arts in an intellectual sense and a disposition that was "civilized" as opposed to "vulgar" or "primitive." Williams refers to the development of culture as an abstract noun indicating the works and practices of intellectual and especially artistic activity as the "modern" permutation. It was this way of using the term *culture* that rock 'n' roll fans and musicians were struggling against.

Young people were aware of the terms of the debate over rock 'n' roll. It was clearly a fight over which meaning of culture would dominate the other. Debbie Otto, a rock 'n' roll enthusiast from Harrisburg, Pennsylvania, also questioned the use of the term *culture*, when she wrote, "President of AFM Mr. Kenin says they [the Beatles] aren't culture. What is culture? Who's to say what culture is? Not you or I." Other young rock 'n' roll fans tried to use relativism in a diplomatic approach. Christine Smith, from Haneoije Falls, New York, wrote to Wirtz, "I enjoy some professional music. Strains from *Camelot, The Sound of Music, South Pacific*, and concerts by Leonard Bernstein are great to me. However, I enjoy some other kinds of music, too, and the Beatles provide that so well."[25]

Kenin's reference to the great violinist Jascha Heifetz as part of his justification for keeping out the Beatles signaled a reversal of sorts in the discourse on culture and union strategy among the AFM leadership that was forged under James C. Petrillo, who was president of the musicians' union from 1940 to 1958. Petrillo had also made many references to Heifetz in the context of statements about culture and union policy, but he made practically the opposite point on the issue of culture and union strategy. Kenin broke from Petrillo and returned to the cultural elitism that characterized Weber's administration between the years 1901 and 1940. For Kenin, it was important for the musicians' union to make clear distinctions between "cultured" and "uncultured" musicians as a way to develop a labor market strategy to protect the jobs of American musicians from the invasion of "non-talented" foreign musicians. But by appropriating a stance of cultural elitism, he was attempting to position the musicians' union as a guardian of high culture in America, and that move is precisely what alienated him from both rock 'n' roll musicians and their fans. For Petrillo, the distinctions between high and low/mass culture were harmful to the union because it was precisely these cultural distinctions between so-called highbrow and lowbrow taste that inevitably create divisions among the rank and file of the musicians' union. Making cultural distinctions between "talented" and "untalented" musicians was, in Petrillo's view, a bad labor market strategy for the union because it bifurcated musicians into a core and peripheral market for music, creating a two-tiered system of labor that inevitably produces unjust inequality among members in the union. Petrillo's often-used rhetorical question on the matter was "Since when is there any difference between Heifetz playing a fiddle and the fiddler in a tavern? They're both musicians."[26]

Referring to Heifetz as a "fiddler" rather than a concert violinist underscored the point. Under Petrillo, the musicians' union considered a "non-talented" fiddler who plays mostly in bars or taverns and Heifetz, a star concert performer, as equally deserving of union protection. One member received the same rights, voice, and treatment as the next: "both are musicians." From Petrillo's point of view, equal treatment of members promotes union solidarity, which in turn creates the necessary conditions for a tight labor market for musicians. Kenin's public criticisms of the Beatles and rock 'n' roll music, however, had brought the musicians' union full circle, back to the cultural elitism that President Weber had codified at the 1901 convention, when the AFM publicly denounced ragtime music. From Petrillo's point of view, it was suicide for a labor union to rank their members into two tiers that corresponded to "deserving" and "less deserving," which for him was essentially what happens when musicians are labeled "talented" and "untalented." Of course Petrillo, like Kenin, would have taken measures to protect the jobs of American musicians under any circumstances, and the Beatles themselves were not members of the American Federation of Musicians when they first arrived, although they did join during their second tour.[27] Still, the question of culture was framed very differently between Kenin and Petrillo. Kenin embraced cultural elitism and sided with the famous rank-and-file members of the union who criticized rock 'n' roll publicly, including Paul Whiteman and Dizzy Gillespie, who had articulated harsh criticisms of the blues and rock 'n' roll music a decade earlier.

It's a matter for debate whether or not the British Invasion really had a negative impact on the job prospects of American musicians. It is doubtful that the Beatles or any of the British rock bands took jobs away from American musicians, because as the teenagers convincingly articulated in their letters to Kenin and Wirtz, the Beatles really were unique and talented. Finding an American replacement was simply out of the question. In April 1964, faced with an impending ban on his clients, Brian Epstein, the manager of the Beatles, took steps to honor the terms of the agreement between the AFM and the BMU. When the Beatles returned to the UK after leaving the United States, Epstein arranged to have U.S. musicians tour with the Beatles and throughout the UK. Epstein also made good on a promise to include U.S. musicians on the ticket of any future Beatles tour in the United States. In the end it was the combination of Epstein's attempts to appease the AFM and the BMU, the record and television industries' pressure on the Department of Labor to facilitate the reentry of the Beatles into the United States through working closely with the Immigration and Naturalization Service, and perhaps most important, the thousands of letters from Beatles fans, that eventually led to the agreement by the AFM and the Department of Labor to allow the Beatles to return in August 1964 as H (i) foreign entertainers. In late May 1964, Willard Wirtz wrote back to Bonnie Wilkins in Scottsdale.

Dear Bonnie:

Thank you and Miss Debbie Page for sending me the petitions urging that the Beatles be allowed to come back to the United States. The determination and ingenuity you demonstrated are very impressive. I also note that thousands of persons have signed your petitions. This is a tremendous showing of interest.

I do not know whether the Beatles will apply to reenter the United States under the part of the law governed solely by the Immigration and Naturalization Service or under the rules where the Department of Labor gives certain information to the INS. In either case, I assume the Beatles would be permitted to enter the United States again.

You may be relieved to know that, while the Government of the United States is old, it is not run by old fogies.

Yours Sincerely,
Willard Wirtz.[28]

Although the AFM failed to keep the Beatles out of America, they were able to ban another popular British band, the Kinks.[29] The Kinks were not as popular as the Beatles. But a number of their singles reached *Billboard*'s top 10, including "You Really Got Me," which went to number 1 in the UK and number 7 in the United States in 1964. In 1965 they had two more singles, "All Day and All of the Night" and "Tired of Waiting for You," reach the top 10 in the United States. The Kinks were banned by the AFM after a few controversial episodes occurred during the band's debut U.S. tour in 1965. The problem occurred when they refused to perform at the Cow Palace in San Francisco on July 4 because the promoter, Betty Kaye, refused to pay the band in cash, which according to Ray Davies, lead singer and bandleader of the Kinks, violated their contract. Kaye then filed a formal complaint with Local 6 of the AFM. Two days prior to the debacle in San Francisco, the Kinks performed on Dick Clark's show *Where the Action Is*, which aired on the ABC network each weekday afternoon between June 28, 1965, and March 31, 1967. As they were preparing to perform, Davies got into a scuffle with a union representative working on the set, which ended with Davies punching the representative in the face. According to Davies, the worker on the set taunted Davies and his bandmates by calling them "communists," "limey bastards," and "fairies." "I remember doing this television spot," recalled Davies, "and this guy kept going at me: 'When the commies overrun Britain, you're really going to want to come here, aren't you?' I just turned around and hit him, about three times. I later found out that he was a union official." On another occasion, Davies's brother Dave had refused to sign union documents regarding another live performance, telling the union official to "fuck off." According to Davies, the union official responded, "You're never gonna work in America again." After the series of confrontations between the Kinks and the union and concert promoters, the AFM withheld necessary work permits for the Kinks until 1969.[30]

According to the AFM, the Kinks were banned on the grounds of "unprofessional conduct." Ted Dreber, who was Kenin's assistant at the time, claims there is no record of the Kinks "on file" at the musicians' union office, but he did acknowledge the Kinks were banned from touring the United States for more than four years based upon the regulations of the Immigration and Naturalization Act.[31] While the details of the incident remain mostly unknown, the Kinks did have a reputation for getting into confrontations with stagehands and other people in the music business at their performances. There is an account of the band chasing a reporter down the street after tangling with him during a press conference. Such a notorious reputation made it relatively uncontroversial for the AFM to ban the Kinks and justify their harsh criticism of rock 'n' roll more generally. Ray Davies's biographer has argued that the AFM banned the Kinks "to make an example of some young English musicians who, the union believed, were taking work from Americans." The Beatles were too popular to harass, and the Rolling Stones, despite their rebellious image, were generally cooperative with officials and promoters. The Kinks, however, were unruly and hardly cooperative, and thus they were an easy target.[32] Another British band that was prevented by the AFM from performing in the United States was the Fortunes, who lost their engagement on the *Ed Sullivan Show* in 1965 because they could not meet the requirements of the labor agreement between the AFM and BMU. According to David Carr, the keyboardist of the Fortunes, "They hung us up because they [the AFM] had to swap us for the Sir Douglas Quintet and another group—they always wanted two groups in England for every one that played here—and while they were dickering, the Sullivan gig came and went. Maybe it wouldn't have made any difference in our career, but you always wonder. It certainly didn't do the Beatles any harm."[33]

It would be wrong to reduce the complexity of the issue to simply a "good guys" (Beatles fans) and "bad guys" (AFM) episode. The conflict over culture between the Beatles' fans and the leadership of the AFM can be understood, in part, as a matter of two sides emphasizing different issues in the manner of incommensurable paradigms. The union and the Beatles' fans were looking at the issue from different perspectives, one primarily economic and the other cultural. From the point of view of Beatles' fans, what may have seemed to be elitism on the part of the AFM leadership stems, in part, from the AFM's craft union consciousness, which is a common phenomenon among all of the craft unions that date back to the founding of the American Federation of Labor in 1886. The role of the craft union is to restrict membership to the union in order to maintain high demand for skilled labor in the given area, which in this case was music performance. The main way craft unions maintain a tight labor market is to restrict membership in the union and monopolize access to training for the particular skill necessary to join a particular craft labor union.[34] The attitude about rock 'n' roll music at the time of the Beatles' ban was that rock 'n' roll was "entertainment," not music, and that rock 'n' roll musicians were rarely "skilled" enough to be members in the union in the first place.

On the other hand, the struggle with the Beatles' fans was not simply a case of incommensurability either, because Kenin himself spoke very disparagingly of the Beatles. Intertwined with the craft union consciousness of the AFM leadership was also a perspective on culture that not only alienated Beatles' fans but actually split the union's rank and file, a problem that goes all the way back to the founding of the AFM in 1896, when the union's rank and file was split between musicians who did not consider themselves "workers" and those who did. As argued in previous chapters, older musicians, who at the time of the founding of the AFM argued against joining, believed it was degrading to belong to a labor union because they believed unions were for manual workers, not for "artists" like themselves. So although it is understandable that Kenin would ask for government help in protecting the jobs of his constituents, ultimately the attack on the culture of rock 'n' roll had the opposite effect: it contributed to public controversy for the union and had a contributing role in the impending decline of the union's influence in the music industry, because the union failed to aggressively organize rock 'n' roll musicians and include them as equals in the culture and structure of the union. In short, the negative representation of the Beatles as "not culture" was part of a larger perspective that framed all of rock 'n' roll as unworthy of equal treatment within the union membership structure.

It is useful here to consider the cultural conflict between rock 'n' roll fans and the AFM from the points of view of F. R. Leavis and Raymond Williams.[35] The issue of mass culture was a significant topic for debate among cultural critics in the twentieth century, including Leavis, who argued that the creation of a mass aesthetic, indeed, of an industry of culture led inevitably toward the standardization and degradation of art and culture more generally. Leavis coined the term *technological-Benthamite* to describe how he viewed the degrading effects that technology and industrialization in capitalist society were having on art and culture. The mass production of cultural objects resulted in what he called a "levelling down." "When we consider, for instance," writes Leavis, "the processes of mass-production and standardization in the form of the Press, it becomes obviously of sinister significance that they should be accompanied by a process of levelling down."[36]

While it is not my contention that the AFM leadership was reading Leavis, their attitude toward the negative effects of mass production was similar to that of Leavis. The issue with the AFM was not the technology of mass production in the press but rather the sound recording. As discussed in chapter 1, the AFM lost tens of thousands of members at the hands of recording technologies that made "talkie" movies possible as well as the disc jockey on radio. The displacement of live musicians in movie houses and in the studios of radio stations devastated the AFM. Still, the AFM was able to fight back, and after their victory in the 1942 strike, the AFM successfully negotiated a contract with the major record labels that included the creation of a fund to be used to support unemployed members of the AFM, who presumably lost their jobs as a result of the application of records. The money was raised from record sales through a royalty payment formula that required the record companies to pay into the fund out of their sales revenue. The *cultural* dimension to the issue of recording technology is that the AFM developed an anti-record aesthetic. Partly as a way to try to save jobs, but also partly as an aesthetic preference, the AFM campaigned for live music during the 1930s and 1940s, developing a public relations strategy that created a public presence for the AFM, where the union advertised widely on the superiority of live music over recorded music. Rock 'n' roll, on the other hand, developed as a record culture. Indeed, rock 'n' roll emerged with the perfection of the mass production of records, especially the 45 RPM single. The record had an impact not only on the culture of rock 'n' roll consumers but also on working-class kids who aspired to play rock 'n' roll and who lacked the financial means to pay for music lessons. On the one hand, in rock 'n' roll culture, the recording is the primary text rather than the live performance. The way in which rock 'n' roll aficionados relate to the music is through records. On the other hand (and equally as important for the culture), records made it possible for working-class youth like George Harrison and Ringo Starr to teach themselves how to play music. Many rock 'n' roll musicians became skilled at their craft without learning how to read music. Conversely, reading music was, from the point of view of the AFM, the essence of the craft of the professional musician. In fact, the AFM required potential members to pass a music reading test (an audition) as part of the process for gaining access to union membership. Many rock 'n' roll bands were excluded from the AFM on the basis of failing the audition. In short, the AFM's position was overdetermined by two factors: a craft union job-consciousness and a perspective on the degrading tendency of mass-produced culture similar to Leavis's, which together shaped an anti-record aesthetic within the culture of the AFM. These aspects helped to frame the AFM's point of view on the controversy that followed the arrival of the British Invasion rock 'n' roll bands in 1964.

Beatles' fans, on the other hand, developed a point of view on culture similar to that of Raymond Williams. For Williams, the division between highbrow and lowbrow culture is not an issue of "levelling down," like it was for Leavis. Rather, the very idea of the masses is a device used by elites to justify their dominance over society. Beatles' fans understood their struggle with the AFM in these terms. Kenin's disparaging remarks that the Beatles were not "culture" was viewed by fans as the principal terrain of the struggle. The AFM's position can be understood as an expression of what Williams refers to as the "effective dominant culture."[37] Rock 'n' roll musicians and listeners, on the other hand, were developing what Williams referred to as an "emergent culture," where new practices, meanings, and values develop outside or in conflict with the dominant culture. From a perspective like Williams', rock 'n' roll culture does not represent a "degradation" of culture, or a levelling down, but an emergent counterculture.

Cultural issues were present, although submerged, within the AFM's discourse on job scarcity during the 1964 episode. The conflict with Beatles fans brought the cultural problem to the surface. Rock 'n' roll became the dominant popular music in America as early as the mid-1950s, and it would have been in their economic interests for the musicians' union to actively organize rock 'n' roll musicians into their union and give them an equal voice. But for reasons having to do with their conservative view on culture, they did not. On the contrary, the union marginalized rock 'n' roll musicians within their organization.

The challenge posed by Paula Victor, Debbie Otto, and Christine Smith and their fellow Beatles fans went beyond the particular issue of the Beatles conflict with the musicians' union. The struggle over the Beatles in some ways foreshadowed the emerging cultural tensions between the counterculture and the increasingly conservative labor movement.[38] The controversy over the Beatles also needs to be placed in a larger context of social protest that characterized the 1960s. The lunch counter sit-ins, the freedom rides of the civil rights movement in the early 1960s, the free speech movement at Berkeley in 1964, and the social upheaval of other student civil disobedience activities that followed had a profound impact on youth culture and rock 'n' roll music in the United States. Social influences worked in the other direction as well, as rock 'n' roll music contributed to the culture of social protest in the 1960s.[39] While the Beatles themselves weren't singing about the civil rights movement or the student free speech movement (at least not in 1964), they did represent cultural change and the oppositional stance of the youth culture against the establishment. Furthermore, the Beatles' first tour took place the same year that the Civil Rights Act was passed, an epoch-changing event in American culture. During that year, Vee Jay Records, an African American-owned record company, released the first Beatles album in the United States, *Introducing... The Beatles*. That album was mostly covers of Little Richard and Chuck Berry songs, and it introduced many white middle-class kids to black rhythm and blues music for the first time, helping to repopularize and "relegitimate" the rich history of black music among white rock 'n' roll fans.

In subsequent years, the innovative recordings of the Beatles, including *Rubber Soul, Revolver*, both released in 1966, and *Sgt. Pepper's Lonely Hearts Club Band* released in 1967, also played a large part in expanding the counterculture in America. In short, for young people in the United States, the Beatles represented change, as young people became a major force in American politics. In the letter by Paula Victor above, she says that culture "consists of all those activities which express the *personality of an age*." Her words pointed to a major source of conflict not only between the musicians' union and Beatles fans but also between the emerging counterculture and the labor movement as a whole in the United States. The "personality of an age" that Ms. Victor refers to was rooted in movements like the civil rights movement, the student free speech movement, the anti–Vietnam War movement, and the emerging counterculture, which all represented a generational/cultural challenge to the established political structure in the United States. From the point of view of the counterculture, the culturally conservative working class had become, by the 1960s, part of the "establishment." The musicians' union and the labor movement bureaucracy represented the "Old" America, the pre-1960s America that was racked with problems of racism, sexism, conservatism, and corruption.

The album *Sgt. Pepper's Lonely Hearts Club Band* became an icon in the counterculture, and it contributed to the cultural distance between rock 'n' roll and the labor union bureaucracy.[40] There is a clear change in direction in the music of the Beatles after Bob Dylan introduced them to marijuana and the American counterculture, which they emphatically embraced. Although John Lennon had publicly denied it, the second track on *Sgt. Pepper's*, "Lucy in the Sky with Diamonds," was a song about an acid trip. The Beatles had attempted to maintain a relatively clean public image after the release of *Sgt. Pepper's*, but when Paul McCartney admitted publicly that the Fab Four had taken LSD, it cemented the connection between rock 'n' roll and drugs. According to McCartney, "It [LSD] opened my eyes. We only use one-tenth of our brains. . . . Just think what we could accomplish if we could tap the hidden part."[41] McCartney's admission made the Beatles once again the center of cultural conflict. The album cover of *Sgt. Pepper's* also created some controversy. The album cover is famous — or infamous, depending on your point of view — for its collection of images of celebrities, including movie stars, Albert Einstein, and Karl Marx. Also on the cover one can see a neat line of marijuana plants at the bottom of the frame, stretching from one side of the picture to the other. The Beatles raised the bar again, only this time with the artistic content of album covers.

Although *Sgt. Pepper's* wasn't burned in massive public bonfires like the Beatles' other albums were in 1966, when Lennon had compared the Beatles to Jesus Christ, McCartney's admission that the Beatles were using drugs once again rallied the ranks of cultural conservatives against rock 'n' roll. Religious leaders were particularly harsh on the Beatles, just as they were in 1966. Billy Graham, the popular television evangelist, took a less hostile approach: he led a public prayer for the Beatles. Other religious figures, however, like David Noebel of the Christian Crusade, led the fringe elements in society who believed that the Beatles were a tool of the communists, using music as a form of hypnotism to capture the minds of American teenagers. In one of his pamphlets from 1965, Noebel argued that the music "isn't 'artform' at all, but a very destructive process. Teenage mental breakdown is at an all-time high and juvenile delinquency is nearly destroying our society. Both are caused in part by emotional instability which in turn is caused in part by destructive music such as rock-and-roll. . . . But no matter what one may think about the Beatles . . . the results are the same—a generation of young people with sick minds, loose morals, and little desire or ability to defend themselves from those that would bury them."[42]

Also in 1967, George Harrison made a well-publicized trip to the Haight-Ashbury district of San Francisco, an area that had become the Mecca for hippies and the counterculture in America. That year, the *Washington Post* ran a series of articles about the rock music scene in the Haight, and it helped create a public stir about the threat of the counterculture and drugs. According to the *Post*, hippies were using rock music and underground radio stations to push dope on the youth of America. Nicolas Hoffman, the author of the *Post* series, claimed that the hippies were conspiring to infiltrate the communication industries via rock music and FM radio as a means of encouraging drug use and taking over the imagination of American youth. While Hoffman's piece was somewhat paranoid in its tone and scope, there was some truth in his allegations that rock musicians were praising the role of drugs in the creation of a new society.

The paranoia and hysteria about drug use and rock music became so widespread that Congress decided to investigate the connection between the music industry, rock music, and drug use. Again the British bands were in the middle of the controversy. Eric Clapton, the guitar virtuoso from the British rock band Cream, said publicly, "Ours is a universal problem; how to find peace in a society which we feel to be hostile. We want to express that search in our music, since that is our most eloquent voice. We need drugs to help us, to free our minds and our imaginations from the prejudices and snobbery that have been bred into us."[43] Clapton's comments were eventually brought to the floor of the Senate for discussion and debate about the supposed epidemic of drug use and its spread via rock music. Vice President Spiro Agnew also entered the national conversation on drugs and rock music. Agnew was among the conservatives who believed that rock musicians essentially brainwashed American teenagers into experimenting with drugs. Speaking at a fund-raising event in Las Vegas, Agnew said:

> We may be accused of advocating song censorship for pointing this out. . . . Have you heard the words of some of these songs? The Beatles have a song, which includes the words, "I get by with a little help from my friends, I get high with a little help from my friends." . . . Until it was pointed out to me, I never realized that "friends" were assorted drugs.[44]

Agnew's comments came three years after the AFM attempted to ban the Beatles from the United States. By then the official voice of the labor union bureaucracy had joined the backlash against rock 'n' roll.

The Beatles' association with the counterculture and John Lennon's outspoken criticisms of American foreign policy alienated and angered the AFL-CIO leadership. The cultural conservatism of the labor movement as a whole, especially their critical attitude toward rock 'n' roll as a vehicle of the counterculture, was made explicit when the AFL-CIO News published an attack on rock 'n' roll in general, and the Rolling Stones in particular, for soliciting drug use as well as all-around delinquent behavior.[45] For the leaders of the AFL-CIO and the rest of the cultural right, rock 'n' roll was associated with long hair, sexual promiscuity, opposition to the Vietnam War, and drug consumption. Rightly so, but for labor leaders, these were problems to be addressed and contained. In general the AFL-CIO leadership supported President Johnson's war plans in Vietnam, and they opposed the libertarian personal politics of the counterculture. On the other side, young people involved in the counterculture and the antiwar movement came to see the labor union aristocracy as part of the problem, part of the establishment in American society, because of the cultural conservatism rampant in the old guard of labor leaders, most of whom were "old white guys in favor of the war in Vietnam and against drug use and sexual freedom."[46] Of course, any kind of embrace of rock music in the late 1960s by the AFM would have been tenuous, since rock music was associated with the counterculture and the movement against the Vietnam War.

The problem of rock 'n' roll and the counterculture was also a problem that labor union leaders had with their own rank-and-file members. Increasingly in the 1960s, young union members embraced the counterculture, which meant smoking pot on and off the job, listening to rock 'n' roll music, and identifying less and less with the workplace and their own union leadership. Labor leaders blamed rock 'n' roll for contributing to the conditions that made it more difficult to keep workers in line. Even managements of the big corporations were concerned that labor leaders were losing control of their rank and file. As Malcolm L. Denise, who was vice president of the Ford Motor Company, complained in 1969:

> A few years ago Reuther and his executive board could map the union's course with confidence. Today they seem uncertain. The reason is a big influx of a new breed of union member—a younger, more impatient, less homogeneous, more racially assertive, and less manipulable member—whose attitudes and desires admittedly are not easily read by a sixty-two-year-old labor leader. . . . For that matter, those attitudes and desires are not always so easily understood by us here, either.[47]

The estrangement of rock 'n' roll musicians from the American Federation of Musicians was one example of the more widespread problem of rank-and-file disenchantment with union leadership in most labor unions in the late 1960s. And, as was the case with the AFM and the major record labels, management at corporations like Ford sided with union leaders against unruly rank-and-file members, especially the subgroup called "hippies." According to Aronowitz:

> Hippie is a self-definition for a large number of young workers who spend some of their time smoking marijuana or using such psychogenic drugs as LSD or mescaline. . . . The hippies are tremendously involved with rock music, especially white acid rock such as the Rolling Stones, the Jefferson Airplane, Janis Joplin, and Bob Dylan. Some of them play instruments and dream of becoming professionals. . . . Being "straight" differs little from being "hip" among young people of Lordstown [a GM factory located in Lordstown, Ohio]. Long hair, marijuana, and rock music is shared by nearly all the young workers in the plant. Still there is a definite distinction between hippies and other young people. They are more aware of alternate political and philosophical ideas.[48]

We know a lot about how "hippies" dropped out of mainstream society in the late 1960s in search of an alternative to the boredom and drudgery of everyday life in the United States, but "hippies" were also a problem for labor leaders concerned with maintaining discipline among their rank and file. The late 1960s was a turning point for the labor movement because it signaled the alienation and disenfranchisement of large segments of rank-and-file members from their unions, as labor leaders repeatedly took sides with management against their own members.

Alienation of young people from the labor movement included rock 'n' roll musicians as much as their fans who were part of the counterculture, and that meant that rock musicians considered the musicians' union irrelevant. For them, unions represented old, conservative white guys, the kind of people who hated rock 'n' roll. As a result, many rock musicians had very little, if any, meaningful interaction with the union. There were instances in the late 1960s where rock musicians were automatically enrolled in the musicians' union if they worked a gig that was a union shop, whether a live venue or a recording session. But for rock musicians, the American Federation of Musicians and its institutions were not part of their culture. That fact was a profound change from a few generations earlier, when jazz and classical music and the musicians' union were part of the same culture.

Because the AFL-CIO—which included the AFM—backed President Johnson's foreign policy, the AFM had to keep a distance from the more radical rock musicians who spoke out against the war, including most famously the self-proclaimed working-class hero, John Lennon.[49] Still, there were chances at creating some kind of rank-and-file solidarity and some kind of organizing strategy among rock musicians in the United States, even if the leadership of the musicians' union kept a distance from the counterculture, because even the most radical American band of the era, the Motor City Five (MC5) from Detroit, was a firm supporter of the AFM.[50] In fact, the MC5 even established an organization within the AFM for young rock musicians who had very little experience with the union. According to John Sinclair, a leader of the counterculture and the antiwar movement, as well as the manager of the MC5, "We were active with Local 5 in Detroit and helped establish a, I forget what we called it exactly, but it was like a 'junior guild' where rock bands could join the union and still play for $50 opening slots. Gary Grimshaw designed the membership cards! We interacted with the Detroit and Ann Arbor (Local 625) outposts in the AFM."[51]

Gary Grimshaw is a Vietnam War veteran turned artist who opposed the war and who designed album covers for the MC5. Grimshaw became famous as the designer of psychedelic posters that promoted some of the most famous live shows of rock stars in the late 1960s, including the Who, Cream, Jimi Hendrix, the Grateful Dead, the Doors, and Jefferson Airplane. When Sinclair was jailed in 1971 for possession of two marijuana joints, Grimshaw organized a rock concert in the effort to get Sinclair out of jail, titled the "John Sinclair Freedom Rally." John Lennon and Yoko Ono performed at the rally along with Stevie Wonder and Bob Seger, both from the same Detroit music scene as the MC5. The case of the MC5 and Local 5 of the AFM is interesting not only because it was a rare situation where rock 'n' roll musicians were attempting to get involved with the musicians' union as active members, but also because it demonstrated that the cultural divide between the counterculture and the labor movement was not entirely unbridgeable. Unfortunately, the MC5 experiment to link up the counterculture with the labor movement was not reproduced on a larger scale, but it does reveal that there may have been opportunities for certain kinds of alliances. The fact that the labor movement failed to find common ground with the counterculture partly explains why the labor movement entered a decade of decline in American politics, as its bureaucracy was increasingly coded as an institution controlled by culturally and socially conservative white men.

The break in culture ultimately led to a break in the music business, too, as the industry changed in profound ways that allowed rock music to grow outside the purview of the musicians' union, as more and more musicians worked without a union contract and without joining the union. In short, the cultural break contributed to the creation of the conditions for the structural break that pushed the musicians' union from atop the perch of the music industry. When the Beatles took the United States by storm in 1964, union musicians like Earl Palmer recognized that the music business was about to change significantly. After the Beatles, the division of labor was radically restructured as more and more rock bands followed the Beatles' model of writing, recording, and performing their own material. The new division of labor meant that demand for session musicians would go into steep decline. According to Palmer's biographer, Tony Scherman, "The fat days didn't last. It's hard for anyone who wasn't a musically inclined youth in the sixties to comprehend the speed with which, in the immediate wake of the Beatles, kids picked up electric guitars. The first of two death knells tolled for studio musicians: self-contained bands that recorded their own material."[52] As the music industry shifted toward the

Beatles' model, the musicians' union found itself on the outside looking in, since for so many years the union had neglected rock musicians.

Notes

An earlier version of chapter 4 was published in *Popular Music* 29, no. 1, as "A Working-Class Hero Is Something to Be."

EPILOGUE. **Tuned In, Turned On, and Dropped Out**

Rock 'n' Roll Music Production Restructures the
Music Industry along Non-Union Lines

Unlike most of the songs nowadays being written uptown in Tin Pan Alley, that's
where most folk songs come from these days.... This song was not written up
there. This song was written somewhere down in the United States.

—BOB DYLAN

When Bob Dylan wrote the lines above, which appear in his 1963 song
"Bob Dylan's Blues," he was commenting on the perceived problem of the
alienation of counterculture music fans and musicians from the corporate-
dominated music industry, which, according to certain perceptions at
that time, was said to follow from the problem of the commodification of
music.[1] Goodman refers to the phenomenon as the "head-on collision of
rock and commerce."[2] Ironically, Dylan and other so-called counterculture
rock 'n' roll musicians were key figures in the corporate transformation of
the division of labor in the music industry that ultimately undermined the
economic potency of musicians across the board for the benefit of the big
companies that dominate the music industry. Dylan may have been correct (to some extent) to claim that he and his generation of counterculture
musicians were on the outside looking in on American society and popular
culture, but they were at the center of the changing *structure* of the business

side of things in the music industry. Rock 'n' roll music may in some cases still be a cultural "threat" to the status quo in society, and in the mid-1950s, rock 'n' roll music posed a legitimate economic threat to the dominant institutions in the music industry, but the corporate response to rock 'n' roll in the late 1960s profoundly changed the structure of the music industry in ways that cannot be considered critical of the political-economic power structure. The corporate strategy of restructuring was possible, in part, due to the position of so-called independent record labels, the supposed home of culturally "radical" and "authentic" music. In short, the major corporations restructured the industry along non-union lines through a strategy of outsourcing the production of records that turned upon the growth of rock 'n' roll music in the 1960s.

Vertical integration of business operations used to be the norm in the recording industry, but that is no longer the operating model. Major record label companies do not supervise all stages of record production under "one roof," including songwriting, publishing, recording, manufacturing, marketing, and distribution. Henry Ford's classic model of vertical integration of business operations and the joining of mass production to mass consumption that became the basic template for all American corporations, including the major record labels, fell apart in the early 1970s. From 1930 to 1960, the major labels dominated all aspects of the division of labor, along the lines of Fordism, a term coined by Gramsci to describe the regime of capital accumulation during the first half of the twentieth century. When the music industry was organized under Fordist principles, at the bottom or beginning of the chain of operations was the Artist and Repertoire (A&R) department, which was in charge of signing artists to the label roster and developing their sound. At the top of the chain were the distribution functions, and in between were the stages of recording, manufacturing, and marketing. Today, production is widely dispersed among independent record companies that largely serve as non-union subcontractors in the labor system, while distribution is tightly controlled by four corporate conglomerates that dominate the business throughout the world.[3]

The transformation of the division of labor through outsourcing work to non-union companies has displaced the musicians' union from the position of power it once had. The loss of union influence has had a negative effect on countless musicians struggling to make a career, because the new business model has translated into lower wages, deteriorating working conditions, and the erosion of benefits for virtually all musicians who have not reached the status of the relatively few rock stars who have been able to find success without help from the union. The great sea change in the organization of business and labor practices occurred in the 1960s, during the heyday of rock music. Rock musicians were the unwitting pawns in the strategy of outsourcing production that created a cheap pool of easily exploitable labor and undermined the power of the AFM. In short, this radical transformation of the music industry pivoted upon rock music and musicians.

Of course rock musicians—who may choose not to join the union, or who may not even know a union exists—are not solely to blame for these changes. On the contrary, the AFM played an important role, because their rejection of rock music on aesthetic grounds, which were rooted in class and race prejudice, facilitated, albeit unintentionally, the ability of corporations to radically restructure the music industry. Since rock musicians were marginalized by the union, the corporations that sought to get a piece of the rock music pie were able to fold rock music into a new business structure that excluded the union. The major record label executives, who were taken by surprise by rock 'n' roll in the 1950s, knew very little about the music. Thus, in order to gain economic control over the independent labels and over rock music, they turned over the creative process to the producers at the independent labels and entered into distribution agreements with them.

Joe Smith, president of Warner Reprise Records in the early 1970s, summed up the new structure of the industry: "The mechanics of a record company are just that—mechanics."[4] Smith and other executives at the majors realized that it was a good business decision to get out of the creative side of music and focus only on the business side, or the bottom line, and that the best way to do that was to focus on monopolizing the distribution end.

The older structure of core and periphery in the economy of music production was completely dismantled. Rock 'n' roll music, which emerged from the periphery of the music industry, eventually entered its core as the old division of labor was dismantled and replaced by a form of outsourcing, which is not unlike the outsourcing that has taken place in most manufacturing industries in the United States in the past few decades. The corporate conglomerates that control the recording industry do so with a monopoly on distribution, leaving the production of recorded music to companies that are more and more resembling independent contractors, and these production companies are increasingly less likely to sign a labor contract with the musicians' union. Working musicians in the new division of labor no longer have control over the conditions of their work like they did in the years of union power between 1900 and 1948. The AFM has suffered under the new division of labor in two ways. First, the demand for session musicians has been in decline, since most rock music recording stars write, perform, and record their own material. Second, many rock bands that record for labels that serve as independent contractors for the majors work without a labor agreement with the musicians' union.

As the majors began, in the late 1960s and early 1970s, to focus more on distribution arrangements rather than the production process, they developed a new so-called open or flexible system of production. The majors began to disperse the recording process among various subsidiaries and increased the number of distribution agreements with labels in their outer orbits, labels they did not own outright. While production was more dispersed than in the 1940s or 1950s, the production companies were still identical with subsidiary labels owned by the majors. In other words, the majors had yet to subcontract production to companies that they did not own. A subsidiary of RCA, like Arista, for example, will use the services of independent producers, but it still controls production, which means that the parent company and subsidiary are obliged to honor the terms of the labor contract with the AFM. In the second wave of mergers, however, the majors stopped purchasing labels and switched to a new strategy of partial purchase, joint venture, or a distribution deal. The more recent trend of joint ventures began in the early 1970s, and it represents the maturation of the post-Fordist model, because the production of the sound recording is farmed out to companies partially owned or not owned at all. It is the dominant model today, and it reveals that the majors exercise control over the music industry via distribution, not production.

The shift to a post-Fordist, postindustrial form of production is the hallmark of the so-called new economy. Postindustrialism refers to the decline of the manufacturing sectors of the U.S. economy. Fewer material goods are produced here in the United States, as companies search for cheaper labor across the border. But dispersed production also occurs, as companies move from the North to the South, where labor is cheaper due to the low rates of unionization among workers. Postindustrialism also refers to a declining commitment by the federal government to support unions and workers' rights. Since the Reagan administration, the government has abandoned the idea that unions are necessary partners in the quest for industrial stability and amicable labor relations between employers and employees.

Post-Fordism refers to the vertical disintegration of corporations and increasing market specialization as the focus for production. The days of mass production and mass consumption in the United States are over. Henry Ford's idea of centralized production and wage-led economic growth no longer has the same kind of influence over economists and policy makers that it once did. Unlike in the Fordist model, in which unions are seen as vital to the economy because they raise wage levels and increase the purchasing power of consumers and therefore boost aggregate demand, unions today are viewed as a drag on the economy. In both cases, the "new" economy does not bode well for unionized workers and workers in general, including professional musicians. Of course, there are good reasons to challenge the backlash of conservatism that has come to dominate economic "wisdom." Many economists believe we need to return to an industrial Fordist model to revive the economy. In the music recording industry, sales are not down as much as in other industries, but for the workers in the music recording industry (the professional musicians), the shift to a post-industrial, post-Fordist pattern of production has had negative economic effects upon them, just like workers in other industries. The post-Fordist model almost invariably translates into poorer working conditions and less pay for professional musicians.[5] The majors are using the indies as subcontractors to cut back on production costs, principally labor costs, a strategy that mimics a widespread pattern of farming out production that cuts across almost every industry in the United States. Just as is the case in other industries, most of the subcontracting companies in the recording industry use non-union workers, and just as in other industries, subcontracting companies in the recording industry do not honor terms and conditions required by the union's labor contract, which is held by the larger contracting company. When a record company signs a labor agreement or contract with the musicians' union, it is referred to as a "signatory" company. The AFM has three contracts with the major record labels in the recording industry that it uses to regulate wages and working conditions throughout the industry. The first contract is the Phonograph Record Labor Agreement, which regulates wage scales and health and pension funds for AFM members. The other two contracts are the Phonograph Record Trust Agreement and the Special Payments Fund, two agreements that raise monies to be used for free public concerts as well as for AFM members in the recording industry.[6] Union companies, then, are signatory companies, but in the words of a well-known lawyer in the recording industry, "all of the majors are signatories, whereas most independent record companies are not."[7] As the market share of the indie labels increases as a result of major label outsourcing of production, the number of nonsignatory labels rises in proportion to the signatory ones. The irony is that the indies, a collective of labels usually viewed as the leaders of an antiestablishment ethos, are in many cases firmly embedded in the establishment as silent partners in the corporate assault on union labor, in this case the musicians' union. I've calculated that in recent years, non-union shops produce recordings for as much as 40 percent of the market for recorded music.[8]

The implications of the history of the reception of rock 'n' roll by the musicians' union point beyond the situation of the American Federation of Musicians and their place in the music industry. Not only is it likely that had the musicians embraced rock 'n' roll and aggressively organized rock musicians, the union would have retained much of its influence that it has since lost in the music industry. If the musicians' union had embraced rock 'n' roll, it might have been able to set an example for the rest of the labor union bureaucracy in bridging the cultural gap between the labor movement and the counterculture. One can only speculate how different the political-economic situation would be today had the labor movement embraced the counterculture.

For a brief moment, the American Federation of Musicians, together with the other militant labor unions who struggled against the major corporations during the turbulent 1940s, was able to reveal the very real possibility of what had hitherto been merely a utopian dream, namely, the promise that technology would free human beings from the burden of toil that follows from economic scarcity. The door to that utopia, which was pried open for just a few years during the 1940s, has since been closed. The desire to make the dream a reality lived on in rock 'n' roll music, but for cultural and political reasons, the American working class was unable to lead us through the door that led down the path to more leisure and less work. After World War II, it was no longer a technical question as to whether or not workers would be able to have more and work less. As Benjamin

Hunnicutt has demonstrated in his book *Work without End,* American political leaders, including some important labor leaders, chose to abandon shorter hours of toil for the "right to work." This is the important legacy of this period in American history and why there remains so much at stake in the work of cultural historians.

NOTES

INTRODUCTION. Union Man Blues

1. See Jay Ruby, "Creedence Clearwater Revival," in *International Musician*, June 1969, 5.

2. The first time the *International Musician* published the words *rock 'n' roll* was in 1968. See Nat Hentoff, "The Pop Explosion," *International Musician*, April 1968.

3. The story of the AFM and the Beatles is covered in more detail in chapter 4.

4. Berry's first union gig was at the Crank Club in St. Louis in the early 1950s. Berry writes in his autobiography that he made twice as much money working union gigs than he did playing non-union establishments. See Berry, *The Autobiography* (New York: Harmony Books), 91–92.

5. In the mid-1940s, the music that we know today as rock 'n' roll was still referred to by musicians who played it — including Louis Jordan — as jump blues. In 1949, it became known as "rhythm and blues." And of course there were other important influences on the formation of rock 'n' roll besides jump blues. Country music, bluegrass, popular swooners like Frank Sinatra and Bing Crosby, the blues, and swing jazz all played an important role in the development of rock 'n' roll. I discuss all these influences in later chapters.

6. The first rock 'n' roll record to appear on the *Billboard* charts was "Crazy Man, Crazy," by Bill Haley and His Comets. I make the case that rock 'n' roll is the music of the American working class rather than exclusively an expression of American "youth" culture as many critics, including Frith (*Sound Effects*) have argued. Certainly youth culture shaped rock 'n' roll in important ways, but the roots of rock 'n' roll music run much deeper than "youth" culture. My interpretation of rock 'n' roll as a working-class phenomenon will be clear in the chapters that follow. Simon Frith, *Sound Effects: Youth, Leisure, and the Politics of Rock-and-Roll* (New York: Pantheon Books, 1981).

7. *International Musician*, October 1968, 23.

8. In chapter 3, I discuss the case of Tommy Dorsey and his extreme dislike of Elvis.

9. For a sociological analysis of the formal aspects of western classical music, see Max Weber, *The Rational and Social Foundations of Music*, trans. Don Martindale et al. (Carbondale: Southern Illinois University Press, 1958).

10. James P. Kraft, *Stage to Studio: Musicians and the Sound Revolution* (Baltimore: Johns Hopkins University Press, 1996).

11. For an analysis of the cultural impact of the division between mental and manual labor in the capitalist mode of production, see Alfred Sohn-Rethel, *Intellectual and Manual Labor: A Critique of Epistemology* (London: Macmillan, 1978).

12. Jacques Derrida, *Margins of Philosophy*, trans. Alan Bass (Chicago: University of Chicago Press, 1982).

13. Neil Leonard, *Jazz and the White Americans: The Acceptance of a New Art Form* (Chicago: University of Chicago Press, 1962).

14. I discuss these strikes in more detail in later chapters.

15. For an excellent analysis of the record aesthetic that contributes to the production of rock 'n' roll culture, see Theodore Gracyk, *Rhythm and Noise: An Aesthetic of Rock* (Durham, NC: Duke University Press, 1996).

16. Rock 'n' roll musicians have made these arguments. For instance, Eric Clapton said that his band, Cream, would never have had the success that it did if it were not for Tom Dowd, the sound engineer who recorded their celebrated album *Disraeli Gears*. According to Clapton, Dowd's influence in the recording studio was just as important as any of the band members. In addition, George Martin, who produced many of the Beatles' albums, became known as the "fifth Beatle" because he played such an important role in the sound engineering of albums like *Sgt. Pepper's*.

17. I am borrowing Walter Benjamin's famous argument from his essay "The Work of Art in the Age of Mechanical Reproduction," which is from the collection of essays published in *Illuminations* (New York: Schocken Books, 1969). Benjamin's argument about the loss of "aura" and the democratizing effect of technology on art was based on photography and its impact on painting, but I think it works equally well with recording technology in the area of music, especially rock 'n' roll. I cover Benjamin's argument in more detail in chapter 2.

18. Kraft, *Stage to Studio*.

19. Peter B. Levy, *The New Left and Labor in the 1960s* (Urbana: University of Illinois Press, 1994); Jefferson Cowie, *Stayin' Alive: The 1970s and the Last Days of the Working Class* (New York: New Press, 2010).

20. Michael Roberts, "Papa's Got a Brand New Bag," in *Rhythm and Business: The Political Economy of Black Music*, ed. Norman Kelley (New York: Akashic Books, 2005).

21. Harrison Bennett and Barry Bluestone, *The Great U-Turn: Corporate Restructuring and the Polarizing of America* (New York: Basic Books, 1988).

22. See Robin D. G. Kelley, "The New Urban Working Class and Organized Labor," in *New Labor Forum: A Journal of Ideas, Analysis, and Debate*, no. 1 (fall 1997).

23. Art Preis, *Labor's Giant Step: Twenty Years of the CIO* (New York: Pioneer, 1964).

24. I am using the term *overdetermined* much in the same way as Althusser does, as a way to avoid the reduction of complex relations to simplified cause-and-effect explanations. *Overdetermined* is used to emphasize how variables like "class" and "race" are not "things" or "things-in-themselves" but rather sets of relations that develop dialectically and become displaced through one another in a variety of specific social contexts.

25. Racism existed in the American Federation of Musicians, much like in other unions, but as white working-class musicians began playing rhythm and blues and rock 'n' roll, class became an equally determining factor in the split inside the union.

26. Clark Halker, "A History of Local 208 and the Struggle for Racial Equality in the American Federation of Musicians," *Black Music Research Journal* 8 (fall 1988): 207–22.

ONE. **Solidarity Forever?**

1. *International Musician*, July 1942.

2. Russell Sanjek, *Pennies from Heaven: The American Popular Music Business in the Twentieth Century* (New York: Da Capo Press, 1996), 51–52.

3. Arnold Seltzer, *Music Matters: The Performer and the American Federation of Musicians* (Metuchen, NJ: Scarecrow Press, 1989), 24.

4. James P. Kraft, *Stage to Studio: Musicians and the Sound Revolution* (Baltimore: Johns Hopkins University Press, 1996), 130.

5. Tim J. Anderson, *Making Easy Listening: Material Culture and Postwar American Recording* (Minneapolis: University of Minnesota Press, 2006), 35.

6. Kraft, *Stage to Studio*, 88–89. I have placed the numbers for both union locals in Minneapolis as well as Atlanta to identify what were once racially segregated locals in those cities.

7. *Official Proceedings of the Annual Convention of the American Federation of Musicians*, 1938 (in Secretary Treasurer's Office of the American Federation of Musicians, 1501 Broadway, Suite 600, New York 10036), 93.

8. Robert D. Leiter, *The Musicians and Petrillo* (New York: Bookman Associates, 1953).

9. Walter Benjamin, *Illuminations*, trans. Harry Zohn (New York: Schocken Books, 1969). I discuss the significance of Benjamin's perspective in the next chapter.

10. Leiter, *The Musicians and Petrillo*, 53.

11. *Official Proceedings*, 1930, 30.

12. Kraft, *Stage to Studio*, 51.

13. Kraft, *Stage to Studio*, 83.

14. Anderson, *Making Easy Listening*, 12.

15. Leiter, *The Musicians and Petrillo*, 60.

16. Ryan, *The Production of Culture in the Music Industry: The ASCAP-BMI Controversy* (New York: University Press of America, 1985), 17–26.

17. Ryan, *The Production of Culture*, 36–37; Sanjek, *Pennies from Heaven*.

18. It may have seemed an odd alliance at first, because to some extent it did not matter to ASCAP members if music played for commercial purposes was recorded or live. ASCAP members would be compensated in both cases. The AFM, on the other hand, was striking the record industry to stop recording music. The eventual transcendence of this potential contradiction in the interests of the AFM and ASCAP was to be worked out in the 1944 labor agreement that created a royalty system for the musicians' union based on record sales.

19. *Official Proceedings*, 1941, 38–40.

20. The radio and record industries remained competitive industries until the 1950s when, after decades of experimentation and investment, RCA introduced television to the mass market. The medium of television immediately took over the popular variety, drama, and music shows from radio, which was left with almost no programming. As a result of television, the radio industry created a symbiotic relationship with the recording industry that remains to this day.

21. See *Overture*, the newspaper of Local 47, American Federation of Musicians, May 1933, 7.

22. Kraft, *Stage to Studio*, 125–30.

23. *New York Times*, August 14, 1940, 21:8.

24. For a detailed account of these strikes, see Art Preis, *Labor's Giant Step: Twenty Years of the CIO* (New York: Pioneer, 1964), Martin Glaberman, *Wartime Strikes: The Struggle against the No-Strike Pledge in the UAW during World War II* (Detroit: Bewick/ Ed, 1980), and Stanley Aronowitz, *False Promises: The Shaping of American Working-Class Consciousness* (New York: McGraw-Hill, 1992 [1973]).

25. Vocal recordings were produced during the AFM's recording ban because singers and vocalists belonged to a separate union, the American Federation of Television and Radio Artists (AFTRA).

26. Although electronic recording processes had dramatically improved the quality of records, live music continued to set the standard for recordings to emulate. The relationship between live and recorded music reversed in the mid-1960s, as recording processes became very elaborate projects. Rock musicians and fans, especially after the Beatles' album *Sgt. Pepper's Lonely Hearts Club Band*, would use the recording as the referent, where live music concerts were to attempt to sound as good as the record. Studio recording became so intricate that producers and sound engineers had considerably more input into aesthetic decisions than they had a decade earlier.

27. Anderson, *Making Easy Listening*, 16.

28. For what remains the most thorough analysis of this phenomenon, see Harry Braverman, *Labor and Monopoly Capital: The Degradation of Work in the Twentieth Century* (New York: Monthly Review Press, 1974).

29. Kraft, *Stage to Studio*, 140.

30. Christopher L. Tomlins, *The State and the Unions: Labor Relations, Law, and the Organized Labor Movement in America, 1880–1960* (Cambridge: Cambridge University Press, 1985).

31. Kraft, *Stage to Studio*, 149.

32. Kraft, *Stage to Studio*, 151.

33. Sanjek, *Pennies from Heaven*.

34. See the *Interlude*, the official newspaper of Local 9, Boston, American Federation of Musicians, November 1940, 7.

35. Mary Austin, "The American Federation of Musicians' Recording Ban, 1942–1944, and Its Effects on Radio Broadcasts in the United States" (master's thesis, North Texas State University, 1980), 60.

36. Tomlins, *The State and the Unions*.

37. Seltzer, *Music Matters*, 52.

38. See the MPTF homepage, http://www.musicpf.org/AboutUs3.html.

39. For an excellent case study, see Bill DiFazio, *Longshoremen: Community and Resistance on the Brooklyn Waterfront* (South Hadley, MA: Bergen and Garvey, 1985).

40. "Editorial Comment," *International Musician*, February 13, 1947.

TWO. Have You Heard the News?

1. *Louis Jordan and His Tympany Five, 1943–1945* (New York: Classics Records, 1996).

2. Glenn C. Altschuler, *All Shook Up: How Rock 'n' Roll Changed America* (Oxford: Oxford University Press, 2003).

3. Civilian Production Administration, *Industrial Mobilization for War: History of the War Production Board and Predecessor Agencies* (Washington, DC: GPO, 1947).

4. George Lipsitz, *Rainbow at Midnight: Labor and Culture in the 1940s* (Urbana: University of Illinois Press, 1994).

5. Information on Jordan's hit singles can be found at http://www.louisjordan.com/charts.aspx.

6. See http://www.rollingstone.com/music/lists/5702/31963.

7. Stuart Hall, "Notes on Deconstructing the Popular," in *People's History and Socialist Theory*, ed. Raphael Samuels (New York: Routledge, 1981), 228.

8. Herbert Gutman, *Work, Culture, and Society in Industrializing America* (New York: Vintage Books, 1976).

9. Arnold Shaw, *Honkers and Shouters: The Golden Years of Rhythm and Blues* (New York: Collier Books, 1978), 64.

10. Bill C. Malone, *Don't Get Above Your Raisin': Country Music and the Southern Working Class* (Urbana: University of Illinois Press, 2002), 4.

11. Indeed, "escape" is particularly important in this context. As Malone notes, most country songs do not directly address work because both the performers and the consumers of country music cannot afford to waste what little leisure time they have on talking about work. Of course, there are important exceptions like the song "Take This Job and Shove It," but it remains the case that most songs focus on issues outside of the workplace. To make his point, Malone quotes Cecil Sharp, who argues that it is understandable why most country and folk singers avoid singing about their work lives,

"seeing that his hours of work are long and arduous, that the laborer should find more recreation in songs of romance and adventure than in those which remind him of his toil." Malone, *Don't Get Above Your Raisin'*, 29.

12. Jose Ortega y Gasset, *Revolt of the Masses* (New York: W. W. Norton, 1994).

13. George Lipsitz, *Time Passages: Collective Memory and American Popular Culture* (Minneapolis: University of Minnesota Press, 1990).

14. Simon Frith, *Sound Effects: Youth, Leisure, and the Politics of Rock 'n' Roll* (New York: Pantheon Books, 1981).

15. I seek to frame my intervention in the ongoing discussions on the significance of the cultural history of rock 'n' roll in terms of "revisionism," similar to the way in which Wald has sought to challenge certain assumptions about how we view the history of rock 'n' roll. Although unlike Wald my intervention specifically focuses on the labor question in rock 'n' roll culture. Elijah Wald, *How the Beatles Destroyed Rock 'n' Roll* (New York: Oxford University Press, 2009).

16. "Work Stoppages Caused by Labor-Management Disputes," *Monthly Labor Review*, May 1946, 720.

17. Theodor Adorno, *Essays on Music* (Berkeley: University of California Press, 2002), 391.

18. See Theodor Adorno, "On the Fetish Character in Music and the Regression of Listening," in *The Culture Industry: Selected Essays on Mass Culture*, ed. J. M. Bernstein (New York: Routledge, 2001).

19. E. P. Thompson, "Rough Music Reconsidered," *Folklore* 103, no. 1 (1992): 3–26.

20. The counterlogic of labor and the cultural struggle against work that animates these musical traditions was shaped by structural changes in society writ large, as well as by more specific structural changes in the music industry, including structural changes that followed from the battles waged by American Society of Composers, Authors and Publishers against the National Association of Broadcasters and their rival organization, Broadcast Music Inc., the strike on the recording industry by the American Federation of Musicians in 1942 and the creation of a new network of independent record label distributors in the mid- to late 1940s. All these structural changes *within* the music industry together with the larger structural changes in the American economy as a whole created a space for rhythm and blues and honky-tonk music to grow and to thrive. Important technological changes also contributed to the development of rhythm and blues and rock 'n' roll, including magnetic tape technology that made sound recording much better, easier, and more affordable. Of course, the invention of the electric guitar itself by Les Paul was also a key ingredient. These technological changes opened up opportunities for working-class people to teach themselves how to play music by listening to records, while the electric guitar was easier to play than the acoustic. Most histories of rock 'n' roll emphasize the structural changes within the music industry without situating these changes in the larger social context of class conflict. I examine the structural changes within the music industry more closely in the next chapter.

21. James Miller, *Flowers in the Dustbin: The Rise of Rock-and-Roll, 1947–1977* (New York: Simon and Schuster, 1999).

22. The most important exception is George Lipsitz's important book, *Rainbow at Midnight*. Unfortunately, Lipsitz's book has been read primarily by labor historians and is less well known among historians of rock 'n' roll. My work is significantly influenced by Lipsitz, and I seek to build upon his argument that "what the mass demonstration and the wildcat strike provided in political life, rock 'n' roll realized in culture" (330).

23. H. M. Douty, "Review of Basic American Labor Conditions," in *Yearbook of American Labor*, ed. Colston E. Warne (New York: Philosophical Library, 1945), 1–11.

24. Douty, "Review," 48–49.

25. "Money and Real Weekly Earnings during Defense, War, and Reconversion Periods," *Monthly Labor Review* 64 (1947): 987–89.

26. Chuck Berry, *The Autobiography* (New York: Harmony Books, 1987), 35.

27. Lipsitz, *Rainbow at Midnight*, 22, 123.

28. Art Preis, *Labor's Giant Step: Twenty Years of the CIO* (New York: Pioneer, 1964), 174–97.

29. John Mowitt has made a similar argument about the significance of drums in rock 'n' roll music. In *Percussion: Drumming, Beating, Striking* (Durham: Duke University Press, 2002), Mowitt presents a fascinating account of drumming by cleverly using terms we usually think of when we discuss the use of drums, like "beating" and "striking," in a very innovative theoretical framework. He deploys the term "striking" in a double sense. On the one hand, he means "striking" in the sense of to "strike" the drum. Because Mowitt discusses drums and their role in labor conflicts, he means to use the term "strike" in a second way as in a labor strike conducted by workers (99–103).

30. The concept of pretension is doubly significant in this theoretical context because not only is the concept used extensively by Marx to explain the changing conditions of class struggle but also because it is in the name of Louis Jordan's band: *tympany*, which means pretentious style. Karl Marx, *Capital, Volume I*, trans. Ben Fowkes (New York: Penguin, 1976).

31. Tosches, *Unsung Heroes of Rock 'n' Roll*, Palmer, *Rock and Roll*. I will address what I see as the weaknesses in Toches' (1999) Palmer's (1995) historical accounts of rock 'n' roll, but my treatment of rock 'n' roll is not intended to be an exhaustive internal history. Other historians discussed above have already provided interesting, lengthy books on the topic. Nick Tosches, *Unsung Heroes of Rock 'n' Roll: The Birth of Rock in the Wild Years before Elvis* (New York: Da Capo Press, 1999). Robert Palmer, *Rock and Roll: An Unruly History* (New York: Crown, 1995).

32. John Chilton, *Let the Good Times Roll: The Story of Louis Jordan and His Music* (Ann Arbor: University of Michigan Press, 1997), 61.

33. Dick Hebdige, *Subculture: The Meaning of Style* (London: Routledge, 1994 [1979]), 3.

34. Robin D. G. Kelley, *Race Rebels: Culture, Politics, and the Black Working-Class* (New York: Free Press, 1994), 163.

35. The quote from *Esquire* magazine can be found in Stuart Cosgrove, "The Zoot Suit and Style Warfare," *History Workshop Journal* 18 (Autumn 1984).

36. Hebdige, *Subculture*, 16. My reading of the zoot suit as text substantially overlaps with the analysis of Hebdige. Although Hebdige's empirical referent is primarily the British working-class subcultures of the 1960s and 1970s, his interpretation of the meaning of the business suit among the teddy boy subculture is remarkably similar to the symbolic dimension of the zoot suit that was embedded in American black and Hispanic working-class subcultures of the 1940s. "The conventional insignia of the business world—the suit, collar and tie, short hair, etc.—were," according to Hebdige "stripped of their original connotations—efficiency, ambition, compliance with authority—and transformed into . . . objects to be desired, fondled and valued in their own right (105)." More generally, the working-class inversion of bourgeois norms that Hebdige interprets in the styles of British subcultures also mirrors to some extent the American postwar working-class subcultures that I am examining. Of particular importance here is Hebdige's remark that beneath the straight world's contempt, "there were different priorities: work was insignificant, irrelevant; vanity and arrogance were permissible, even desirable qualities" (54).

37. Kelley, *Race Rebels*, 173.

38. See "Zoot Suit Riots," an episode of the video documentary series *American Experience*.

39. See the liner notes written by Chuy Varela that accompany the 2002 re-release of "Pachuco Boogie," on *Arhoolie Records*, El Cerrito, California.

40. The lyrics appear in Louis Jordan, "Inflation Blues," from *Louis Jordan and His Tympany Five, 1946–1947* (New York: Classics Records, 1998).

41. Howlin' Wolf's account appears in the video documentary *The Howlin' Wolf Story*, directed by Don McGlynn (New York: Blue Sea Productions and © BMG Music, 2003).

42. *The Howlin' Wolf Story*.

43. Lipsitz, *Rainbow at Midnight*, 305.

44. Jordan's quote is from the liner notes to the CD *Louis Jordan and His Tympany Five, 1943–1945*.

45. "Let the Good Times Roll," appears on *The Best of Louis Jordan* (New York: MCA Records, 1975).

46. Martin Glaberman, *Wartime Strikes: The Struggle against the No-Strike Pledge in the UAW during World War II* (Detroit: Bewick/Ed, 1980).

47. Nelson Lichtenstein, *Labor's War at Home: The CIO in World War II* (Cambridge: Cambridge University Press, 1983).

48. "Saturday Night Fish Fry," *Best of Louis Jordan*.

49. Glaberman, *Wartime Strikes*.

50. Glaberman, *Wartime Strikes*, 32.

51. R. J. Smith, *The Great Black Way: L.A. in the 1940s and the Lost African American Renaissance* (New York: PublicAffairs, 2006).

52. Smith, *The Great Black Way*, x.

53. Buddy Collete with Steven Isoardi, *Jazz Generations: A Life in American Music and Society* (New York: Continuum, 2000), 64.

54. Collete, *Jazz Generations*, 275.

55. Clora Bryant et al., *Central Avenue Sounds: Jazz in Los Angeles* (Berkeley: University of California Press, 1998), 315.

56. Quoted by Tony Collins, *Rock Mr. Blues: The Life and Music of Wynonie Harris* (Winter Haven, FL: Big Nickel Publications, 1994).

57. Albert Murray, *Stompin' the Blues* (New York: Da Capo Press, 2000 [1976]), 25.

58. Miller, *Flowers in the Dustbin*, 27.

59. In Bryant's *Central Avenue Sounds*, the jazz drummer William Douglas, who played with Earl Hines, Benny Goodman, T-Bone Walker, and others, recounts a brawl between Wynonie Harris and the bassist Dorcester Irving. "One night Wynonie Harris, the great blues singer, kept cracking on Dorcester Irving," recalled Douglas. "Next thing Irving pulled the peg out of his bass and went after him. He had Wynonie begging for his life. It was really funny (240)."

60. See http://rockhall.com/inductees/syd-nathan/bio/.

61. Steve Chapple and Reebee Garofalo, *Rock-and-Roll Is Here to Pay: The History and Politics of the Music Industry* (Chicago: Nelson Hall, 1977); Rick Kennedy and Randy McNutt, *Little Labels—Big Sound: Small Record Companies and the Rise of American Music* (Bloomington: Indiana University Press, 1999).

62. John Broven, *Record Makers and Breakers: Voices of the Independent Rock 'n' Roll Pioneers* (Urbana: University of Illinois Press, 2010). My focus on the independent labels has to do with the division of labor in the music industry in terms of the use of the indies as non-union subcontractors, rather than the question of how much credit the indies should be given in contributing to the emergence of alternative forms of music that have historically been ignored by the majors.

63. I cover this issue in more detail in the next chapter.

64. I realize there are perhaps many more important musicians and recording artists that could be included in my historical analysis of rock 'n' roll, but for the sake of space I have chosen the recording artists I find most appropriate for the arguments I am making about the working-class content of early rock 'n' roll. This section is not intended to be an exhaustive history of rock 'n' roll.

65. T-Bone Walker's "Stormy Monday" appears on *T-Bone Blues* (New York: Atlantic Records 1988).

66. For an excellent reading of Hank Williams's music, see George Lipsitz, *Rainbow at Midnight*, 303–34.

67. Hank Williams, *The Ultimate Collection* (Nashville: Mercury Records, 2002).

68. Charles Hamm, *Yesterdays: Popular Song in America* (New York: W. W. Norton, 1983), 379.

69. Gutman, *Work, Culture, and Society in Industrializing America*.

70. Andre Millard, *America on Record: A History of Recorded Sound* (Cambridge: Cambridge University Press, 1995).

71. James P. Kraft, *From Stage to Studio: Musicians and the Sound Revolution* (Baltimore: Johns Hopkins University Press, 1996).

72. Russell Sanjek, *Pennies from Heaven: The American Popular Music Business in the Twentieth Century* (New York: Da Capo Press, 1996), 355.

73. Roy Rosenzweig, *Eight Hours for What We Will: Workers and Leisure in an Industrial City, 1870–1920* (Cambridge: Cambridge University Press, 1985).

74. Benjamin's essay is reprinted in *Illuminations*, trans. Harry Zohn (New York: Schocken Books, 1969).

75. Benjamin, *Illuminations*, 221, 228.

76. Benjamin, *Illuminations*, 232.

77. Cavaliere's quote is from episode one of the video documentary *The History of Rock-and-Roll* (Time-Life Video and Television and Warner Bros. Entertainment, 2004).

78. See http://www.rollingstone.com/music/lists/5702/31963/32407.

79. Altschuler, *All Shook Up*, 15.

80. My emphasis on radio in this section has to do with how radio helped to spread rock 'n' roll and working-class pretensions by integrating the airwaves, but by the 1950s radio had already had a profound impact on the social relations of production as capitalism entered a new formation in the South. For example, Roscigno and Danaher have demonstrated that radio and the music that aired on independent radio stations played a crucial role in the spread of textile strikes throughout the South in the late 1920s. The structural position of the technology of radio is another example of Benjamin's appropriation of the Marxist argument that the forces of production develop in *contradiction* to the relations of production in the formation of stages of capitalism. Vincent J. Roscigno and William F. Danaher, *The Voice of Southern Labor: Radio, Music, and Textile Strikes, 1929–1943* (Minneapolis: University of Minnesota Press, 2004).

81. Miller, *Flowers in the Dustbin*, 37.

82. This relationship became known as payola, a topic I discuss in the next chapter.

83. Michael T. Bertrand, *Race, Rock, and Elvis* (Urbana: University of Illinois Press, 2000), 172.

84. The best biography of Elvis is Peter Guralnick's *Last Train to Memphis: The Rise of Elvis Presley* (New York: Little, Brown, 1994).

85. Tina Turner's quote appears in the documentary *The History of Rock-and-Roll*.

86. Arnold Shaw, *The Rockin' 50s* (New York: Da Capo Press, 1974), 162.

87. *The History of Rock-and-Roll*.

88. Burgess's comments on cotton picking can be seen in the video documentary *Good Rockin' Tonight: The Legacy of Sun Records*, directed by Bruce Sinofsky (Educational Broadcasting Corporation and SLM Productions, 2001).

89. Bertrand, *Race, Rock, and Elvis*, 99.

90. Greil Marcus, *Mystery Train: Images of America in Rock-and-Roll Music* (New York: Plume Books, 1997), 132.

91. Marcus, *Mystery Train*, 134.

92. Marcus, *Mystery Train*, 137.

93. Richards's quote appears during an interview for the documentary film *Chuck Berry: Hail! Hail! Rock'n'Roll*, directed by Taylor Hackford (Universal City Studios, 1987).

94. "Too Much Monkey Business," from the *Chuck Berry Box Set* (Chicago: Chess Records, 1989).

95. It is interesting to note that Brian Setzer, of the Stray Cats, has put together a very successful big band in the spirit of the 1940s swing bands. In some ways, Setzer has gone full circle in popular music by making the big band a viable commercial enterprise. Setzer performed "Summertime Blues" with his big band for the film *La Bamba*, about 1950s pop culture phenomenon Richie Valens, starring Lou Diamond Phillips. Sezter played the role of Eddie Cochran for that particular scene. I find this somewhat ironic, given the topic of my next chapter.

96. My reading of the electric guitar is the minority position in academic interpretations of its significance in popular culture, and it is at odds in many ways with the majority position, which is best represented by Steve Waksman's book, *Instruments of Desire*. Waksman's account has become the authoritative perspective on the role of the electric guitar in shaping musical experience in American popular culture. Waksman's superbly researched book is certainly valuable, but he focuses on how the electric guitar was used to maintain inequality and reproduce exploitation in the music industry in particular and America popular culture in general. Steve Waksman, *Instruments of Desire: The Electric Guitar and the Shaping of Musical Experience* (Cambridge, MA: Harvard University Press, 1999).

Waksman looks at how Les Paul's work on the development of the instrument was framed by gender difference and ultimately reproduced the male fantasy of domination over women in the domestic sphere. His discussion of Led Zeppelin and hard rock focuses on the ways in which bands like Led Zeppelin appropriated the music of nonwestern culture in a colonial manner. In short, the argument is that popular, white rock 'n' roll musicians are colonialists, racists, and sexists.

Waksman's account overlaps with many other books that deal with the problem of misogyny and racism in rock 'n' roll, but there is no analysis of class difference *within* white culture in rock 'n' roll. On the contrary, "whiteness" is presented as a monolithic category. Class conflict between "whites" escapes his treatment of the electric guitar in shaping musical experience and in the history of rock 'n' roll more generally. Waksman has an interesting chapter on Chuck Berry's use of the guitar, but at times Waksman treats Berry as a victim, downplaying his role as an agent who changed the music industry. The history of rock 'n' roll looks very different if the emphasis in on agency rather than victimhood.

My point of view is influenced by rock critics like Ellen Willis (1991), who while being a feminist is not willing to downplay the liberating aspects of rock 'n' roll. In her analysis of rock 'n' roll Willis starts from assuming exploitation but looks for conditions of possible resistance and moments where freedom is a real possibility. Susan

Fast (2001) provides a different view of Led Zeppelin that is more along the lines of Willis' point of view and diverges significantly from Waksman's interpretation of Led Zeppelin as merely "colonialists." Ellen Willis, *Beginning to See the Light: Sex, Hope, and Rock-and-Roll* (Hanover, NH: Wesleyan University Press, 1992); Susan Fast, *Inside the Houses of the Holy: Led Zeppelin and the Power of Rock Music* (New York: Oxford University Press, 2001).

97. Robert Walser, "The Body in Music: Epistemology and Musical Semiotics," *College Music Symposium* 31 (1991).

98. Both of these theoretical paradigms, according to Walser, reproduce the Cartesian dualism that separates the mind from the body, where the body is excluded or marginalized in explanatory discourses that seek to discover the meaning of music. On the one hand, the problem with applying the methods of structural linguistics to the study of music is that the ineffable quality of music is lost. On the other hand, the argument made by transcendentalists—which does address the ineffable quality of music—is equally problematic because it leads to the reification and mystification of music by situating it "outside" of social context.

99. Walser emphasizes this point by arguing that musicians have long understood the nonpropositional nature of what they do.

100. Walser, "The Body in Music," 120.

101. Johnson is quoted by Walser, "The Body in Music."

102. Parker's quote is in Bin Sidran, *Black Talk* (New York: Da Capo Press, 1982). Duke Ellington's phrase is the title of one of his compositions from 1932.

103. Walser, "The Body in Music," 121.

104. Walser, "The Body in Music," 123.

105. For an analysis of the sign as a potential terrain of class struggle, see V. N. Volosinov, *Marxism and the Philosophy of Language*, trans. I. R. Titinuk (Cambridge, MA: Harvard University Press, 1986).

106. Lawrence Levine, *Highbrow/Lowbrow: The Emergence of Cultural Hierarchy in America* (Cambridge, MA: Harvard University Press, 1991).

107. Williams is quoted by Steven Baur, "Music, Morals, and Social Management: Mendelssohn in Post–Civil War America," *American Music* 19, no. 1 (2001): 116.

108. For an analysis of the consolidation of the capitalist class in the second half of the nineteenth century, see Sven Beckert, *The Monied Metropolis: New York City and the Consolidation of the Capitalist Class, 1850–1896* (Cambridge: Cambridge University Press, 2001).

109. For an analysis of how the spatial relations of the urban form in modernity reproduce the social relations of production in monopoly capitalism, see Lefebvre, *The Production of Space*. trans. Donald Nicholson-Smith (New York: Blackwell, 1991).

110. Levine, *Highbrow/Lowbrow*, 116.

111. Antonio Gramsci, *Selections from the Prison Notebooks*, trans. Quintin Hoare and Geoffrey Nowell Smith (New York: International, 1971).

112. Steven Baur, "Music, Morals, and Social Management."

113. For an excellent discussion of how the work ethic was used to legitimate the rule of the bourgeoisie over the working class, see Daniel T. Rodgers, *The Work Ethic in Industrializing America, 1850–1920* (Chicago: University of Chicago Press, 1979).

114. Baur, "Music, Morals, and Social Management," 115. What makes Gramsci's (1971) concept of "hegemony" preferable to orthodox Marxists' discussion of the sources and applications of political power is that Gramsci does not view culture as a mere reflection of the class position of the agents who produce it. Rather, he sees culture — or the "superstructure" to use technical terms in Marxist theory — as relatively autonomous from the economic base. What this means for Baur is that it would be a mistake to say that the renewed interest in European classical music among the industrialists and financiers of the Gilded Age was a conspiracy on the part of the bourgeoisie to legitimate and maintain their political-economic power by way of the production of ideology in the culture industry: books, newspapers, and music (live performances and sheet music). Rather, as Baur argues, acknowledging "the role of Protestantism in reinforcing a moral outlook that served the interests of industrial capitalism need not imply collusion between religious leaders and industrialists. The functioning of a hegemonic system does not depend on such collusion, as long as the dominant belief system reinforces established economic and social relationships. Gramsci used the term *historical bloc* to refer to groups that coalesce through commitments to similar ideological principles, whether acting independently or in concert" (75). It would also be wrong to use the term *hegemony* to argue that the capitalist class enjoys complete dominance in any given social formation. "Hegemony theory," argues Baur "acknowledges the relative autonomy of the individuals and groups involved in the process of cultural production. Because it must be articulated, produced, disseminated, and received through the actions of real individuals, ideology is subject to constant negotiation and is therefore always evolving" (72).

115. Baur, "Music, Morals, and Social Management," 84.

116. Baur, "Music, Morals, and Social Management," 105.

117. Craig H. Roell, *The Piano in America, 1890–1940* (Chapel Hill: University of North Carolina Press, 1989), 4.

118. For an excellent analysis of the history of the work ethic in the United States, see Rodgers, *The Work Ethic in Industrializing America*.

119. "Old Fashioned Piano Teacher Gives Way to Studio and Radio," *New York Times*, June 28, 1925, sec. 9, p. 2.

120. For a history of the cultural significance of the piano in American culture from 1890 to 1940, see Roell, *Piano in America*.

121. Coolidge's quote is found in Roell, *Piano in America*, 1.

122. See the description of Fats Domino in *Rolling Stone Magazine* available on their website, http://www.rollingstone.com/music/lists/100-greatest-artists-of-all-time-19 691231/fats-domino-19691231.

123. Rick Coleman, *Blue Monday: Fats Domino and the Lost Dawn of Rock 'n' Roll* (New York: Da Capo Press, 2007).

124. Peter Stallybrass and Allon White, *The Politics and Poetics of Transgression* (Ithaca, NY: Cornell University Press, 1986), 192–93.

125. Stallybrass and White, *The Politics and Poetics*, 191.

126. Lewis's performance can be seen on episode two of the video documentary *The History of Rock-and-roll* (Time-Life Video and Television and Warner Bros. Entertainment).

127. W. T. Lhamon Jr., *Deliberate Speed: The Origins of a Cultural Style in the American 1950s* (Cambridge, MA: Harvard University Press, 2002 [1990]), 78.

128. Lhamon Jr., *Deliberate Speed*, 78.

129. I return to the issue of the trickster figure in the next chapter.

130. Lhamon Jr., *Deliberate Speed*, 79.

131. Lhamon Jr., *Deliberate Speed*, 79.

132. Lhamon Jr., *Deliberate Speed*, 82–83.

133. Bertrand, *Race, Rock, and Elvis*, 119.

134. Bertrand, *Race, Rock, and Elvis*, 121.

135. For a good analysis of the contribution that Jackson and other women made to the history of rockabilly, see David Sanjek, "Can a Fujiyama Mama Be the Female Elvis?" in *Sexing the Groove*, ed. Sheila Whiteley (New York: Routledge, 1997).

136. Sanjek, "Can a Fujiyama Mama Be the Female Elvis?" 139.

137. Jackson's account comes from the liner notes on her album, *Wanda Jackson: Queen of Rockabilly* (London: Ace Records, 2000).

138. The lyrics to "Hot Dog!" appear on *Wanda Jackson: Queen of Rockabilly*.

139. See http://video.google.com/videoplay?docid=4393703873579135322#.

140. Wanda Jackson's record sales figures can be found on the website for the Rock and Roll Hall of Fame Museum, http://rockhall.com/inductees/wanda-jackson/bio/.

141. *History of Rock-and-roll*, video documentary.

142. Sanjek, "Can a Fujiyama Mama Be the Female Elvis?' 149.

143. Malone, *Don't Get Above Your Raisin'*.

144. It is also important to challenge the received wisdom that the 1950s was a period of relative stability between labor and capital or an era of political consensus. Indeed, the phrase "the silent generation," which was coined by *Time* (November 5, 1951) to describe what was perceived as the relative affluence-driven "consensus" or political "apathy" of the generation born between 1925 and 1945, revealed a half-truth at best. *Time* stated that this generation desired "conventional" values and that "the most startling claim about the younger generation is its silence . . . [and] this generation wants a good, secure job . . . and with it a kind of suburban idyll." For evidence to the contrary, see the chapter by Aronowitz, "The Unsilent Fifties," in *False Promises*.

145. Miller, *Flowers in the Dustbin*, 31.

1. Trenier's account can be found in Nick Tosches, *Unsung Heroes of Rock 'n' Roll: The Birth of Rock in the Wild Years before Elvis* (New York: Da Capo Press, 1999).

2. In *Central Avenue Sounds*, the pianist Art Farmer recounts an incident involving Big Jay McNeely, who gave up performing bebop in order to pursue a career in rhythm and blues. "I remember one night I was in the Downbeat," says Farmer, "and Big Jay McNeely was working across the street at the Last Word. He came out in the street with his horn and came all the way across Central Avenue and walked into the Downbeat with his horn, playing it, honking, whooping and hollering. And the owner . . . he said, 'Get the horn! Someone get the horn!' That was the funniest thing. Because the Downbeat was the bebop club that night, and this guy [McNeely]—he was like the enemy." Clora Bryant et al., *Central Avenue Sounds: Jazz in Los Angeles* (Berkeley: University of California Press, 1998), 275.

3. Scott DeVeaux, *Birth of Bebop: A Social and Musical History* (Berkeley: University of California Press, 1997), 7–8.

4. DeVeaux, *Birth of Bebop*, 344.

5. Gillespie's comment appears in Eric Porter, *What Is This Thing Called Jazz? African American Musicians as Artists, Critics, and Activists* (Berkeley: University of California Press, 2002), 58.

6. DeVeaux, *Birth of Bebop*, 351.

7. *Esquire*, June 1957, 55.

8. Tony Scherman, *Backbeat: Earl Palmer's Story* (Washington, DC: Smithsonian Institution Press, 1999), 46–51.

9. Scherman, *Backbeat*, 59.

10. Dizzy Gillespie, *To Be or Not to Bop* (New York: Da Capo Press, 1985), 287.

11. *Esquire*, June 1957, 143.

12. There are numerous accounts of the history of racism in the music industry. For the best narratives, see Steve Chapple and Reebee Garofalo, "Black Roots, White Fruits: Racism in the Music Industry," in their book *Rock 'n' Roll Is Here to Pay: The History and Politics of the Music Industry* (Chicago: Nelson-Hall, 1977). See also Frank Kofsky, *Black Music, White Business: Illuminating the History and Political Economy of Jazz* (New York: Pathfinder Press, 1998).

13. Norman Kelley, *R&B, Rhythm, and Business: The Political Economy of Black Music* (New York: Akashic Books, 2002).

14. Bryant et al., *Central Avenue Sounds*, 248.

15. *Esquire*, June 1957, 55.

16. *Esquire*, June 1957, 141.

17. See John Cohen's liner notes to the album *George Davis: When Kentucky Had No Union Men* (Washington, DC: Folkways FA 2343, 1967).

18. *George Davis: When Kentucky Had No Union Men.*

19. Colin Escot, *Hank Williams: The Biography* (Boston: Little, Brown, 2004), 260.

20. DeVeaux, *Birth of Bebop*, 347.

21. Scherman, *Backbeat*, 75.

22. DeVeaux, *Birth of Bebop*, 343.

23. DeVeaux, *Birth of Bebop*, 340.

24. Richards's remarks appear in the liner notes to the album *Robert Johnson: King of the Delta Blues* (New York: Columbia Records, 1997).

25. Carl Dahlhaus, *Nineteenth-Century Music* (Berkeley: University of California Press, 1989).

26. Of course the bebop musicians were not the first jazz musicians who attempted to move their interpretation of jazz toward classical music in an effort to elevate the music. In the 1920s, Paul Whiteman was experimenting with his own version of creating highbrow jazz interpretations using elements of classical music, particularly his famous "Experiment in Modern Music" concert in 1924, when he commissioned Gershwin's *Rhapsody in Blue*, which premiered at New York's Aeolian Hall. Whiteman specified to Gershwin that he wanted a "jazz concerto." Among those in the audience were the notable composers John Phillip Sousa and Sergei Rachmaninoff.

27. *New York Post*, March 17, 1963.

28. See http://news.bbc.co.uk/2/hi/entertainment/2965225.stm.

29. Bryant et al., *Central Avenue Sounds*, 154–59.

30. Buddy Collete with Steven Isoardi, *Jazz Generations: A Life in American Music and Society* (New York: Continuum, 2000), 114.

31. Porter, *What Is This Thing Called Jazz?* 108.

32. DeVeaux, *Birth of Bebop*, 14–15.

33. DeVeaux, *Birth of Bebop*, 360.

34. Porter, *What Is This Thing Called Jazz?* 106–107.

35. *Esquire*, June 1957, 55.

36. DeVeaux, *Birth of Bebop*, 435.

37. Donald Spivey, *Union and the Black Musician: The Narrative of William Everett Samuels and Chicago Local 208* (Lanham, MD: University Press of America, 1984), 41.

38. Spivey, *Union and the Black Musician*, 37.

39. For an excellent discussion of the serious limitations of craft union tactics, see Jonathan Cutler and Stanley Aronowitz's essay "Quitting Time," in *Post-Work* (New York: Routledge, 1998).

40. I discuss this issue in more detail in the epilogue.

41. DeVeaux, *Birth of Bebop*, 345.

42. For the best scholarly account of the complexity and cultural significance of minstrelsy in American history, see Eric Lott, *Love and Theft: Blackface Minstrelsy and the American Working Class* (New York: Oxford University Press, 1993). Lott persuasively demonstrates that class formation in the United States was intimately bound up with race and profoundly mediated by race relations. Similarly, David R. Roediger, *The Wages of Whiteness: Race and the Making of the American Working Class* (New York:

Verso, 1996 [1991]), argues that the self-conscious creation of the identity "working class" in the United States depended upon the exclusion of the Other. In short, American workers made themselves into a class by excluding "blackness" from their cultural imaginary. I seek to complicate the issue by emphasizing another layer of complexity to issue of class and culture in American history, namely, how race is mediated by class. I intend my discussion of rock 'n' roll in the musicians' union to supplement, not contradict, the exceptionally important work of Lott and Roediger.

43. John Chilton, *Let the Good Times Roll: The Story of Louis Jordan and His Music* (Ann Arbor: University of Michigan Press, 1997), 52.

44. Chilton, *Let the Good Times Roll*, 65.

45. DeVeaux, *Birth of Bebop*, 340.

46. Chilton, *Let the Good Times Roll*, 143.

47. Chilton, *Let the Good Times Roll*, 144.

48. African American trickster tales entered popular culture with the publication of Charles Waddell Chestnutt's story "The Goopherd Grapevine," which was first published by the *Atlantic Monthly* in 1887. For an extended academic discussion on the issue, see Henry Louis Gates Jr., *The Signifying Monkey* (New York: Oxford University Press, 1989).

49. Chilton, *Let the Good Times Roll*, 145.

50. Sammy Davis Jr.'s account appears in the liner notes of *Louis Jordan and His Tympany Five, 1946–1947* (New York: Classics Records, 1998).

51. Liner notes of *Louis Jordan*.

52. As argued in the previous chapter, cultural distinctions between highbrow and lowbrow art legitimates, in ideology, class stratification in the economic and political realm, because it places responsibility for class stratification on individuals rather than the structure or system of class relations. Highbrow and lowbrow are terms that were used originally to refer to the shape of the skull, which is supposed to be a signifier of intelligence. Bourgeois ideology also implicitly claims that the working-class cultural emphasis on the body and bodily pleasure is a result of a lack of intelligence.

53. Scherman, *Backbeat*, 149.

54. Scherman, *Backbeat*, 91.

55. Scherman, *Backbeat*, 89, 105, and 117.

56. I cover their criticisms of rock 'n' roll in more detail below.

57. In fact, the name change was racially motivated. As a strategy to make rhythm and blues music seem less threatening to white, middle-class America, key figures in the music industry promoted the new term "rock 'n' roll" to give the impression that white performers were responsible for the production of the music, when in fact most of the early white pop stars who recorded rock 'n' roll songs, like Pat Boone, were actually covering songs written by black recording artists like Little Richard.

58. *DownBeat*, March 23, 1955, 1.

59. "Musicians Argue Values of Rock-and-Roll," *DownBeat*, May 30, 1956, 12.

60. *Esquire*, June 1957, 143.

61. Hal Espinosa, who is now the president of AFM Local 47, in Los Angeles, told me that when he was a young rank-and-file member of the union, "We didn't consider rock 'n' roll performers to be legitimate musicians. We considered them more as entertainers. . . . We also thought rock 'n' roll was a passing fad." Interview with the author, February 15, 2006.

62. Anonymous Local 47 member, interview by author, Los Angeles, February 15, 2006.

63. Quincy's quote appears in the video documentary series *The History of Rock-and-Roll* (Burbank: Time-Life Video, 1995).

64. H. Wiley Hitchcock, *Music in the United States: A Historical Introduction* (Englewood, NJ: Prentice-Hall, 1988), 54–55.

65. "Musicians Argue Value of Rock-and-Roll Music," *DownBeat*, May 30, 1956.

66. For a fascinating discussion of Charlie Christian and the history of the electric guitar in rock music, see Steve Waksman, *Instruments of Desire: The Electric Guitar and the Shaping of Musical Experience* (Cambridge, MA: Harvard University Press, 1999). Waksman made a good choice by putting Chuck Berry on the cover of his book.

67. According to George Lipsitz, *Rainbow at Midnight: Labor and Culture in the 1940s*. Urbana: University of Illinois Press, 1994): "A creative tension between European and African harmonies gave blues its distinctive sound. When musicians accustomed to the African five-tone scale played or sang music designed for the European eight-tone scale, it sounded better to them when they flattened or bent certain sounds, thus creating 'blue' notes. To those trained in European harmony, the resulting music seemed to involve flattening the third, fifth, or seventh steps of the eight-tone scale, but a more accurate description would recognize that blues musicians used their own system of harmony and chord progressions. The musicologist Robert Walser points out that the use of blue notes by African Americans displays an understanding of pitch as an expressive parameter in direct contrast to the rigid European system of fixed pitches" (307).

68. Lipsitz, *Time Passages*, 113.

69. Michael Roberts, "Papa's Got a Brand-New Bag," in *Rhythm and Business: The Political Economy of Black Music*, ed. Norman Kelley (New York: Akashic Books, 2005).

70. See Michael T. Bertrand, *Race, Rock, and Elvis* (Urbana: University of Illinois Press, 2000).

71. Bertrand, *Race, Rock, and Elvis*, 201.

72. Bertrand, *Race, Rock, and Elvis*, 202.

73. Bertrand, *Race, Rock, and Elvis*, 209.

74. Bertrand, *Race, Rock, and Elvis*, 203.

75. *History of Rock-and-Roll*.

76. Bertrand, *Race, Rock, and Elvis*, 101.

77. *Pittsburgh Courier*, February 2, 1957, 22.

78. *Pittsburgh Courier*, February 2, 1957, 10.

79. Amiri Baraka, *Blues People: Negro Music in White America* (New York: Quill William Morrow, 1999 [1963]), 169.

80. Quoted in Linda Martin and Kerry Segrave, *Anti-Rock: The Opposition to Rock 'n' Roll* (New York: Da Capo Press, 1993), 63.

81. "Rock-and-Roll Called a 'Communicable Disease,'" *New York Times*, March 28, 1956.

82. For the details on how ASCAP achieved their monopoly, see John Ryan, *The Production of Culture in the Music Industry: The ASCAP-BMI Controversy* (Lanham, MD: University Press of America, 1985).

83. Neil Leonard, *Jazz and the White Americans: The Acceptance of a New Art Form* (Chicago: University of Chicago Press, 1962), 118–19.

84. Ryan, *The Production of Culture in the Music Industry*, 65, 69.

85. Arnold Shaw, *The Rockin' 50s* (New York: Da Capo Press, 1974).

86. *Hearings before the Subcommittee on Communications of the Committee on Interstate and Foreign Commerce, United States Senate, Eighty-Fifth Congress, Second Session, Pursuant to an Amendment to the Communications Act of 1934, S. 2834*, 543, 547–48.

87. *Hearings*, 105–106.

88. See William K. and Nancy H. Young, *The 1950s* (Westport, CT: Greenwood Press, 2004).

89. Freed's quote appears in Glenn C. Altschuler, *All Shook-Up: How Rock 'n' Roll Changed America* (New York: Oxford University Press, 2003), 33.

90. *Allegro: Official Newspaper of Local 802, AFM*, October 1955, 1.

91. See Amendment of the Communications Act of 1934: Hearings before the Subcommittee on Communications of the Committee on Interstate and Foreign Commerce, Senate, 85th Cong., 2nd sess., on S. 2834, March 11, 12, 13, 19, 20, April 15, 16, 17, May 6, 7, 20, 21, July 15, and 23, 1958, 968–69.

92. *Variety*, 204:54, October 17, 1956.

93. Brackett, *Pop, Rock, and Soul Reader*, 108. On May 16, 1960, *Life* ran a story by Peter Bunzel titled, "Music Biz Goes Round and Round: It Comes Out Clarkola." In the article Bunzel reveals the rather incestuous and perhaps corrupt business practices of Dick Clark, making the case that Clark was a much more crooked businessman than Alan Freed. Bunzel's piece is reprinted in David Brackett, *The Pop Rock and Soul Reader*, 3rd ed. (New York: Oxford University Press, 2013).

94. Brackett, *Pop, Rock, and Soul Reader*, 109.

95. Both quotes taken from the video documentary *The History of Rock-and-Roll*, episode 2 (Burbank: Time-Life Video, 1995).

96. Trent Hill, "The Enemy Within: Censorship in Rock Music in the 1950s," In *Present Tense: Rock & Roll and Culture*, ed. Anthony DeCurtis (Durham, NC: Duke University Press, 1992), 66.

97. Reebee Garofalo, *Rockin' Out: Popular Music in the USA* (Boston: Allyn and Bacon, 1997).

98. Richard A. Peterson and David G. Berger, "Cycles in Symbol Production: The Case of Popular Music," in *On Record: Rock, Pop, and the Written Word*, ed. Simon Frith and Andrew Goodwin (New York: Routledge, 1990).

99. Garofalo, *Rockin' Out*, 160–61.

100. Jacqueline Warwick, *Girl Groups, Girl Culture: Popular Music and Identity in the 1960s* (New York: Routledge, 2007), x.

101. Hill, "The Enemy Within."

102. Garofalo, *Rockin' Out*, 167.

103. "'Only the Best Is Good Enough' A.F. of M. Tells Congress Cultural Committee," *International Musician*, October 1963.

104. See *Variety*, September 7, 1966, 54.

105. *Esquire*, June 1957, 55.

FOUR. **A Working-Class Hero**

1. National Archives and Records Administration (NARA), record group 174, stack area 530, row 47, shelf 7, box 164 "Beatles."

2. I have tried to find a list of these so-called unique musicians, but I haven't been able to find any specific list or definition of exactly who they were. It seems the unions had an unspoken agreement on who would count as cultured.

3. NARA, "Beatles."

4. NARA, "Beatles."

5. NARA, "Beatles."

6. "'Only the Best Is Good Enough' A.F. of M. Tells Congress Cultural Committee," *International Musician*, October 1963, 7. See also my discussion of the AFM's testimony before Congress in the previous chapter.

7. See Peter B. Levy, *The New Left and Labor in the 1960s* (Urbana: University of Illinois Press, 1994).

8. NARA, "Beatles."

9. NARA, "Beatles."

10. NARA, "Beatles."

11. Dick Hebdige, *Subculture: The Meaning of Style* (London: Routledge, 1994 [1979]).

12. NARA, "Beatles."

13. NARA, record group 174, stack area 530, row 47, compartment 48, shelf 7, box 165, "Employment Security."

14. See the previous chapter for a discussion of the payola scandal and its effect on the sale of rock 'n' roll records.

15. The success of the Beatles came with some sense of bitter irony, however, for although the Beatles helped to legitimate rock 'n' roll, and therefore indirectly participate in the political process of recognizing the value of African American culture, their arrival meant that many black recording artists were pushed off the record charts.

16. Steve Chapple and Reebee Garofalo, *Rock 'n' Roll Is Here to Pay: The History and Politics of the Music Industry* (Chicago: Nelson-Hall, 1977), 70.

17. Jones's quote is from *The History of Rock-and-Roll*, episode 3, "Britain Invades, America Fights Back" (Burbank: Time-Life Video, 1995).

18. NARA, "Employment Security."

19. NARA, "Employment Security."

20. *Variety*, March 25, 1964.

21. NARA, "Employment Security."

22. "Keeping Out the Beatles," by Victor Riesel in NARA, "Beatles."

23. NARA, "Beatles."

24. Raymond Williams, *Keywords: A Vocabulary of Culture and Society* (New York: Oxford University Press, 1985), 87.

25. NARA, "Beatles."

26. *New York Times*, August 14, 1940, 21:8.

27. On their second U.S. tour the Beatles did join the AFM, but they were never encouraged to be active members or participate in any way with the union. On the contrary, they were forced to join based on union rules governing traveling bands in the States. Begrudgingly, the union allowed the Beatles to tour.

28. NARA, "Beatles."

29. Loraine Alterman, "Who Let the Kinks In?" *Rolling Stone*, December 13, 1969.

30. Thomas M. Kitts, *Ray Davies: Not Like Everybody Else* (New York: Routledge, 2008), 60–61.

31. I haven't been able to find any "official" documents regarding the ban on the Kinks, but Ray Davies does talk about it in his autobiography, *X-Ray: The Kinks* (Woodstock, NY: Overlook Press, 1994).

32. Kitts, *Ray Davies*, 61.

33. Carr was interviewed for *Music Magazine*, a publication of the Freelance Musicians' Association. Kubernik's words can be found in the article "The American Federation of Musicians Is Not Your Father's Union Anymore—for Better or for Worse," *Music Magazine*, October 1998, The State of the Union. The article can be found online at http://freelancemusicians.org/fathers.html.

34. On the question of craft unionism and "job consciousness" in the AFL, see Selig Perlman's classic statement in *The Theory of the Labor Movement* (Philadelphia: Porcupine Press, 1928).

35. Of course, the issue of the impact of technology on culture should also be approached from the points of view found in both Walter Benjamin and Theodor Adorno, which I covered in chapter 2.

36. F. R. Leavis, *Education and the University* (London: Chatto and Windus, 1961), 147.

37. Raymond Williams, *Culture and Materialism* (New York: Verso, 2005 [1980]).

38. For an extended analysis of the cultural conflict between the labor union bureau-

cracy and the counterculture, see Levy, *The New Left and Labor*, and Jefferson Cowie, *Stayin' Alive: The 1970s and the Last Days of the Working Class* (New York: New Press, 2010).

39. See, for instance, Ron Eyerman and Andrew Jamison, *Music and Social Movements: Mobilizing Traditions in the Twentieth Century* (Cambridge: Cambridge University Press, 1998).

40. Perhaps it is ironic that Sgt. Pepper's also became a seminal text in the art rock movement and contributed to the development of a certain cultural elitism within rock music. Art rock ideologues mirrored the beboppers in some ways when they struggled to distinguish rock (art) from pop music, which was said to lack the artistic value of "rock." I also found in my interviews with AFM leaders that the rank and file of the AFM began to take rock 'n' roll seriously only *after* the release of *Sgt. Pepper's*.

41. McCartney was originally quoted in *Queen Magazine*, a UK-based publication. The quote was later used in *Life*, June 16, 1967, in an article by Thomas Thompson, "The New Far-Out Beatles."

42. David A. Noebel, *Communism, Hypnotism, and the Beatles* (Tulsa, OK: Christian Crusade, 1965).

43. J. L. Buckley, "The Record Industry and the Drug Epidemic," *Congressional Record—Senate*, November 21, 1973, 37853.

44. Agnew's words from the Las Vegas speech are published in Jon Weiner, *Come Together: John Lennon in His Time* (New York: Random House, 1984), 139–40.

45. Edward Morgan, "A Different View of Protesting Youth," *AFL-CIO News*, January 14, 1967, 5. Cited by Levy, *The New Left and Labor*.

46. For a detailed discussion of the overall conservatism of the labor movement, see Paul Buhle, *Taking Care of Business: Samuel Gompers, George Meany, Lane Kirkland, and the Tragedy of American Labor* (New York: Monthly Review Press, 1999). For a look at the relationship between the counterculture and the labor movement, see Levy, *The New Left and Labor*.

47. Denise's words are cited by Stanley Aronowitz, *False Promises: The Shaping of American Working-Class Consciousness* (New York: McGraw Hill, 1992 [1973]), 34.

48. Aronowitz, *False Promises*, 30–31.

49. For a look at the AFL-CIO's take on the threat of rock 'n' roll and the counterculture, see Levy, *The New Left and Labor*, 232.

50. John Sinclair, "Rock-and-Roll Dope #5," *Guitar Army Street Writings*, 1972.

51. Correspondence with the author, March 19, 2006.

52. Tony Scherman, *Backbeat: Earl Palmer's Story* (Washington, DC: Smithsonian Institution Press, 1999), 126.

EPILOGUE. Tuned In, Turned On, and Dropped Out

1. The perspective described here is not mine. It is, to some extent, the view of sociologists of culture like Eyerman and Jamison, who argue that "the use of punk songs in

television commercials can serve as a kind of counterexample [to Bob Dylan's 'authentic' music]. While it is true that punk can in some sense be thought of as an alternative or countercultural movement, punk music was from the very beginning commercial, and the punk 'style' began as a fashion which could be bought and tried on. This is quite different from the social and political space opened up by social movements of the 1960s. . . . It is not impossible to imagine a Dylan song being used to sell a commercial product, even in a topical song like 'Blowin' in the Wind.'" It is much more difficult, however, to imagine the same for 'Only a Pawn in Their Game'. . . . The difference lies in the unambiguous nature of the lyrics and the forcefulness of their presentation. They are clearly political songs." Ron Eyerman and Andrew Jamison, *Music and Social Movements: Mobilizing Traditions in the Twentieth Century* (Cambridge: Cambridge University Press, 1998), 166.

I do not agree with the argument put forth here, that because punk was or is "commercial" that it is not or cannot be "political." The band Rage Against the Machine is an obvious example that "commercially" oriented music can be explicitly political. This point of view provided by Eyerman and Jamison, which overlaps in significant ways with a simplistic Marxist analysis that claims "authentic" resistance to capitalism can only come from the margins of society—not within the commercially oriented, for-profit music industry—has of course undergone sustained criticism in recent years. The works of Antonio Gramsci (*Prison Notebooks*) and the appropriation of Gramsci by Stuart Hall (*Culture, Media, Language*), Dick Hebdige (*Subculture*), and their colleagues working in the area of cultural studies have systematically reconfigured the Marxist theory of culture and point of view on the popular culture industry. I do not seek to enter into the debate on the question of whether or not recording artists can produce "critical" or "radical" music while signed to a corporate-owned major record label. Rather, I seek to add another perspective to the conversation, which is how the structural transformation of the music recording industry has been made possible, in part, by cultural factors having to do with certain interpretations of the role of "independent" record labels in the music industry.

2. Fred Goodman, *The Mansion on the Hill: Dylan, Young, Geffen, Springsteen, and the Head-on Collision of Rock and Commerce* (New York: Vintage Books, 1998).

3. Michael Roberts, "Papa's Got a Brand New Bag," in *Rhythm and Business: The Political Economy of Black Music*, ed. Norman Kelley (New York: Akashic Books, 2005).

4. Steve Chapple and Reebee Garofalo, *Rock-and-Roll Is Here to Pay: The History and Politics of the Music Industry* (Chicago: Nelson-Hall, 1977), 175.

5. For more on post-Fordism, see Michel Aglietta, *Theory of Capitalist Regulation* (New York: Verso, 1979), Mike Davis, *Prisoners of the American Dream* (New York: Verso, 1984), and Ash Amin, *Post-Fordism* (New York: Blackwell, 1994).

6. I describe the function and history of these funds below.

7. The term *signatory* refers to a record company that signs a labor agreement with the American Federation of Musicians. All of the major record labels have signed labor agreements, or contracts, with the AFM, and as such, they are referred to as signatory

labels. The quote above is from Lawrence J. Blake in *The Musician's Business & Legal Guide*, ed. Mark Holloran (Upper Saddle River, NJ: Prentice-Hall, 1996).

8. Exact figures on the percentage of the market that represents CDs recorded by non-union record labels is almost impossible to calculate because of the myriad relationships between the gigantic number of record labels and the rapid turnover of company ownership. My calculations are based on data from *Billboard* magazine. I tallied data from the largest and most successful independent labels that did not hold a contract with the union.

BIBLIOGRAPHY

Archives

Hearings before the Subcommittee on Communications of the Committee on Interstate and Foreign Commerce, United States Senate, Eighty-Fifth Congress, Second Session, Pursuant to an Amendment to the Communications Act of 1934. Washington, 1958.
National Archives and Records Administration:
> Record Group 174, stack area 530, row 47, shelf 7, box 164 "The Beatles."
> Record Group 174, stack area 530, row 47, shelf 7, box 165 "Employment Security."
Official Proceedings of the Annual Convention of the American Federation of Musicians, in Secretary Treasurer's Office of the American Federation of Musicians, 1501 Broadway, Suite 600, New York 10036.

References

Adorno, Theodor. *The Culture Industry.* New York: Routledge, 2001 [1991].
————. *Essays on Music.* Berkeley: University of California Press, 2002.
AFL-CIO. "Elected Leadership Task Force on Organizing." In *Organizing for Change, Changing to Organize.* 1996.
Aglietta, Michel. *A Theory of Capitalist Regulation.* New York: Verso, 1979.
Alterman, Loraine "Who Let the Kinks In?" *Rolling Stone Magazine,* December 13, 1969.
Althusser, Louis. "Ideology and Ideological State Apparatus." In *Lenin and Philosophy and Other Essays,* trans. Ben Brewster. New York: Monthly Review Press, 2001.
Altschuler, Glenn C. *All Shook Up: How Rock 'n' Roll Changed America.* New York: Oxford University Press, 2003.
Amin, Ash. *Post-Fordism.* New York: Blackwell, 1994.

Anderson, Tim J. *Making Easy Listening: Material Culture and Postwar American Recording*. Minneapolis: University of Minnesota Press, 2006.

Aronowitz, Stanley. *False Promises: The Shaping of American Working-Class Consciousness*. New York: McGraw-Hill, 1992 [1973].

———. *Roll Over Beethoven: The Return of Cultural Strife*. Hanover, NH: Wesleyan University Press, 1993.

Attali, Jacques. *Noise: The Political Economy of Music*. Trans. Brian Massumi. Minneapolis: University of Minnesota Press, 1985.

Austin, Mary. "The American Federation of Musicians' Recording Ban, 1942–1944, and Its Effects on Radio Broadcasts in the United States." Master's thesis, North Texas State University, 1980.

Baraka, Amiri. *Blues People: Negro Music in White America*. New York: Quill William Morrow, 1999 [1963.]

Baur, Steven. "Music, Morals, and Social Management: Mendelssohn in Post–Civil War America." *American Music* 19, no. 1 (2001): 64–130.

Beckert, Sven. *The Monied Metropolis: New York City and the Consolidation of the Capitalist Class, 1850–1896*. Cambridge: Cambridge University Press, 2001.

Benjamin, Walter. *Illuminations*. Trans. Harry Zohn. New York: Schocken Books, 1969.

Berry, Chuck. *The Autobiography*. New York: Harmony Books, 1987.

———. *The Chess Box Set*. MCA Records, 1988.

Bertrand, Michael T. *Race, Rock, and Elvis*. Urbana: University of Illinois Press, 2000.

Braverman, Harry. *Labor and Monopoly Capital: The Degradation of Work in the Twentieth Century*. New York: Monthly Review Press, 1974.

Broven, John. *Record Makers and Breakers: Voices of the Independent Rock 'n' Roll Pioneers*. Urbana: University of Illinois Press, 2010.

Broyles, Michael. *Music of the Highest Class: Elitism and Populism in Antebellum Boston*. New Haven, CT: Yale University Press, 1992.

Bryant, Clora, et al. *Central Avenue Sounds: Jazz in Los Angeles*. Berkeley: University of California Press, 1998.

Buhle, Paul. *Taking Care of Business: Samuel Gompers, George Meany, Lane Kirkland, and the Tragedy of American Labor*. New York: Monthly Review Press, 1999.

Burnett, Robert. *The Global Jukebox: The International Music Industry*. New York: Routledge, 1996.

Chanan, Michael. *Repeated Takes: A Short History of Recording and Its Effects on Music*. New York: Verso, 1995.

Chapple, Steve, and Reebee Garofalo. *Rock-and-Roll Is Here to Pay: The History and Politics of the Music Industry*. Chicago: Nelson-Hall, 1977.

Chilton, John. *Let the Good Times Roll: The Story of Louis Jordan and His Music*. Ann Arbor: University of Michigan Press, 1997.

Coleman, Rick. *Blue Monday: Fats Domino and the Lost Dawn of Rock-and-Roll*. New York: Da Capo Press, 2007.

Collete, Buddy, with Steven Isoardi. *Jazz Generations: A Life in American Music and Society*. New York: Continuum, 2000.

Collins, Tony. *Rock Mr. Blues: The Life and Music of Wynonie Harris*. Winter Haven, FL: Big Nickel, 1994.

Commons, John R. "The Musicians of St. Louis and New York." In *Labor and Administration*. New York: Augustus M. Kelley, Bookseller, 1964.

Cosgrove, Stuart. "The Zoot-Suit and Style Warfare." *History Workshop Journal* 18 (autumn 1984).

Cowie, Jefferson. *Stayin' Alive: The 1970s and the Last Days of the Working Class*. New York: New Press, 2010.

Cutler, Jonathan, and Stanley Aronowitz, eds. *Post-Work*. New York: Routledge, 1998.

Dahlhaus, Carl. *Nineteenth-Century Music*. Berkeley: University of California Press, 1989.

Davies, Ray. *X-Ray: The Kinks*. Woodstock, NY: Overlook Press, 1994.

Davis, George. *When Kentucky Had No Mining Men*. Smithsonian Folkways, 2010 [1967].

Davis, Mike. *Prisoners of the American Dream*. New York: Verso, 1984.

Derrida, Jacques. *Margins of Philosophy*. Trans. Alan Bass. Chicago: University of Chicago Press, 1982.

DeVeaux, Scott. *The Birth of Bebop: A Social and Musical History*. Berkeley: University of California Press, 1997.

DiFazio, Bill. *Longshoremen: Community and Resistance on the Brooklyn Waterfront*. South Hadley, MA: Bergen and Garvey, 1985.

Draper, Alan. *Conflict of Interests: Organized Labor and the Civil Rights Movement in the South, 1954–1968*. Ithaca, NY: Cornell University Press, 1994.

"Editorial Comment: Lest Ivory Tower Temp." *International Musician* 13 (February 1947).

Escott, Colin. *Good Rockin' Tonight: Sun Records and the Birth of Rock-and-Roll*. New York: St. Martin's Press, 1991.

———. *Hank Williams: The Biography*. Boston: Little, Brown, 2004.

Eyerman, Ron, and Andrew Jamison. *Music and Social Movements: Mobilizing Traditions in the Twentieth Century*. Cambridge: Cambridge University Press, 1998.

Fast, Susan. *Inside the Houses of the Holy: Led Zeppelin and the Power of Rock Music*. New York: Oxford University Press, 2001.

Forbath, William E. *Law and the Shaping of the American Labor Movement*. Cambridge, MA: Harvard University Press, 1991.

Frith, Simon. *Sound Effects: Youth, Leisure, and the Politics of Rock-and-Roll*. New York: Pantheon Books, 1981.

Frith, Simon, and Andrew Goodwin. *On Record: Rock, Pop, and the Written Word*. New York: Pantheon, 1990.

Gans, Herbert J. *Popular Culture and High Culture: An Analysis and Evaluation of Taste*. New York: Basic Books, 1999.

Garofalo, Reebee. *Rockin' Out: Popular Music in the USA*. Boston: Allyn and Bacon, 1997.

Gates, Henry Louis, Jr. *The Signifying Monkey*. New York: Oxford University Press, 1989.

George, Nelson. *The Death of Rhythm and Blues*. New York: Penguin, 1988.

Gillespie, Dizzy. *To Be or Not . . . to Bop*. New York: Da Capo Press, 1985.

Gillet, Charlie. *The Sound of the City: The Rise of Rock-and-Roll*. New York: Pantheon Books, 1983.

Gitler, Ira. *Swing to Bop: An Oral History of the Transition in Jazz in the 1940s*. New York: Oxford University Press, 1985.

Glaberman, Martin. *Wartime Strikes: The Struggle against the No-Strike Pledge in the UAW during World War II*. Detroit: Bewick/Ed, 1980.

Goldfield, Michael. *The Decline of Organized Labor in the United States*. Chicago: University of Chicago Press, 1987.

Goodman, Fred. *The Mansion on the Hill: Dylan, Young, Geffen, Springsteen, and the Head-on Collision of Rock and Commerce*. New York: Vintage Books, 1998.

Gordon, David M., et al. *Segmented Work, Divided Workers: The Historical Transformation of Labor in the United States*. Cambridge: Cambridge University Press, 1982.

Gracyk, Theodore. *Rhythm and Noise: An Aesthetic of Rock*. Durham, NC: Duke University Press, 1996.

Gramsci, Antonio. *Selections from the Prison Notebooks*. Trans. Quintin Hoare and Geoffrey Nowell Smith. New York: International, 1971.

Gray, Lois, and Ronald L. Seeber, eds. *Under the Stars: Essays on Labor Relations in Arts and Entertainment*. Ithaca, NY: Cornell University Press, 1996.

Griffith, Barbara. *The Crisis of American Labor: Operation Dixie and the Failure of the CIO*. Philadelphia: Temple University Press, 1988.

Guralnick, Peter. *Last Train to Memphis: The Rise of Elvis Presley*. Boston: Little, Brown, 1994.

Gutman, Herbert. *Work, Culture, and Society in Industrializing America*. New York: Vintage Books, 1976.

Halker, Clark. "A History of Local 208 and the Struggle for Racial Equality in the American Federation of Musicians." *Black Music Research Journal* 8 (fall 1988): 207–22.

Hall, Stuart. *Culture, Media, Language: Working Papers in Cultural Studies, 1972–1979*. New York: Routledge, 1991.

———. "Notes on Deconstructing the Popular." In *People's History and Socialist Theory*, ed. Raphael Samuels. New York: Routledge, 1981.

Hamm, Charles. *Yesterdays: Popular Song in America*. New York: W. W. Norton, 1983.

Harrison, Bennett. *Lean and Mean: The Changing Landscape of Corporate Power in the Age of Flexibility*. New York: Basic Books, 1994.

Harrison, Bennett, and Barry Bluestone. *The Great U-Turn: Corporate Restructuring and the Polarizing of America*. New York: Basic Books, 1988.

Hebdige, Dick. *Subculture: The Meaning of Style*. London: Routledge, 1994 [1979].

Hentoff, Nat. "The Pop Explosion." *International Musician*, April 1968.

Hill, Trent. "The Enemy Within: Censorship in Rock Music in the 1950s." In *Present Tense: Rock & Roll and Culture*, ed. Anthony DeCurtis. Durham, NC: Duke University Press, 1992.

Hitchcock, H. Wiley. *Music in the United States: A Historical Introduction*. Englewood, NJ: Prentice-Hall, 1988.

Holloran, Mark, ed. *The Musician's Business and Legal Guide*. Upper Saddle River, NJ: Prentice-Hall, 1996.

Hunnicutt, Benjamin. *Work without End: Abandoning Shorter Hours for the Right to Work*. Philadelphia: Temple University Press, 1988.

Jackson, Wanda. *Queen of Rockabilly: The Very Best of the Rock 'n' Roll Years*. Nashville Records and Ace Records, 2000.

Johnson, Mark. *The Body in the Mind: The Bodily Basis of Meaning, Imagination, and Reason*. Chicago: University of Chicago Press, 1987.

Jordan, Louis. *Louis Jordan and His Tympany Five, 1941–1943*. Classics, 1994.

———. *Louis Jordan and His Tympany Five, 1943–1945*. Classics, 1996.

———. *Louis Jordan and His Tympany Five, 1946–1947*. Classics, 1998.

Kelley, Norman. *R&B, Rhythm, and Business: The Political Economy of Black Music*. New York: Akashic Books, 2002.

Kelley, Robin D. G. "The New Urban Working Class and Organized Labor." *New Labor Forum*, no. 1 (fall 1997).

———. "The Riddle of the Zoot: Malcolm Little and Black Cultural Politics during World War II." In *Race Rebels: Culture, Politics, and the Black Working Class*. New York: Free Press, 1994.

———. "Without a Song: New York Musicians Strike Out against Technology." In *Three Strikes: Miners, Musicians, Salesgirls, and the Fighting Spirit of Labor's Last Century*. Boston: Beacon Press, 2001.

Kennedy, Rick, and Randy McNutt. *Little Labels—Big Sound: Small Record Companies and the Rise of American Music*. Bloomington: Indiana University Press, 1999.

Kitts, Thomas M. *Ray Davies: Not Like Everybody Else*. New York: Routledge, 2008.

Kofsky, Frank. *Black Music, White Business: Illuminating the History and Political Economy of Jazz*. New York: Pathfinder Press, 1998.

Kraft, James P. *Stage to Studio: Musicians and the Sound Revolution*. Baltimore: Johns Hopkins University Press, 1996.

Lash, Scott, and John Urry. *The End of Organized Capitalism*. Madison: University of Wisconsin Press, 1987.

Leavis, F. R. *Education and the University*. London: Chatto and Windus, 1961.

Lefebvre, Henri. *The Production of Space*. Trans. Donald Nicholson-Smith. New York: Blackwell, 1991.

Leiter, Robert D. *The Musicians and Petrillo*. New York: Bookman Associates, 1953.

Leonard, Neil. *Jazz and the White Americans: The Acceptance of a New Art Form.* Chicago: University of Chicago Press, 1962.

Levine, Lawrence. *Highbrow/Lowbrow: The Emergence of Cultural Hierarchy in America.* Cambridge, MA: Harvard University Press, 1991.

———. "Jazz and American Culture." In *The Jazz Cadence of American Culture,* ed. Robert G. O'Meally. New York: Columbia University Press, 1998.

Levitt, Martin Jay. *Confessions of a Union Buster.* New York: Crown, 1993.

Levy, Peter B. *The New Left and Labor in the 1960s.* Urbana: University of Illinois Press, 1994.

Lhamon, W. T., Jr. *Deliberate Speed: The Origins of a Cultural Style in the American 1950s.* Cambridge, MA: Harvard University Press, 2002 [1990].

Lichtenstein, Nelson. *Labor's War at Home: The CIO in World War II.* Cambridge: Cambridge University Press, 1983.

Lipsitz, George. *Rainbow at Midnight: Labor and Culture in the 1940s.* Urbana: University of Illinois Press, 1994.

———. *Time Passages: Collective Memory and American Popular Culture.* Minneapolis: University of Minnesota Press, 1990.

Lott, Eric. *Love and Theft: Blackface Minstrelsy and the American Working Class.* New York: Oxford University Press, 1993.

Lynd, Alice, and Staughton Lynd. *Rank-and-File: Personal Histories by Working-Class Organizers.* New York: Monthly Review Press, 1973.

Malone, Bill C. *Don't Get Above Your Raisin': Country Music and the Southern Working Class.* Urbana: University of Illinois Press, 2002.

Marcus, Greil. *Invisible Republic: Bob Dylan's Basement Tapes.* New York: Henry Holt, 1997.

———. *Mystery Train: Images of America in Rock-and-Roll Music.* New York: Plume Books, 1997.

Martin, Linda, and Kerry Segrave. *Anti-Rock: The Opposition to Rock 'n' Roll.* New York: Da Capo Press, 1993.

Marx, Karl. *Capital, Volume I.* Trans. Ben Fowkes. New York: Penguin, 1976.

———. *The Grundrisse: Foundations of the Critique of Political Economy.* Trans. Martin Nicolaus. New York: Penguin Books, 1973.

McGlynn, Don, dir. *The Howlin' Wolf Story.* Blue Sea Productions and BMG Music, 2003.

McLeod, Kembrew. "Genres, Subgenres, Sub-Subgenres, and More: Musical and Social Differentiation within Electronic/Dance Music Communities." *Journal of Popular Music Studies* 13 (2001): 59–75.

Millard, Andre. *America on Record: A History of Recorded Sound.* Cambridge: Cambridge University Press, 1995.

Miller, James. *Flowers in the Dustbin: The Rise of Rock-and-Roll, 1947–1977.* New York: Simon and Schuster, 1999.

"The Mission of Music." *Harper's New Monthly Magazine* 51 (October 1875): 738–39.

Moody, Kim. *An Injury to All: The Decline of American Unionism.* New York: Verso Press, 1988.

Mowitt, John. *Percussion: Drumming, Beating, Striking.* Durham, NC: Duke University Press, 2002.

Murray, Albert. *Stompin' the Blues.* New York: Da Capo Press, 2000 [1976].

Nietzsche, Friedrich. *On the Genealogy of Morals.* Trans. Walter Kaufman. New York: Vintage Books, 1967.

Noebel, David A. *Communism, Hypnotism, and the Beatles.* Tulsa, OK: Christian Crusade, 1965.

Ortega y Gasset, Jose. *Revolt of the Masses.* New York: W. W. Norton, 1994.

Paddison, Max. *Adorno's Aesthetic of Music.* Cambridge: Cambridge University Press, 1998.

Palmer, Robert. *Rock and Roll: An Unruly History.* New York: Crown, 1995.

Peretti, Burton W. *The Creation of Jazz: Music, Race, and Culture in Urban America.* Urbana: University of Illinois Press, 1992.

Perlman, Selig. *The Theory of the Labor Movement.* Philadelphia: Porcupine Press, 1928.

Peterson, Richard A. *Creating Country Music: Fabricating Authenticity.* Chicago: University of Chicago Press, 1997.

Peterson, Richard A., and David G. Berger. "Cycles in Symbol Production: The Case of Popular Music." In *On Record: Rock, Pop, and the Written Word,* ed. Simon Frith and Andrew Goodwin. New York: Routledge, 1990.

Porter, Eric. *What Is This Thing Called Jazz? African American Musicians as Artists, Critics, and Activists.* Berkeley: University of California Press, 2002.

Preis, Art. *Labor's Giant Step: Twenty Years of the CIO.* New York: Pioneer, 1964.

Rawick, George P. *From Sundown to Sunup: The Making of the Black Community.* Westport, CT: Greenwood Press, 1972.

Roberts, Michael. "Papa's Got a Brand-New Bag." In *Rhythm and Business: The Political Economy of Black Music,* ed. Norman Kelley. New York: Akashic Books, 2005.

Rodgers, Daniel T. *The Work Ethic in Industrial America, 1850–1920.* Chicago: University of Chicago Press, 1979.

Roediger, David R. *The Wages of Whiteness: Race and the Making of the American Working Class.* New York: Verso, [1991] 1996.

Roell, Craig H. *The Piano in America, 1890–1940.* Chapel Hill: University of North Carolina Press, 1989.

Roscigno, Vincent J., and William F. Danaher. *The Voice of Southern Labor: Radio, Music, and Textile Strikes, 1929–1943.* Minneapolis: University of Minnesota Press, 2004.

Rosenzweig, Roy. *Eight Hours for What We Will: Workers and Leisure in an Industrial City, 1870–1920.* Cambridge: Cambridge University Press, 1985.

Ruby, Jay. "Creedence Clearwater Revival." *International Musician,* June 1969, 5.

Ryan, John. *The Production of Culture in the Music Industry: The ASCAP-BMI Controversy.* Lanham, MD: University Press of America, 1985.

Sanjek, David. "Can a Fujiyama Mama Be the Female Elvis?" In *Sexing the Groove*, ed. Sheila Whiteley. New York: Routledge, 1997.

Sanjek, Russell. *Pennies from Heaven: The American Popular Music Business in the Twentieth Century*. New York: Da Capo Press, 1996.

Scherman, Tony. *Backbeat: Earl Palmer's Story*. Washington, DC: Smithsonian Institution Press, 1999.

Seltzer, George. *Music Matters: The Performer and the American Federation of Musicians*. Metuchen, NJ: Scarecrow Press, 1989.

Shaw, Arnold. *Honkers and Shouters: The Golden Years of Rhythm and Blues*. New York: Collier Books, 1978.

———. *The Rockin' 50s*. New York: Da Capo Press, 1974.

Shipton, Alyn. *Groovin' High: The Life of Dizzy Gillespie*. New York: Oxford University Press, 1999.

Smith, R. J. *The Great Black Way: L.A. in the 1940s and the Lost African American Renaissance*. New York: PublicAffairs, 2006.

Sohn-Rethel, Alfred. *Intellectual and Manual Labor: A Critique of Epistemology*. London: Macmillan, 1978.

Solt, Andrew, dir. *The History of Rock-and-Roll, Episode 1: Rock-and-Roll Explodes*. Warner Bros. Home Video, 1995.

Southern, Eileen. *The Music of Black Americans: A History*. New York: W. W. Norton, 1971.

Spivey, Donald. *Union and the Black Musician: The Narrative of William Everett Samuels and Chicago Local 208*. Lanham, MD: University Press of America, 1984.

Stallybrass, Peter, and Allon White. *The Politics and Poetics of Transgression*. Ithaca, NY: Cornell University Press, 1986.

Tate, Greg S. Foreword to *Rip It Up: The Black Experience in Rock-and-Roll*, ed. Kandia Crazy Horse. New York: Palgrave. 2004.

Thompson, E. P. "Rough Music Reconsidered." *Folklore* 103, no. 1 (1992): 3–26.

———. "Time, Work-Discipline, and Industrial Capitalism." *Past and Present* 38, no. 1 (1967): 56–97.

Tomlins, Christopher L. *The State and the Unions: Labor Relations, Law, and the Organized Labor Movement in America, 1880–1960*. Cambridge: Cambridge University Press, 1985.

Tosches, Nick. *Unsung Heroes of Rock 'n' Roll: The Birth of Rock in the Wild Years before Elvis*. New York: Da Capo Press, 1999.

Volosinov, V. N. *Marxism and the Philosophy of Language*. Trans. I. R. Titinuk. Cambridge, MA: Harvard University Press, 1986.

Waksman, Steve. *Instruments of Desire: The Electric Guitar and the Shaping of Musical Experience*. Cambridge, MA: Harvard University Press, 1999.

Wald, Elijah. *How the Beatles Destroyed Rock 'n' Roll*. Oxford: Oxford University Press, 2009.

Walker, T-Bone. *T-Bone Blues*. Atlantic Records, 1988.

Walser, Robert. "The Body in Music: Epistemology and Musical Semiotics." *College Music Symposium* 31 (1991).

Ward, Ed, Geoffrey Stokes, and Ken Tucker. *Rock of Ages: The Rolling Stone History of Rock & Roll*. New York: Rolling Stone Press/Summit Books, 1986.

Warwick, Jacqueline. *Girl Groups, Girl Culture: Popular Music and Identity in the 1960s*. New York: Routledge, 2007.

Weber, Max. *The Rational and Social Foundations of Music*. Trans. Don Martindale et al. Carbondale: Southern Illinois University Press, 1958.

Weiner, Jon. *Come Together: John Lennon in His Time*. New York: Random House, 1984.

Welch, Walter L., Burt Stenzel, and Leah Brodbeck. *From Tinfoil to Stereo*. Gainesville: University Press of Florida, 1994.

Whiteman, Paul, and Mary Margaret McBride. *Jazz*. New York: J. H. Sears, 1926.

Wilentz, Sean. *Chants Democratic: New York City and the Rise of the American Working Class, 1788–1850*. New York: Oxford University Press, 1984.

Williams, Hank. *The Ultimate Collection*. Mercury Records, 2002.

Williams, Raymond. *Culture and Materialism*. New York: Verso, 2005 [1980].

———. *Keywords: A Vocabulary of Culture and Society*. New York: Oxford University Press, 1985.

Willis, Ellen. *Beginning to See the Light: Sex, Hope, and Rock-and-Roll*. Hanover, NH: Wesleyan University Press, 1992.

Young, William K., and Nancy H. Young. *The 1950s*. Westport, CT: Greenwood Press, 2004.

INDEX

International Workers of the World (IWW), 14

Introducing . . . The Beatles (Beatles), 193

"Irate AFM Flips Lid over Invasion of Rocking Redcoats *Sans* Culture" (*Variety*), 181

Irving, Dorcester, 217n59

"Is You Is or Is You Ain't My Baby" (Jordan), 50–51

"I Wanna Hold Your Hand" (Beatles), 178

Izenhall, Aaron, 134

Jackson, Alan, 95

Jackson, Wanda, 2, 68, 81, 106–10

James, David, 148

jazz: AFM's core membership and, 6–8, 13, 117–18; classical music's relation to, 5, 117–29, 135–37, 168–69, 224n26; class identification and, 3, 7–8, 114–23, 138–39, 141–48, 187; racial discourses and, x, 114–15, 152–53; rhythm and blues's origins and, 113–14. *See also* AFM (American Federation of Musicians); bebop musicians; culture

Jazz and the White Americans (Leonard), 153

Jim Crow laws, 50, 111, 147, 149

John Birch Society, 165, 171–72

"Johnnie B. Goode" (Berry), 94, 107

Johnny Johnson Trio, 93

"John Sinclair Freedom Rally" (concert), 199

Johnson, Johnny, 93–94

Johnson, Lyndon B., 173, 182, 196, 198

Johnson, Mark, 97–98

Johnson, Patsy, 170–71

Johnson, Robert, 52–53, 124–25

Jones, Deacon (character), 47, 132–33

Jones, Jo, 70

Jones, Quincy, 141–42, 179

Jones, Thad, 139

Joplin, Janis, 1

Jordan, Louis: Berry and, 92, 94–95; jump blues and, 46–47, 53, 93, 132, 134–35, 137, 209n5; performative elements of, 41–42, 47–48, 58–59, 70, 94, 115, 132–34; working class concerns of, 41–43, 50–51, 62–63, 65–68, 77, 81–82

jukeboxes, 16, 20–21, 31–35, 44, 75, 82–85, 107, 150

jump blues: bebop's relation to, 114–18, 125–27, 136–37; clothing and dance styles of, x, 54, 59–62, 121–22, 136–37, 216n36; origins of, 47, 53, 67, 70, 113–14; working class pretensions and, 46, 53–57, 65–66, 81–82. *See also* Jordan, Louis; performativity; rock 'n' roll

Juvenile Jungle (film), 157

"Keeping Out the Beatles" (Riesel), 181–83

"Keep on Churnin'" (Harris), 74

Kefauver, Estes, 156

Kelley, Robin D. G., xii, 51, 59–60, 62

Kenin, Herman, 9–10, 12, 163–74, 177–87, 189–90, 192–93

Kennedy, Rick, 73

Keywords (Williams), 185

KFVD (station), 88

KFWB (station), 63

King, Albert, 76, 93

King, B. B., 76, 149

King, Martin Luther, Jr., 150

King Records, 74, 112

Kinks, the, 178, 188–89

Krupa, Gene, 3, 29, 38

KTSP (radio station), 27, 29

Ku Klux Klan, 149

labor movement: anti-labor legislation and, 38, 205–7; automation and technology and, xii, 16–17, 26–40; conservatism of, 11–12, 167–73, 182–87, 192–95, 197–99; craft unions and, 5–6, 8–10, 14–15, 115–18, 120–21, 129–32, 189–90, 192; culture wars and, ix, xi, 11–12, 167–72, 180–87, 190–92; decline of, xi, 16–17, 201–7; gender and, xi, 14–15, 43, 55; great migration and, 50, 53, 55, 67, 77, 87–90; leadership's relations with rank-and-file and, 3, 5, 8–11, 25–30, 49–50, 56, 157–58, 167–72, 196–98; race and, xi, 14–15, 53–56, 64–67, 70–71, 126, 152–54; strikes and, 16–20, 23–40, 49–50, 56–57, 63–67, 70–71, 191; workers' exclusions from, xi, 3, 12, 14, 122, 142–48, 151–52, 168–69; World War II and, 20–21, 42, 53–57, 61–62, 70–71, 78–82. *See also* AFM (American Federation of Musicians); recording industry; rock 'n' roll

Lackey, Terry M., 174

Lafargue, Paul, xii

Lawler, Kristin, xii

141, 178; rock 'n' roll genealogy and, 2, 68, 75, 89, 138–39; Wanda Jackson and, 107–8; working class background of, 53, 77, 81, 89–92, 105, 107, 145, 147–48, 150–51, 159

pretensions, 46, 53–60, 76–82, 96–98, 107, 112, 123–24, 215n30

Protestant work ethic, 45–46, 67–68, 81–82, 94, 100–106, 146–48

"Proud Mary" (CCR), 1

Quinichette, Paul, 133–34

Rabbit Foot Minstrels, 47

race and racialization: the body and, 96–98, 103–5, 128–30, 141, 149, 220n98; class practices and, 3, 14, 43, 48, 59–62, 64, 66, 75, 77–82, 88, 105, 107, 118–19, 122–32, 148–49, 224n42; great migration and, 50, 53, 55, 67, 77, 87–90; jazz's complexity and, 114–20, 125; labor movement and, xi, 3, 11–12, 53–54, 70–71; music genres and, 5, 8–9, 132–33, 158–60; performativity and, 98–105, 110–11, 115–16, 127–28; recording industry and, x, 9, 15, 45, 112, 119–20, 225n57; rock 'n' roll's identifications with, 7, 43–44, 50–51, 74–75, 77–82, 93–98, 110–11, 146–51, 157–58, 160–62, 193; segregation and, 50–51, 59–60, 147, 149; World War II and, 118–20. See also class; minstrel shows; performativity; rock 'n' roll; working class

radio (medium), 24–28, 37–40, 82–89, 147–62, 212n20, 218n80

Rage Against the Machine, 230n1

ragtime music, 8, 183

Rainbow at Midnight (Lipsitz), x, 215n22

Randolph, A. Phillip, 70–71, 118

rank-and-file (of unions): cultures of, 5, 180–87, 190; leadership's relationship to, 3, 8–10, 26–27, 30, 56, 157–58, 196–98; militancy of, 30–31, 49–50, 56–57, 68. See also AFM (American Federation of Musicians); labor movement

"Ration Blues" (Jordan), 41–43, 50–51, 62

Ravel, Maurice, 125–27

Rawick, George, xii, 1

RCA Victor, 37, 148, 204, 212n20

reading (of music), 5–6, 15, 118, 129–31, 143, 192

Reagan, Ronald, xi, 205

Rebel without a Cause (film), 156

Reconstruction, 50

"Re-conversion Blues" (Jordan), 51

Recording and Transcription Fund (RTF), 37–40

recording ban of 1942, 16, 19–21, 25–40, 214n20

recording industry: AFM's relation to, 10–11, 16–17, 20–25, 31–40, 201–7; division of labor in, 163–64, 199, 202–3; independent labels and, 13, 36, 73, 86, 88, 98, 140, 161, 163–64, 201–7, 217n62, 230n1; payola hearings and, 151–65, 227n93; race and racialization in, x, 9, 15, 112–15, 119–20, 225n57; structure of, 5, 16, 131, 160–63, 201–7, 230n1; Tin Pan Alley and, 64, 78, 81–82. See also AFM (American Federation of Musicians); rhythm and blues; rock 'n' roll

Recording Musicians Association (RMA), 136

records: musical training and, 5, 10, 84, 86; rock 'n' roll culture and, 5–6, 9–10, 12, 44, 82–86, 140, 158–59, 191–92. See also jukeboxes

Red Hot 'n' Blue (radio show), 86–87

Revolver (Beatles), 193

Rhapsody in Blue (Gershwin), 224n26

rhythm and blues: class struggle and, 3, 16, 43–45, 51–52, 64–70, 89–93, 111, 115, 136; jazz's relation to, 113–15, 130–38; jukebox culture and, 83–85; lyrics of, 41–42, 115–16; origins of, 70–72, 114; popularization of, 82–112; race and, 43–44; radio and, 82–83, 86–87; rock 'n' roll genealogy and, 2, 6, 43, 72–75, 157–58

Richards, Keith, 93, 124–25

Richbourg, John R., 88

Riesel, Victor, 181–83

"Right or Wrong" (Jackson), 110–11

"Riot in Cell Block No. 9" (Robins), 110

"Rip It Up" (Little Richard), 68, 110

rising expectations, 46, 59–60, 107. See also pretensions

Robins, the, 110

Robinson, Bill, 116

rockabilly (genre), 53, 69, 89–93, 107–10, 148–49

"Rock Around the Clock" (Haley), 96, 138, 156